...ed Tensions

PITT LATIN AMERICAN SERIES

Catherine M. Conaghan, *Editor*

Unresolved Tensions BOLIVIA

PAST AND PRESENT

JOHN CRABTREE AND LAURENCE WHITEHEAD

UNIVERSITY OF PITTSBURGH PRESS

Published by the University of Pittsburgh Press,
Pittsburgh, Pa., 15260
Copyright © 2008, University of Pittsburgh Press
All rights reserved
Manufactured in the United States of America
Printed on acid-free paper

10 9 8 7 6 5 4 3 2 1

Library of Congress Cataloging-in-Publication Data
Crabtree, John, 1950–
  Unresolved tensions : Bolivia past and present /
John Crabtree and Laurence Whitehead.
      p. cm. — (Pitt Latin American series)
  Includes bibliographical references and index.
  ISBN-13: 978-0-8229-4355-6 (cloth : alk. paper)
  ISBN-10: 0-8229-4355-7 (cloth : alk. paper)
  ISBN-13: 978-0-8229-6006-5 (pbk. : alk. paper)
  ISBN-10: 0-8229-6006-0 (pbk. : alk. paper)
    1. Bolivia—Politics and government—1982– 2. Bolivia—
Economic conditions—1982– 3. Bolivia—Race relations.
I. Whitehead, Laurence. II. Title.
  F3327.C73 2008
  306.20984—dc22   2008016330

CONTENTS

ACKNOWLEDGMENTS

The editors would like to thank a number of people and institutions for their help in making this book a reality. In the first place, thanks go to the Warden and Fellows of Nuffield College for allowing us to use their premises for the original conference that formed the basis for this book. We would also like to thank the United Nations Development Program (UNDP) in La Paz for their help and encouragement, as well as for hosting a follow-up meeting and helping to finance a Spanish-language edition of this book. A particular debt of gratitude goes to the British Embassy and the Department for International Development (DfID) in La Paz for helping cover the traveling expenses of key speakers to the Oxford conference, as well as to the Foreign and Commonwealth Office (FCO) in London for helping out with the costs of translation. But special thanks are due to all of those who have contributed to this volume and for the time and effort this has involved. John Crabtree translated the majority of the chapters from Spanish.

N

PERU

BRAZIL

PANDO
• Cobija

BENI
• Trinidad

LA PAZ

A M A Z O N I A

Lake
Titicaca

H I G H L A N D

⊛ La Paz

COCHABAMBA
• Cochabamba

SANTA CRUZ
• Santa Cruz

Oruro
•

V A L L E Y S

A L T I P L A N O

ORURO

• Sucre

GRAN CHACO

Potosí •

CHUQUISACA

POTOSÍ

PARAGUAY

CHILE

Tarija
•

TARIJA

Laguna
Verde

0   50   100 mi
0 50 100 150 km

ARGENTINA

Bolivia: Political Divisions. Map by Bill Nelson.

Introduction

A Story of Unresolved Tensions

JOHN CRABTREE

There could be no dispute over the verdict of the 2005 presidential elections in Bolivia. Juan Evo Morales—known to most as plain "Evo"—won, with nearly 54 percent of the vote. A fair election result, it avoided the need for a run-off vote in Congress. The movement backing his candidacy—for it was more a movement than a party as conventionally defined—the MAS (Movimiento al Socialismo—Instrumento Político), won 70 of the 130 seats in the lower house. It only narrowly missed winning a majority in the Senate, which heavily overrepresents the less-populous lowland departments.

Although universal suffrage dated back more than half a century, the advent of democratic politics was much more recent. Only in 1982 did Bolivia emerge from nearly two decades of intermittent military rule. In every democratic election since the 1980s, the electorate had split in fragments, with the eventually victorious candidate winning only a relatively small minority of votes. No previous democratically elected president had won by an absolute majority on the first round, and no democratically elected Congress had produced such a majority for a single party. Until 2005, electoral contests had resulted in awkward (and sometimes dishonorable) coalitions held together by the rewards of office. The system of party rule, or *partidocracia*, came to be seen as venal and corrupt. The scale of Morales's victory therefore conferred on him a mantle of legitimacy that his predecessors had conspicuously lacked.

Internationally, Evo's victory also attracted interest. It was one of a number of contests in a year of electoral activity in Latin America, which saw a swing to the left in many countries that challenged some of the assumptions of liberalizing economic and political reform. The Bolivian MAS, unlike parties elsewhere whose popular base seemed to be in decline, managed to bring together the country's social movements and give them political expression. Evo's victory reflected the extent of dissatisfaction with the meager social benefits of the economic policies in this South America's poorest nation. First introduced in the mid-1980s, these were once heralded by the World Bank as being a model for other countries to follow. Also, Evo was widely seen as the first "indigenous" head of state in a country where a "white minority" had previously monopolized political leadership. Though the reality was more complicated, the symbolism was compelling. His personal story—the rise from the humblest of origins to the presidency—was particularly striking. And his ties to the ranks of the country's coca farmers (*cocaleros*), among its most combative and organized social movements, raised questions about the policies that the new government would follow, not least with respect to the United States. Not only was he the man whose presidential election a U.S. ambassador had attempted to blackball as a threat to U.S. relations with Bolivia, but his relationship with Cuba's Fidel Castro and Venezuela's Hugo Chávez provided further confirmation to the outside world of the resurgence of an anti-U.S. Left in Latin America.

Morales's victory thus represented a break with the past. It promised a more direct and participatory schema of democratic representation, with an increased role for popular mobilization. It highlighted the quest for new economic policies and the reassertion of the state in policymaking. It proffered a new relationship between Bolivia and the outside world, based less on exploitation and more on respect. Arguably, it also represented a coming together of two traditions in Bolivian politics—a constitutional one and one of popular mobilization—both with histories going back to the earliest days of the republic (Whitehead 2002). The new government promised to rewrite the constitution in such a way as to enable previously excluded groups—notably the country's indigenous population—to play a leading role in politics. Among its first actions was to announce the election of a constituent assembly to undertake this task. Elected by a similar margin only slightly less than Evo's vote in 2005, the assembly was inaugurated in August 2006 with a majority of its members (but less than the two-thirds needed to ratify the new constitution) coming from the ranks of the MAS. The job allotted to the *constituyentes* was nothing less than to "refound" the republic. The challenge of writing a document that would heal Bolivia's previous political, social, economic, and geographic rifts was ambitious indeed, particularly in a country where democratic institutions were fragile and where those who had won power through the ballot box set out to use that power to bring about profound changes in the structure and workings of Bolivian society.

The new government took office after a period of heightened political conflict and social mobilization. The first years of the twenty-first century had seen empowered social movements take on the political elite and win. Bolivia became something of a laboratory for the study of social movements, providing useful indicators as to their strength and weakness (Crabtree 2005). Pivotal was the so-called Cochabamba water war of 1999–2000, which had forced the government of the day into a humiliating volte-face on its policies of privatization. Then, in 2003, a coalition of social movements—led by the urban neighborhood committees in El Alto—brought down the government of Gonzalo "Goni" Sánchez de Lozada. Goni had come to symbolize the sort of business politics that had exacerbated the country's social and ethnic inequalities, and his forced resignation was evocative of the sort of popular protagonism that had characterized earlier periods in Bolivian history.

Although the social movements that had emerged as political actors in the first years of the twenty-first century were organizationally fragmented and ideologically inchoate, they were united in their opposition to the sort of liberalizing economic policies that had predominated in Bolivia since 1985 and of which Goni had been the main architect. They were also brought together by the new tide of indigenous politics (even though this meant different things to different groups) and by the conviction that the country's raw materials should be developed in ways that would benefit all Bolivians—especially the poorest, more indigenous sectors. The issue of Bolivian control over the gas industry thus became emblematic, a point which the new government was quick to seize upon by forcing foreign gas companies to renegotiate their contracts on terms more favorable to domestic Bolivian interests.

However, in spite of the margin of Evo's victory in 2005 and the power shift it entailed, this did not bring an end to political conflict. As the policy tide turned, the new conservative opposition quickly resorted to a combination of constitutional and extra-parliamentary pressure to stymie aspects of the government's program. The shoe was, in a sense, on the other foot. The main motor of opposition, coming as it did from lowland Santa Cruz, used its regional influence to put pressure on the new government, demonstrating an ability to mobilize large demonstrations in support of its perceived interests. Other departments, too, followed this lead, demanding greater political autonomy from the central government. Methods of direct action included marches, road blockades, and hunger strikes, tools used to great effect by the social movements prior to 2005. Through a combination of such shows of force and the skillful use of other arenas open to it, the new opposition forced the government to back down on important issues. It wielded its influence within the Constituent Assembly and by boycotting the final proceedings, it undermined the new constitutional text's claim to be a document of consensus. Finally, it demanded de facto autonomy for Santa Cruz and other eastern departments.

The difficulties of governing the country soon were thus quickly made clear to the new regime, notwithstanding its own legitimacy and popularity among large sectors of the population.

Not only did it find itself having to deal with challenges from elite groups in the lowlands, but it had to face up to other instances of conflict among different interests that otherwise supported it. These could quickly flare into violent confrontation. Often they concerned access to or control over natural resources. A showdown between mineworkers at Huanuni in October 2006—unionized employees on the one hand and self-employed *cooperativistas* on the other—left many dead. The two groups struggled to wrest control over one of Bolivia's richer mineral deposits. Similarly, a dispute over provincial borders in Tarija in April 2007 led to the temporary suspension of gas exports to Argentina. Each province vied to establish its jurisdiction over one of Bolivia's most productive gas wells. A month later, indigenous groups and peasant colonists found themselves in conflict over land titles in a part of La Paz department reputedly rich in hydrocarbons. Such disputes exposed the government's difficulties in imposing solutions on its own supporters. Nor was the significance of such instances lost on critics of Morales further to the left, who saw the new government failing to meet revolutionary expectations.

Why is Bolivia such a conflictual country? Why does it exhibit such acute problems of governability—problems present elsewhere in Latin America but not to the same degree? The answer would seem to reside, at least in part, in the relationship between the state and society in a country where the power exerted by one over the other is far from uniform. As it has evolved over time, the state in Bolivia is highly concentrated in some areas and all but absent in many others. It is a state with many of what Guillermo O'Donnell (1993) called "brown areas," where the writ of centralized authority does not run very far. It is a state that does not exert national authority in a homogenous way. Indeed it has been called a "Swiss cheese state," a state full of holes (UNDP 2007). At the same time, social organization is also far from being homogenous, with pockets where social actors enjoy enormous influence and are well able to organize their own agendas and impose these on weak state authorities. Historically, the highly politicized Bolivian mineworkers were exemplary in this respect; today their successors are probably to be found among the *cocaleros,* the inheritors of a trade-union tradition that has few parallels elsewhere in Latin America. In many respects, the strength of social organization—founded on strong communitarian traditions—has flourished precisely because of the uneven strength of the state and the opportunities to which this has given rise.

This relationship between state and society is also, of course, far from static over time. There have been periods of outright conflict and others of relative peace, periods where the state has exerted greater control over society and ones where the opposite has been true. Over the last fifty years, the political reach of the state has widened, and the areas where it is wholly absent have diminished. Among other things, the development of improved communications has meant that there are no longer so many isolated communities cut off from the rest of the country. Reforms such as Popular Participation in the 1990s helped build a state presence in parts of the country where it had scarcely existed previously. In spite of such reforms, however, the state frequently found itself hard pressed to exert its authority over recalcitrant social movements. Social organization has remained strong, resistant to co-optation, and frequently prepared to counter force with force. It is, of course, an open question whether, under Evo Morales, state and society will eventually enter into a new period of greater harmony and collaboration. The experience of the MAS government's first two years in office suggested that this bridging of the gap may be a far harder task to accomplish than many had predicted at the outset.

This book seeks to offer some explanations about the nature of political conflict in Bolivia by focusing on some of the main issues that have emerged in recent years. Ostensibly concerned with the present and the future, these conflictual issues also involve differing interpretations of the past (both the near past and the more distant past) and how it relates to the present. Though a good deal of the book touches on history, this tends to be selective history—not necessarily a historian's history—that illuminates the concerns of the early twenty-first century. The past is repeatedly evoked—sometimes inaccurately and sometimes selectively—to justify the pretensions of the present. Rather than just chart political developments since Morales's election as such, this volume seeks to examine the way in which current events respond to a set of much deeper historical issues arising from the country's patterns of economic and political development. Hopefully, these will help the reader to understand some of the complexities of Bolivian politics and the key debates that emanate, debates which of course have wider ramifications for the rest of Latin America and indeed other parts of the developing world. Rather than present a single interpretation, the book seeks to air these debates that are defining (and dividing) Bolivia's political and intellectual elites in what seems to be an increasingly polarized situation. In so doing, it seeks to deepen our understanding of these enduring discrepancies.

It is, of course, difficult to judge the lasting historical significance of changes taking place in the present. Preoccupation with the present can distort the lens through which we view the significance of change, and indeed, it may only be possible to provide a proper analysis two or three generations hence. Analyzing the present in the present is always fraught with dangers. It is impossible to know how future generations will judge the importance of what is going on in Bolivia today, just as it was impossible for those immersed in the 1952 revolution to perceive the full significance of that event for subsequent Bolivian history. Much will depend on how the unresolved tensions we have highlighted here are, eventually, addressed. But, whatever the outcome of Evo's government, future generations may well see this as an important turning point; much as 1952 was, where some of the changes now taking place have their roots.

The authors of this volume include some of the foremost analysts of the Bolivian scene. Most came and contributed papers to a conference organized by Laurence Whitehead and myself at Nuffield College, Oxford, in May 2006, with a second round of discussions held the following August in La Paz. Like other observers of the Bolivian scene, we were concerned to try to make sense of fast-moving political developments—developments that seemed to have the potential for far-reaching change. But in particular, we were interested in how analysts with different perspectives and from different academic disciplines would place the current situation within a broader sweep of Bolivian history and consider aspects often overlooked by commentators of the current scene. Although not entirely a meeting of minds, there was broad consensus at the conference that the then-fledgling government of Evo Morales represented an important new departure in the country's history—one with the potential to build a new order but also the potential to further exacerbate existing contradictions.

The book is therefore organized around the six major issues of ethnicity, regionalism, state-society relations, constitutional reform, economic development, and globalization. These controversial themes encapsulate many of the discussions that currently underlie Bolivian politics, although clearly there are many linkages to be found between them. Each section of the book is preceded by a short introduction written by the editors and designed to contextualize the issues involved. In each we have sought to contrast different interpretations of past and present, often fairly radically different, with a view to elucidating the various positions adopted in Bolivia today. We hope this will encourage further intellectual debate and help to overcome problems by improving the understanding of their origins.

PART I

The issue of ethnicity has emerged as a powerful force in recent Bolivian politics, more so than in most other Latin American countries. The rise of Evo Morales and his spectacular election victory in December 2005 has been emblematic of the importance of ethnicity, and from the very beginning his government made clear that its proposal to refound the republic would signify the implementation of a proindigenous agenda. This appointment of well-known *indigenista* figures to the cabinet reinforced this commitment, although nonindigenous figures were also present, and the large electoral base of the Movimiento al Socialismo (MAS) was ethnically very mixed. The Constituent Assembly, elected in July 2006, provided further evidence of the new salience of *indigenismo* in Bolivian politics; a large percentage of the *constituyentes* elected came from indigenous backgrounds, and the transformation that they hoped to bring about involved a "new deal" for Bolivia's indigenous population. There has therefore been a tendency to portray policy in distinctly ethnic terms.

However, ethnicity has also created major and overt new cleavages. It has become one of the dividing lines between the MAS and the opposition, with some elements of the latter concerned by the implications of the *indigenista* agenda, certainly in its more far-reaching forms. Ethnic considerations have suffused other conflictual issues, such as the country's longstanding regional tensions, which in places like Santa Cruz is expressed in the desire for greater autonomy and has contained some racist connotations. In response, the MAS and its supporters have criticized the opposition as simply seeking to perpetuate a status quo from a bygone era that seeks to sustain white superiority. The bitterness of the debates within the Constituent Assembly reflects the lack of common ground on the issue of ethnicity.

The issue, and the politics that go with it are, of course, rendered far more complicated by the lack of clarity about what the *indigenista* agenda actually consists of. There is no clear agreed statement of this, apart from a general desire to right the wrongs of centuries and to break down areas of exclusion. For some, the *indigenista* challenge is to rid Bolivia of all vestiges of neocolonialism, including, for example, the power of the Catholic Church. For others, it has more to do with establishing ethnic rights in areas such as landholding, legal procedure, and bilingual education. In other contexts, it has more to do with control over the exploitation of natural resources.

The issue is rendered still more complicated by the different realities facing Bolivia's many ethnic groups, and the varying agendas that therefore emerge. Not only do the political stances of Bolivia's lowland indigenous groupings differ markedly from those of the highlands, but there are differences, rivalries, and mutual suspicions between Aymaras and Quechuas, for instance, and between different subgroups among them. There is certainly no one organization that speaks for the whole, in the way that the Central Obrera Boliviana (COB) used to speak for the labor movement. Perhaps one of Evo Morales's more important assets is that he is not seen as the representative of a particular ethnic group; although he is Aymara, he has spent much of his working life in the Quechua-speaking Chapare. He does not seek to speak as the advocate of any specific ethnic interest. Indeed, his markers of identity are quite plural, and his government has formulated many of its projects in Spanish.

Another source of complication in understanding social movements in Bolivia is trying to grasp the heterogeneity of their organizational make-up, particularly the relationship between *sindicalismo* and *indigenismo.* The specific admixture of these elements varies from place to place, but in many places—even in some *ayllus* of the Altiplano—ethnic consciousness is suffused with some of the deep-rooted traditions of class politics for which Bolivia (not so long ago) was famous. At the same time, in places like Santa Cruz, a world away from the traditions of the *ayllu,* class politics among migrant workers are deeply affected by considerations of ethnicity. The politics of ethnicity are affected by the experience of migration and the changes this entails on the mindset of those involved. The transfer of lifestyles from the rural to the urban context, or from one region to another, affects how peoples of different ethnic origins see themselves and their relationship to others in society.

The three contributions to this part of the book seek to discuss these complexities, albeit from different points of view. Xavier Albó, an anthropologist, probably more than anyone else in Bolivia over the last fifty years has ruminated over and written about the nature of the Bolivian peasantry in its various forms. One of the cofounders of CIPCA (Centro de Investigación y Promoción del Campesinado), a Jesuit-run development and research center that has promoted popular organization and evaluated the growth of rural *indigenismo* at least since the emergence of Katarismo in the 1970s, Albó opens his chapter with the observation that the 2001 census established clearly that indigenous peoples constitute the majority of Bolivia's population and that there is an intimate connection between ethnicity and social status. He looks at the rise of ethnic politics and its relationship with the neoliberal reforms of the 1980s and 1990s, and how these scuppered *clasista* politics but helped foster *indigenismo.* For him, Evo Morales represents the *indio alzado*—the confrontational Indian, as opposed to the servile one—but within a situation where his scope for pursuing his agenda is tightly circumscribed by political realities.

Carlos Toranzo, in contrast, takes issue with Albó's starting point, challenging the idea that Bolivia is essentially an indigenous country and the claim derived from the 2001 census that indigenous people constitute 62 percent of the total population. This interpretation has also been taken up by those who dislike the *indigenista* agenda and see it as an aberration of democratic practice. He argues that, in reality, Indian and mestizo identities often overlap. Toranzo furthermore criticizes the more extreme versions of *indigenismo,* which he associates with the desire to establish Aymara hegemony over the whole country, irrespective of the rights or traditions of other forms of ethnicity. Toranzo's reading of history therefore differs from that of the *indigenistas,* and he attacks the idea that the national revolution of 1952, in its attempt to create a homogenous *campesinado,* was necessarily based on perpetuation of neocolonialism wrapped up in a myth about democratization. He sees in the 1952 revolution the key milestone on the road to building a democratic nation, a road that began with the Chaco War in the early 1930s. This nation involved de facto the bringing together of a fragmented society within a process of multiple *mestizajes.* He also argues that 1952 opened up an economic space (previously restricted) in which those of indigenous background could engage in business and prosper, ceasing to be *indígenas* in the traditional sense of the word. Thus, it is not surprising that he takes issue with the 2001 census findings, highlighting instead other survey findings that suggest that Bolivia—far from being a country of *indigenas*—is a country of mestizos of one form or another. Nevertheless, as Albó also acknowledges, it is quite possible for a person to be at once *indígena* and mestizo when it comes to answering censuses or other research surveys, and the preference for Spanish over an indigenous language does preclude self-identification *indígena* or *originario.*

The issue of multiple identities is also taken up by Diego Zavaleta as key to understanding how Bolivians from different walks of life perceive themselves, those around them, and society in general. He argues that different identities become paramount depending on the circumstances people find themselves in and the organizational forms their various different activities take. Based on the findings of the CRISE survey, undertaken by the University of Oxford in 2006, he finds himself much closer to the 2001 census results than some of the other surveys cited by Toranzo. He concludes that Bolivia is indeed primarily indigenous in its social make-up, but that this observation actually tells us very little in terms of people's attitudes and allegiances. The CRISE study establishes that ethnicity is but one of a range of identities that people have, and that therefore giving it the salience it has come to enjoy in recent times is perhaps a distortion of reality. Other types of identity include religion, gender, region and—of course—class. These different types of identity are naturally closely interrelated. This points to the conclusion that what is important is to establish the precise weighting that people give to one sort of identity over another at a particular point of time, and beyond that to know how those weightings change over time. The issue of ethnicity is, therefore, far from clear-cut.

The "Long Memory" of Ethnicity in Bolivia and Some Temporary Oscillations

XAVIER ALBÓ

This chapter highlights the persistence of ethnicity in Bolivian politics and society when viewed over the long term, intertwined with such other key factors as the development of a national state and class conflict. The 2001 census provides the most recent data on how Bolivians classify themselves ethnically. This census asked people over the age of fifteen to state which ethnic group they thought they belonged to. Around 31 percent considered themselves to be Quechua, 25 percent Aymara (the largest populations of both groups found in the western Andean region of the country), and a further 6 percent identified themselves as belonging to one of thirty-one smaller indigenous (*originario*) groups, distributed mainly through the lowlands.[1] Of these, the three largest were Chiquitanos (2.4 percent), Guaranís (1.6 percent), and Mojeños (0.9 percent). In other words, nearly two-thirds (62 percent) of the population said they belonged to one or another of these ethnic groups.

It is worth pointing out that the 1900 census (Bolivia 1901) included a fairly similar question, although it did not specify particular ethnic groups. It concluded that the population was 13 percent white, 51 percent indigenous and 27 percent mestizo. This was the last time that a census used this last category; at the time, the office which carried out the census remarked, "In a short space of time, in view of the progressive laws of statistics, the indigenous race will be, if not removed entirely from the scene, at least reduced to a small fraction" (ibid., vol. 2, 36; cf. pp. 31–32).

When we established CIPCA (the Centro de Investigación y Promoción del Campesinado) in 1971, we chose the term *campesinado* (peasantry), as opposed to any reference to indigenous peoples. From the time of the MNR (Movimiento Nacional Revolucionario) revolution in 1952, this had been the expression in common usage. But thirty years after the founding of CIPCA, fifty years after the revolution, and fully one hundred years after the census

13

officer foretold the disappearance of the indigenous population—62 percent of all Bolivians identified themselves as belonging to an indigenous or *orginario* people. For many, the term *indígena* is more pejorative than mestizo, and it is for this reason that many define themselves both as Quechua or Aymara and at the same time as mestizo. However, those who identified themselves as mestizo in the 2001 census did so in a different sense than in 1952. For most, it no longer implies a denial of their belonging to one of these *originario* peoples (Seligson 2006, 13–19).

The greatest concentration of indigenous people is to be found in the western Andean region (ranging from 66 percent in Chuquisaca to 84 percent in Potosí), an area that accounts for two-thirds of the total indigenous population. However, regional development in the lowlands and the cities of eastern Bolivia, which accelerated in the years after the 1952 revolution, attracted numerous waves of migrants, and in these areas today a significant proportion of the population is of Andean origin.[2] As a consequence of migration, more than half of those who say they are Quechua, Aymara, or members of the main lowland indigenous groups now live in cities, where they are more inclined to feel that they are also mestizos.[3] Here, they do not necessarily speak to one another in their language of origin, especially those of the younger generation.

The data quoted above show that although major changes have taken place over the last century, there have also been some important underlying historical continuities. In spite of the obvious social changes that have taken place, especially since the time of the Chaco War (1932–1934), it becomes clear that here we confront Fernand Braudel's concept of long historical cycles. Both at the local level and among indigenous peasant movements, Silvia Rivera has termed these as "the long memory" (beyond the "short"), principally the centuries-old survival of colonialism and neocolonialism. We will look at this across three periods of time: under colonial society and its neocolonial aftermath, under the revolutionary state as it emerged after 1952 with its "peasant" agenda, and with the reemergence of ethnic politics as of the end of the 1960s.

Colonial and Neocolonial Society

The importance of the Audiencia of Charcas, the precursor of modern Bolivia, resided in its mines and the abundance of its indigenous labor force. The forced labor draft known as the *mita* was the institution that effectively linked the two.[4] A dual society was welded together by the *mita* and other forms of taxation. Channeled through indigenous colonial authorities (given the Caribbean name of *caciques* by the Spaniards), these taxes legitimized the persistence of indigenous peoples for the Spanish crown, each with their own culture, organization, and territory. This was the essence of what Tristan Platt (1982) termed the "colonial pact." It was precisely the weakening of this pact as a consequence of the mid-eighteenth-century Bourbon reforms that led to the indigenous risings of Túpac Amaru in Cusco and the Kataris in Charcas between 1780 and 1784. These were events that remained alive in the collective memory of the descendents of those defeated.

After these rebellions were put down, the Spanish crown proceeded to abolish the system of caciques. However, neither then, nor during the period that followed Bolivia's independence in 1825 (itself stimulated by the indigenous rebellion), was the colonial system broken as such. Rather, the asymmetries and systems of exploitation became more evident. Moreover, with the recovery of silver mining, the new state no longer required the indigenous system of taxation (preserved as the euphemistically named *contribución territorial*). Community lands were increasingly acquired to feed the expanding hacienda system of agricultural estates, with former *comuneros* (members of indigenous landholding communities) being transformed into peons. A century after independence, the surface area belonging to communities and kinship groups (known as *ayllus*) had shrunk to less than half its previous dimensions, provoking endless rebellions among these communities that were met in turn by repression and even massacres by the army. This helps explain why, when the army was sent to the Chaco in the war against Paraguay, many communities and even hacienda peons took advantage of the situation to widen the scope of what had become an undeclared indigenous war.

This transformation of the colonial pact into an even more asymmetric pattern of exploitation helped to consolidate what we now call a "neocolonial" society. What both societies had in common was the confrontation of a small but dominant elite (considered to be descendents of the original Spanish *conquistadores* and colonists and identified with the culture and history of Europe) against a majority who were the descendents of those peoples who had previously inhabited these lands. The latter were referred to first as *naturales,* and then as *indios* (because of Columbus's initial confusion as to where he had landed) or *indígenas.* They were also referred to as *originarios* (descended from the original inhabitants) and *agregados* (in-migrated from other indigenous communities) if they continued to live in *ayllus* and communities, or as *yanaconas* (and, during the republic, *pongos*) if they had moved into direct dependence on Spanish landlords and their hacendado successors or into other forms of service in the city.

Mestizos, meanwhile, a growing group in the middle, were of two main types. They initially consisted of biological mixed-race individuals, people of mixed Spanish and indigenous blood who tended to form part of the "republic of Spaniards." However, little by little, the prevalent form of *mestizaje*, or mixture, became cultural: people who were biologically indigenous but who had lost contact with their rural origins and who wanted to create a new identity for themselves. This sort of intermediate status gained importance under the new republic, to the extent that it came to distinguish itself from another culturally mestizo subaltern group termed *cholo* (Barragán 1990). This group was closer to those indigenous groups from which they too had emerged. *Cholos* did not identify themselves as such, since this was a disrespectful term conferred on them by others. A classic but gloomy description is to be found in the essay by Alcides Arguedas entitled "Pueblo enfermo" (1909).

The colonial and neocolonial regime was somewhat different in the eastern lowlands of Bolivia. This was due to a number of factors, such as lower population density, the dispersion of and differences between a multiplicity of ethnic groups, and the absence of mining. Ethnic relationships were therefore much more varied. Some groups had no contact with one another, while others coexisted in a state of constant warfare, such as that between the Guaranís and Chiriguanos. At the other end of the spectrum, members of ethnic groups were exploited on haciendas. And we should not forget the specific way in which some entered the colonial world through religious missions and settlements. During the republican era, new points of contact emerged as a consequence of the opening up of the rubber extraction industry and its corollary the war in Acre (of 1903), as well as expeditions to conquer new lands and peoples. Later on, the Guaraní people became ensnared in the Chaco War, a conflict in no sense of their own making. The aftermath of the war saw rapid expansion of livestock ranching throughout the Guaraní territory.

But it would be wrong to conclude, as some seem to think, that the political class during this long period of colonial and neocolonial rule was constituted solely by a dominant white minority, possibly enlarged by mestizo allies, and that indigenous peoples (who constituted the great majority of the population) simply adopted a passive, prepolitical posture. That this may have been what the elite hoped for is another matter. The continuous struggles and rebellions of indigenous peoples, both during the colonial period and then under the republic, are evidence of constant political activity. Also highly political (from a rather different point of view) was the role played by *caciques* and other indigenous authorities, albeit from a position of inferiority—providing, as they did, the linkage between the "republic of *indios*" and that of white people. We have already mentioned how the general uprising of 1780–1784, which threatened the colonial regime as never before, also had the unexpected effect of acting as a wake-up call to the *criollo* elite, demonstrating the real possibility of independence. Very few indigenous people were ever invited to take part in the wars of independence, however.

When the new republican state sought to establish itself without the involvement of indigenous peoples, these populations continued to respond politically. They resisted the subjugation of their territories, as well as taking part in the various conflicts prompted by *criollo* politicians who wanted to take power for themselves. Enraged by the need to defend their threatened lands, they repeatedly allied themselves with different emergent political groups, even though time after time this trust was betrayed once these groups established themselves in power. This is what happened, for example, when they supported the overthrow of General Mariano Melgarejo in 1871, following his expropriation of lands previously belonging to indigenous communities. Again in 1899, indigenous groups rallied to support the insurrection of liberals based in La Paz against conservatives in Sucre. It also happened a third time, two decades later, in 1921 during Bautista Saavedra's republican revolution against the liberals (Albó and Barnadas 1995, fig. 31). On that occasion, they went so far as to form an alliance between Saavedra's Republican Party and a new *"cacique"* movement, so called to commemorate the former *caciques* of colonial times (Choque amd Ticona 1996, 35–45).[5]

Ideological justifications for a hierarchical and discriminatory society varied in some respects between the colonial period and the neocolonial republic, but in ways that led in fairly similar directions. Notwithstanding the stratified heritage of Spanish society, with some almost sacred flourishes (God was on the Spaniards' side), there was a debate during the early part of the colonial period about the human condition of the *indios*. Although it was agreed that Indians were indeed human, they were confronted by a series of restrictions on their juridical standing: for example in holding public or religious office. The process of *mestizaje* tended to generate a sophisticated layering of castes (Szeminski 1983), depending on the mix of white, indigenous, and even black (even though the latter were never numerous in Charcas/Bo-livia). By contrast, the first century of the republic saw the rise of so-called social Darwinism, which, with its veneer of science, exalted the superiority of the white race (Demelas 1981). The subordination of former *comuneros* within the hacienda system was seen as a boon to the indigenous population that would help them overcome the limitations of their race.

To sum up, the asymmetric dualism of colonial society persisted, and in some respects became even more pronounced, with the advent of republican neocolonialism. However, the counterpart to this was the persistence of re-sistance among the *originario* peoples thus dominated. From its origins, Bo-livian multiculturalism was such that it sustained the blatant asymmetries of neocolonial society. This is its founding structure, the "original sin" that, in one way or another, continues to shape its historical destiny.

The 1952 State and the Campesinos

Bolivia's defeat at the hands of Paraguay in the Chaco War presaged a pro-found national crisis and precipitated the search for a new kind of country. Some traits of this were already made clear in the 1938 Constituent Assem-bly (Barragán 2005, 359–71). However, the real change came about with the bloody 1952 revolution, spearheaded by the MNR, whose chief, Víctor Paz Es-tenssoro, assumed the presidency. Thus it was that the "1952 state" came into being, and with it some significant but secondary modifications; it would last until it was finally dismantled in 1985.

The 1952 state represented the longest and most successful attempt in Bolivian history to fashion a governing structure that was at once relative-ly solid and inclusive of the population as a whole. It contrasts with what George Gray (2006a) has called "the [Bolivian] state as a modus vivendi." In economic terms, this period saw the emergence of state-owned compa-nies or corporations. The first of these was the Bolivian Mining Corporation (Comibol), the fruit of the nationalization of the mines. This was followed by the founding of YPFB (Yacimientos Petroleros Fiscales Bolivianos) in the oil sector and a number of others under the aegis of the Bolivian Development Corporation (CBF). Inspired by the PRI in Mexico and by Peronism in Ar-gentina, the regime tended toward the consolidation of an omnipresent and all-powerful party—the MNR—to which a variety of social organizations became appendages. Having come to power with the support of the police against the army, the MNR complemented the former by creating a feared mechanism known as "political control" (*control politico*) and replaced the latter with "popular militias" principally made up of miners and peasants armed with old Mausers from the Chaco War. Subsequently, a new military academy was inaugurated in the vain hope of building a new army faithful to the revolution.

The 1952 national revolution brought about a series of transformations in the public and social spheres. For our purposes, the following stand out: the introduction of universal suffrage, even for illiterate indígenas who still constituted the great majority of the population; the expansion of rural education in ways that did not question the notions of the traditional Spanish-language educational system as a civilizing force; and new forms of peasant unionization, encouraged by the government and backed up by the presence of a substantial number of peasant representatives in Congress. With the support, and sometimes at the behest, of these new peasant unions, agrarian reform managed to dismantle the traditional system of hacienda agriculture in the highlands. Yet at the same time, these reforms created the basis for a new dual agrarian structure on the agricultural frontier. This frontier expanded in the eastern lowlands, the consequence of a strategy of self-sufficiency, modernization, and agricultural diversification, with large units of landholding cheek by jowl with small-scale peasant migrants (*colonizadores*). Thus it was that the counterrevolutionary face of the MNR began to gestate in the eastern lowlands, with the development of a new landowning and agroindustrial oligarchy, the beginnings of what would become one of the country's most important structural conflicts.

In the western highlands, agrarian reform converted the campesinos into the regime's most solid and stalwart allies, militantly opposed to any attempt to subvert the new state. Moreover, "peasant super-states," in which peasant union leaders assumed the main duties of the state, came into being in some areas. These areas included the Quechua-speaking Valle Alto in Cochabamba, which had long resisted landlordism and where the agrarian reform decree (and the future law) had first been promulgated (Dandler 1984), as well as the Quechua-speaking valleys of northern Potosí and the Aymara region around Achacachi, near Lake Titicaca. The peasant organizations enjoyed notable degrees of autonomy but were unquestioning in their loyalty to the MNR. Particularly notorious was the popular regiment of the peasant militia from Ucureña, the town where the agrarian reform was launched. This force was always present whenever there was any sort of uprising against the government, not just in Cochabamba but also more distant parts, such as the mining districts, where they confronted unrest from workers who had distanced themselves from the government and its agenda, and Santa Cruz, where they helped suppress rebel landowners in what amounted to the first of open breach between *collas* (highlanders) and *cambas* (people from the eastern lowlands) (Albó and Barnadas 1995, 217–26; Albó 1999, 467–71).

However, there was a price to be paid for this incorporation of the rural sector, as the state came to ignore and, indeed, actively suppress the cultural identities of Bolivia's rural population. Under the legitimate pretext of eliminating racial discrimination against *indios*, these came to be referred to as just campesinos, and their communal organizations were transformed into peasant unions, even though there were no landlord bosses left, nor any clear demands such as the recovery of lost lands. At least during the early years of the agrarian reform, peasants largely accepted this change—often with pride—even in areas where there had never been landlords or haciendas. They saw it as the way to free themselves from past forms of exploitation and discrimination and become full and modern citizens of the state.

Notwithstanding such changes, the new state was not always successful in meeting its objectives, whether due to conflict between its various component parts, to economic and management problems within Comibol and other state companies, or to the government's growing fiscal dependence on the United States and the rightward shift to which this gave rise—notably in the wake of the Cuban Revolution of 1959.

The MNR finally fell from power with the 1964 coup d'état of General René Barrientos, Paz Estenssoro's vice president during his second term in office. Although the coup ushered in a sequence of military regimes, these nevertheless maintained the basic structure of the 1952 state. Barrientos made it quite clear from the outset that he would maintain—even deepen—agrarian reform. He consolidated the so-called Military-Campesino Pact, which he had signed as vice president during the MNR government. Adopting a populist posture, he was acclaimed as "supreme leader" of the *campesinado* during his frequent visits to peasant communities. The military governments that followed Barrientos lacked this charismatic flair, but the majority of the peasantry regarded them as allies. They saw them as leaders following in the tradition of the MNR, which had bestowed on them the agrarian reform; little consideration was given to the fact that the military had overturned the party of the national revolution and had curtailed the democratic system.

The 1952 state, and the ideology on which it was based, was not therefore just a simple reproduction of the neocolonialism that had preceded it. Well over a century after the country's independence, there was at least a widespread recognition that all within its borders were members of the Bolivian nation-state. No longer were people just Bolivians in a formal sense; they felt themselves to be such. But in spite of the considerable effort made politically to incorporate indigenous peoples as campesinos in ways that were more equitable and formal than before—imbuing in them a sense of liberation—the new state basically preserved the old colonial structure through time-honored means, as well as ways that were new and rather more subtle.

This structure was no longer built on the exclusion and direct exploitation on haciendas; rather, it depended on a deep and persistent inequality between rural and urban areas, particularly in terms of access to common goods and services. In a more ideological sense, the 1952 state deprived people of their *originario* identity, this being the necessary price for achieving full citizenship. To be sure, the ideal of the 1952 state was to build a society that was more inclusive, but also more homogenous, through the adoption of mestizo culture. Society was no longer to be *indígena*, but rather subject to a common culture ever closer to that of the dominant *criollo*/white society with its civilizing mentality. The means to this end was the state school system (which had expanded to the most remote corners of rural Bolivia), the peasant unions supported by the *comandos* of the MNR, and the system of military service which rested essentially on recruiting young people of rural origin.

Paradoxically then, a system originally designed to overcome ethnic discrimination—and thus welcomed by those affected—ended, boomerang-like, by creating yet another form of cultural discrimination. Years later, Juan Condori Uruchi, a young Aymara university student who had not lived through this phase, expressed this lucidly in the following terms: "They told us that we would be liberated if we ceased to be *indios.* We believed them, and almost without realizing it, bit by bit, we found ourselves reduced to a mere social category—'campesinos'—and by this means we are losing our condition as Aymara people."[6]

The Reemergence of Ethnicity

Condori's comment reflects the first inklings of a deeper understanding of the sociocultural structure and of the collective subconscious, the "long memory." Two dynamics were at work here. The first, frustration with the unfulfilled promises of the 1952 revolution, was perhaps the more negative.

In spite of the efforts of the dominant *criollo* society to inculcate greater equality, the marginalization of rural and popular society persisted. People continued to consider themselves second-class citizens, a feeling that became rather more pronounced during the years of military government. The second was rather more positive and had to do with a growing awareness of cultural identity. This was assisted by the establishment of a network of educational radio stations, mostly run by institutions linked to the Catholic Church. By retransmitting in indigenous languages, often with a high level of audience participation, these contributed to developing (sometimes without really meaning to do so) a new sense of belonging among Aymaras and Quechuas. These came to realize that their numbers were much more extensive than they had previously thought from their experience in the small communities where they lived. The presence of privately run promotion projects was also influential, as well as the contribution of particular researchers and intellectuals committed to highlighting the cultural and ethnic dimension. Fausto Reinaga, a militant writer (1969), stands out among the latter. In spite of its colonial-style "civilizing" approach, expansion of the educational system contributed to opening the eyes of those reaching secondary and even university levels.[7]

The movement known as Katarismo was the first real expression of this new spirit. It began at the end of the 1960s, its primary adherents young Aymara students who had one foot in the countryside and the other in the city and who had not personally experienced the earlier period of agrarian reform. Significantly, the main geographical nucleus of Katarismo was in precisely those *originario* communities that, two centuries earlier, had fostered the rebellion of Túpac Katari, the great anticolonial hero of the 1780s from whom the movement took its name. The Kataristas would invoke the slogan "We are not the 1952 campesinos any more." And elaborating on their hero's supposed last words, they would proclaim, "Túpac Katari has returned, and we are millions."

The meteoric rise of Katarismo during and after the Banzer dictatorship (1971–1978) and its consolidation in the first few years after Bolivia's return to democracy (1982–1983) has been dealt with elsewhere, notably by Rivera (1983 and 2003, 148–84); Albó (1985) and Hurtado (1986). Here I limit myself to highlighting some of the characteristics of this process, both internal and external.

Internally, it implied the dismantling of the Military-Campesino Pact and the end to the ideas and illusions it had imbued among peasant organizations for over a decade. In a broader sense, it also implied going beyond the "short memory" (Rivera 2003, 179) that extended no further than the 1953 agrarian reform and the hopes this had created for homogenous citizenry based on the 1952 state. In its place, it invoked a long memory that harked back to the (neo)colonial state and the need to destroy it. It was by no means a coincidence that this paradigm shift happened at a time when the leadership of the peasant movement was undergoing change. During the period of the short memory, leadership came mainly from the former haciendas of Cochabamba, some dating back to colonial times, as well as from the Achacachi region in the Altiplano, where haciendas had also prevailed, at least since the expropriation of indigenous lands in the nineteenth and early twentieth centuries. By contrast, the leaders of the Kataristas, who revived the long memory, came primarily from the same indigenous communities and *ayllus* where Túpac Katari had been active in the 1780s.

Two other landmarks deserve a mention. In 1982, just after democracy was restored, the Confederación Indígena del Oriente Boliviano (CIDOB) was set up, an organization that, over the years, managed to bring together all the smaller ethnic groups from the lowlands. Then in 1983, the second congress of the Confederación Sindical Unica de Trabajadores Campesinos de Bolivia (CSUTCB) produced and disseminated its political thesis (CSUTCB 1983), stating for the first time:

"Enough of integration and cultural homogenization. . . . We want . . . the construction of a plurinational and pluricultural society which, upholding the unity of the state, combines and develops the diversity of the Aymara, Qhechwa, Tupiguaraní, and Ayoreode nations, and all the others who integrate it."

It is important to note that this whole process of recovering ethnic consciousness was something essentially endogenous to Bolivia, taking place as it did well before the ethnic factor began to loom large on the international scene. In this respect, the sort of initial resistance expressed by the Central Obrera Boliviana (COB) to incorporating the Katarista leaders is revealing, influenced as it was at the time by an exclusively class-based paradigm that dominated the international arena. Indeed, when Bolivia returned to democracy in 1982, the COB was reluctant even to accept the use of native languages under the SENALEP (Servicio Nacional de Alfabetización y Educación Popular) literacy program.

The fall of the Berlin Wall in 1989 and the collapse of the Soviet Union in 1991 were key international milestones in the crisis of the class-based approach that had prevailed over most popular movements, including those of Latin America, and in the adoption of a more ethnic paradigm. The significance of ethnicity was given salience by the many ethnic conflicts that broke out in the countries of the former Soviet Union and Eastern Europe. By this time, the Katarista agenda was already well developed, and even the less numerous lowland ethnic peoples had come together in the CIDOB.

These changes in the international paradigm had an important impact in transforming the perceptions of traditional parties in Bolivia—both on the left and the right. These had previously regarded the initiatives of the Kataristas and others like them as the dilettante taste of a few crackpots. They had tended to see *indigenismo* as confirming the "primitivism" of the peasantry, or even as a dangerous sort of deviationism that could end up in racism. The powerful mineworkers' movement, led by the COB, used such ideological arguments to justify its vanguard role over the peasantry and the "*indiecitos*"—the "little Indians" whose ownership of land rendered them essentially petit bourgeois. Such theoretical justifications were effectively underpinned by the colonial mentality of the state, both before and after 1952.[8]

With all the changes that took place in Eastern Europe, the parties of the Left—some more quickly than others—woke up to the importance of the ethnic dimension. But before this, other movements appeared on the scene that were more populist in nature than the Kataristas and CIDOB. They included Conciencia de Patria (Condepa), led by the self-styled "Compadre" Carlos Palenque. Condepa emerged in 1988 to become a significant force in Aymara politics in La Paz. A year later, the Unión Cívica Solidaridad (UCS), founded by the beer magnate Max Fernández, made its appearance and developed into a movement of more national scope than Condepa. Although Fernández avoided ethnic or ideological rhetoric, he was characterized by political analysts as a *cholo* politician. Some parties of the Right also incorporated elements of ethnic discourse.[9] Among the last to do so was the MNR, or more precisely its presidential candidate in the 1993 elections, Gonzalo Sánchez de Lozada. Prompted by public opinion survey findings, Sánchez de Lozada decided to invite Víctor Hugo Cárdenas, an Aymara Katarista, to be his vice presidential running mate. Thus it was that, for the first time, an indigenous leader became the country's vice president (Albó 1994). Whether this choice was a merely piece of opportunism or in fact an acknowledgment of the political importance of the ethnic factor, from this point onward ethnicity was something that could no longer be ignored.

It is worthwhile pausing a moment to analyze how this old and new paradigm—which connects with a long historical cycle that goes back at least to the colonial period—adapted itself to the new scenario of the Bolivian state in the late twentieth century. As of 1985, by means of a simple decree (no. 21060), the state of that emerged after 1952 gave way to a new paradigm. The so-called New Economic Policy embraced the neoliberal model of globalization in vogue at the time throughout Latin America (see chapters 12 and 13).

The economic shock that set these changes in motion was made easier to bear—even for popular sectors—by the climate of uncertainty created by galloping inflation and devaluation between 1982 and 1985, and the social chaos and lack of effective government that resulted. Stringent monetary stabilization helped generate a degree of greater tranquility among the population, even though the social cost was high. Perhaps the most problematic aspect was the "relocalization" (a euphemism for mass layoffs) of most of the workers in the state mining industry. Whether by design or not, this policy caused mineworkers to lose the hegemony they had enjoyed previously as the proletarian vanguard of the popular movement. A similar fate also beset other workers, with less-efficient labor hemorrhaging into the much more precarious informal economy. This sort of economic instability had always been a feature of the indigenous peasant sector and, consequently, it was less affected by the economic crisis of the 1980s and its aftereffects; indeed, the *campesinado* acquired a greater degree of protagonism within the popular movement. As time passed, peasants were joined by other informal workers, whose numbers were swollen by rural-urban migrants and displaced mineworkers.

During Sánchez de Lozada's first term (1993–1997), when vice president Cárdenas also presided over the Congress, a number of second-generation reforms were approved. These had two main logics to them. On the one hand, policies associated with the New Economic Policy were reinforced; on the other, there was a greater preoccupation with social and, indeed, indigenous affairs. So far as the latter were concerned, the 1994 constitutional reform defined the country as "multiethnic and pluricultural" (Article 1), while Article 171 introduced the concept of the TCO (*tierra comunitaria de origen*, or indigenous territory). This article recognized the main attributes of indigenous peoples and their territory in concordance with Agreement 169 of the International Labor Organization (ILO), ratified by Bolivia in 1991 in the wake of the historic march by lowland indigenous peoples to La Paz. As a corollary to the New Economic Policy, the Law of Capitalization (1994) privatized former state companies on the lines of joint ventures and gave profits from them a social function in the shape of the Bonosol, which extended benefits to those aged 65 or more. The spectacular increase in proven gas reserves (in large part anticipated in advance by YPFB) was a consequence of the generous terms extended to multinational oil and gas companies.[10]

Three further laws passed at this time were particularly relevant to this dialectical relationship between the two logics. On the one hand, the 1994 Education Reform Law was spurned by the teachers because it withdrew various privileges they had gained in the past and weakened their job stability; at the same time, it introduced the principle of interculturality and bilingual teaching throughout the educational system. This clearly favored the indigenous population and, had it been implemented to the letter, would have had positive effects in helping to build a more pluricultural country. Similarly, the 1996 INRA (Instituto Nacional de Reforma Agraria) Law both helped open up the land market to the benefit of large agricultural concerns and, paradoxically, introduced the TCOs as a form of landholding for indigenous peoples. Then the 1994 Popular Participation Law, reflecting the demands of grassroots organizations, helped develop and strengthen municipal government across the country. It gave powers and resources to rural municipalities which had previously existed only on paper. It also gave a legal standing to grassroots OTBs (*organizaciones territoriales de base*, territorial base organizations), as well as oversight roles to, among others, indigenous communities and peasant unions (failing fully to realize that the latter were also often "indigenous").

From the outset, there were many who asked whether these concessions toward ethnicity were part of a strategy on the part of global powers to weaken the state and thereby impose their liberal economic model—a bit like the strategy of bread and circuses of ancient Rome—or whether it was more a response to pressure from below by indigenous peoples seeking to achieve recognition. In all probability, it was a bit of both. Without such pressure, it is unlikely that the government or international donors would have thought it necessary to go down this road. In Bolivia, the World Bank initially resisted the intercultural, bilingual approach of the educational reform on the grounds of financial inefficiency, rather like the way that the COB had opposed the approach of the SENALEP program years before on the grounds that it was not grounded on principles of class. However, it also seems to be the case that, once the power groups had accepted the need to respond to this sort of pressure, they did everything possible to ensure that it supported their interests. Indeed, they saw it as a way of deflecting attention away from class struggles toward more cultural concerns. Thus it was that the fear of the *indio alzado* (the resurgent Indian) pushed the state, and even international financial agencies, to make concessions toward the *indio permitido* (the tolerated Indian).[11]

Here some credit must go to Cárdenas, with his origins among the *indios alzados* of the Kataristas. His skill as president of the Congress led that body to pass a number of measures that favored indigenous groups, despite the fact that parliament was clearly ill-disposed to do so. It was also from his office as vice president and from a new National Office for Ethnicity, Gender, and Generations that the first steps were taken toward what, in 1997, was to become the Consejo Nacional de Markas y Ayllus del Qullasuyu (Conamaq). Still, Cárdenas paid a high price for his role in a government whose economic model was neoliberal and whose leader, over the years, came to be seen to represent the very antithesis of national interests. Cárdenas pushed and shoved, managing to open up the state to the *indio permitido,* but then he found himself overwhelmed in the surge of the *indio alzado* (of which he was once one).

Initially, at least, the popular movement referred to these second-generation laws as *leyes malditas* (cursed laws) imposed by the World Bank. But this view changed to some extent when they were put into effect. This was particularly true of Popular Participation, which soon became referred to as a *ley bendita* (a blessed law), because it helped switch a significant percentage of state resources toward rural areas for the first time. And despite inevitable corruption and mistakes made along the way, Popular Participation quickly became a key instrument in helping build popular power at the local level. Thus it was that in the December 1995 municipal elections, the first to take place after the passage of the new law, more than five hundred peasants and *indígenas* were elected as municipal councilors (*concejales*) or, in some cases, mayors. In the 2000 municipal elections, that number rose to over one thousand, or 65 percent of the total number of seats (Albó and Quispe 2004, 35).

One of the most notable things about the 1995 municipal elections was the emergence of the Asamblea por la Soberanía de los Pueblos (ASP/IU), which would later become the MAS (Movimiento al Socialismo). Peasant organizations in Cochabamba, under the leadership of Evo Morales, the leader of the coca growers' association, had sufficient political instinct to see that the Law of Political Participation—which some still saw as *maldita*—provided them with a means to construct a political instrument, albeit at the local level. They quickly sought to register their party with the electoral court, skillfully dodged the legal objections made by merging with an already-existing party, and less than a year after it was founded they topped the poll among the rural municipalities of Cochabamba.

This was the beginning of the rise of the MAS. In the 1997 elections, when Hugo Banzer emerged as president following a run-off vote in Congress, the MAS managed to elect four deputies: all *indígenas*/peasants and all from Cochabamba. By April 2000, rejection of neoliberal globalization had become more widespread. It started with the "water war" in Cochabamba and was followed up by a string of roadblocks across the Altiplano (led by the Aymara Felipe Quispe) and in the coca-producing Chapare (led by Morales). In January 2002, Congress expelled Evo, accusing him (without foundation) of being responsible for the deaths of two policemen in a clash with the coca growers. This maneuver, however, had the opposite effect: it cast him into the limelight, and in the presidential elections of the following July he came in second, a mere 1.4 percentage points behind Sánchez de Lozada. Between the MAS and Felipe Quispe's Movimiento Indígena Pachakuti (MIP), *indígenas*/peasants came to occupy nearly a third of the seats in Congress. A little more than a year later, a series of protests against the new government's gas policies (considered to be overly favorable to the interests of foreign companies) culminated in massive roadblocks and demonstrations, mainly in and around the city of El Alto. The violent response of the government helped tilt the advantage in the protestors' favor, forcing Sánchez de Lozada to resign the presidency and then flee the country. Following two transition governments—led by Carlos Mesa and Eduardo Rodríguez, respectively (by constitutional succession)—fresh elections in December 2005 ended in the landslide victory for Evo and the MAS. Not since the return to democracy in 1982 had a government been elected by such a large margin.

Much of the symbolic political capital accumulated since then by Morales and the MAS comes from his being the first militant *indígena* ever elected president in Bolivia—or, for that matter, anywhere in Latin America.[12] However, his electoral support did not come only from the indigenous sector; he was supported by other social movements, including the *cocaleros*, trade unions (both campesino unions and urban workers), and neighborhood associations (*juntas vecinales*). He also appealed to the traditional Left, which had been displaced politically since 1985, and even to concerned sectors of the middle class.

Beyond such symbolic appeal, Morales's program combined an ethnic discourse (synthesized by proposals for a plurinational and intercultural country) and a more traditional left-wing one that sought to improve the distribution of resources and opportunities at home while at the same time increasing the state's scope for maneuver and autonomy vis-à-vis multinational business interests and the foreign countries backing them.[13] To this end, the MAS government has taken important steps toward rebuilding a powerful and unitary state. In many respects, this harks back to the 1952 model, but it also projects a new message regarding ethnicity and the need to destroy all vestiges of neocolonialism. It thus seeks to combine the plurinational quality of the new state with one that is strong and unitary.

Internationally, the government found itself on an unusually favorable footing, both economically (given the high prices of gas and other commodities) and politically (in view of the leftward shift in many other Latin American countries). Domestically, however, the growing confrontation between the western highlands and valleys, the poorest part of the country and home to the majority of the population, and the more affluent power groups able to rally support in the lowland crescent (the *media luna*, or half moon usually understood to comprise the departments of Santa Cruz, Tarija, Pando, and Beni), has created a difficult situation. As José Luis Roca shows in chapter 4, this polarization has a long history behind it. To some extent it was mitigated by the strengthening of municipalities under the Law of Popular Participation, but it returned with new force during the short and weak administration of Carlos Mesa (2003–2005). Mesa's period in office revealed the stark opposition between the 2003 "October Agenda" strongly supported in El Alto and the western part of the country and the 2004 "July Agenda" of Santa Cruz and the *media luna*. Arguably, this is a contradiction that has been unnecessarily exacerbated by some of the positions adopted by the MAS government.

This conflict demands analysis of the meaning of autonomy within a state that is at once unitary and plurinational. What emerges is that, in practice, there are a range of different sorts of autonomy: the departmental autonomies demanded by the *media luna*, municipal autonomies inspired by the Law of Popular Participation, and the indigenous territorial autonomies defended by the government. Each has different powers and responsibilities that are yet to be properly defined. This task of definition was central to the work of the Constituent Assembly, which starkly revealed the conflicting agendas of the ruling MAS majority, perhaps overly dazzled by the 54 percent majority it won in the July assembly elections, and an opposition minority determined to recover the ground lost to the MAS. This is the paradox of a government that came to power through democratic, electoral means, winning a substantial majority but which, failing to remove its opponents from the field, found itself unable to carry out its plans. This contrasts, for example, with the situation in 1952 when, following the bloody revolution that destroyed the opposition, the MNR imposed its own agenda.

Some Recurrent Dialectical Traits

To conclude, this section will briefly highlight some of the dialectical tensions that tend to repeat themselves through history and which help us detect some of the continuities that underlie widely varying conjunctures. The first two are, in my opinion, the most fundamental; the others are complementary.

The first tension is between ethnic identity—or identities—and a unifying national identity. In remotest times, there was a diversity of ethnic identities. These only crystallized around specific territorial notions following the patterns of settlement that took place during the colonial period. This period also saw a dilution of ethnic particularities through the emergence of a more generic polarization between white Spaniards and *criollos,* on the one hand, and *indios* and indigenous groups on the other. There was thus an implicit convergence between different ethnic peoples around the fundamental contradiction of the colonial period and its neocolonial aftermath.

This therefore is the oldest and most enduring conditioning factor affecting both politics and social formation in Bolivia. Neither biological *mestizaje* during the colonial period nor the subsequent period of cultural *mestizaje,* which after 1952 became the ideological backdrop of Bolivian national identity, has managed to replace it—as the reemergence of ethnic politics from the 1960s onward makes plain.

A legal corollary of this first tension is the search for greater complementarity between individual citizen rights—which point toward national unity—and collective rights, among which the specific rights of each indigenous group loom large. Indigenous peoples thus have a double demand: to be first-class citizens, without discrimination on the basis of ethnic origins, while at the same time having their right to be different respected. In other words, they want to be equal while maintaining their different cultural identities. This can also have consequences for territoriality and the degree of unity and autonomy within a territory, not just with respect to departments and municipalities but also to other criteria derived from their identity and organization as indigenous peoples.

The second tension is between ethnicity and class. This relates to the way in which the (neo)colonial structure came about. The polarization between the Spanish-*criollo* on top and the indigenous beneath already had many of the contradictory elements of a ruling class versus an exploited one. How this was explained in terms of class conflict is rather more recent, linked to new ways of interpreting politics, society, and the economy that were introduced in Europe during the course of the nineteenth century. But the way in which such ideas arrived and adapted themselves to the reality of Latin America—from Mexico down to the southern tip of Chile—has maintained this dialectical tension. At the beginning of the twentieth century, these new Marxist currents involved a degree of synthesis when it became clear that the *indio* was the poorest of the poor. Influenced by the thinking of José Carlos Mariátegui in Peru, this was highlighted in Bolivia by people such as Tristán Marof and José Antonio Arze.[14] Later on, however, because of the greater degree of internationalism of the Marxist-inspired parties, the tendency was to view class struggle as the fundamental contradiction. The ethnic contradiction was relegated to something superstructural, or even as something dangerously racist.

The rediscovery of the cultural wealth of poor indigenous people came about first through the work of artists and literary figures. One such was the novelist and student of Quechua, Jesús Lara, who was also the Communist Party's presidential candidate in 1951. More recently there has been the filmmaker Jorge Sanjinés. But it was also the achievement of *originario* peoples themselves. In spite of being organized in peasant unions, they began to appreciate the importance of different cultural ideologies, especially during the decadence of the 1952 state during the period of the military regimes. They began to insist on the importance of their diverse cultural indentities, seeing themselves as distinct ethnic peoples and not just as generic *indios* or *indígenas.* It was only much later that the international concern for ethnicity arose, a product of the collapse of socialism in Europe and Asia and the abandoning of class as the only model for interpreting social reality. The risk was that in the debacle, the baby would be thrown out with the bath water, and one would fall into a kind of reductionism through reference to the ethnic pole alone. This is what appeared to happen in Bolivia and other Latin American countries when governments and neoliberal-inspired international agencies began to incorporate multiethnicity and pluriculturalism into their various constitutional arrangements (Sieder 2002). At the same time, they imposed a neoliberal vision which veered toward reducing the size of the state and banishing ideas of class. It is from this that the distinction arises between the *indio permitido,* accepted by the state, and the *indio alzado,* rebellious and revolutionary in ways that the dominant society cannot tolerate.

These changes and continuities over time do not constitute contradictory perspectives where only one is correct. Nor do they constitute a chronological evolution from ethnicity to modern class-based politics, or vice versa. A metaphor that used to be common years ago among the Kataristas states: ethnicity and class are the two eyes through which to understand reality, or the two feet with which to move through it. It is precisely the emergence of Evo and the MAS into government that has led the bull to be grasped by the horns, both in domestic policy and in terms of international relations. His government and the Constituent Assembly needed to exercise caution in using these two eyes, two hands, and two feet when it came to interpreting and transforming Bolivia's complex national reality.

On the way, other complementary dialectical tensions have emerged that relate to the two foregoing. Here I would highlight two. The first, in effect the third of our tensions, is the rural-urban tension. A catalyst here is the fact that it is in rural areas where both poverty and indigenousness is concentrated, both demographically and culturally. The cities, on the other hand, concentrate greater wealth and the hegemony of a nonindigenous culture that is open to other cultural influences (whether new or not) emanating from ever more pervasive globalization. This contradiction in the past often led to the perverse and scientifically unsustainable conclusion that the rural sector was poorest precisely because it was most influenced by ancient cultures; the solution therefore was to civilize them and extend cultural *mestizaje:* in other words, to help them abandon their own culture and bring them within the dominant Hispanic-*criollo* one.

In recent decades, an important variant has emerged within this tension, as a consequence of the huge increase in migration, first from the countryside to the cities or to the advancing agricultural frontier, and more recently from Bolivia to other countries. The net effect of this is that the majority of those who define themselves as belonging to indigenous groups now live in urban areas, often (but not always) in their poor peripheries. Over the long run, second- and third-generation migrants undergo significant changes in their sense of what it is to be *originario,* losing their links with their place of family origin. Still, there are also many who continue to identify themselves as such, even though they no longer speak an indigenous language, and who say they are mestizos at the same time. Many also keep a foot in both areas, as if the city was now another "eco-socioeconomic" resource for their people to make use of. The city of El Alto is the most notable example, although not the only one by any means. Of its population, 74 percent identified themselves as Aymara in the 2001 census, even though only 48 percent speak Aymara (an additional 3 percent speak Quechua). The proportion is lower among the younger generation. It is for this reason that El Alto, which only fairly recently achieved its administrative independence from La Paz, acts as a sort of hinge between the urban metropolis of La Paz/El Alto and the surrounding Aymara countryside where nearly 40 percent of its population was born. It was for this reason that the popular upsurge in October 2003, of which El Alto was the focal point, has been described by many as an "Aymaran rebellion." To some extent, therefore, the strength of migratory flows shifts the rural-versus-urban contradiction to one of rural plus impoverished and ethnically defined urban peripheries versus wealthier, more central, and *criollo* urban areas.

The fourth tension is regionalism. This has polarized into the contradiction between *collas* and *cambas* or, if you will, between the Andean west and the *media luna* that includes both the eastern lowlands and Tarija. These regional antagonisms are of long standing, to the point that some commentators believe they are the main contradiction in the country. Thus it is that the demand for autonomy is so key to the *media luna.* In its current form, this dualism has taken on a new aspect which, according to some, could—if not handled properly—break asunder the viability of Bolivia as a country.

Simplifying things and resisting the temptation to include other equally relevant variables, this tension is not unconnected to the two fundamental ones mentioned previously. The ecological, cultural, socioeconomic, and political differences between the Andean macroregion and the lowlands go back to precolonial times and have persisted with only minor changes (such as the grouping of Tarija with the departments of the eastern lowlands for cultural and economic reasons, even though its most populated portions are ecologically Andean in nature). These are also reasons that go a long way to explaining the present polarization between the Andean west and the *media luna*. In class terms, the control exercised by the elites of the *media luna* over natural resources is fundamental, from land through to hydrocarbons. There are many more rich people in the lowlands than in the western part of the country, long impoverished by the decline of mining and the loss of links to maritime commerce. If on top of this we add, in ethnic terms, the dominance of Hispanic-*criollo* culture in the *media luna* over that of fragmented and dispersed lowland ethnic minorities and migrants from the Andes, it becomes clear why this polarization finds an echo among other sectors of the population—even within the lowlands, where it had never been challenged before.

These are not the only dialectical tensions that have emerged over the centuries. For example, there is a persistent dilemma between unity and factionalism within social and ethnic movements. There are the regional movements mentioned above. The growing impact of globalization, which among other things reflects itself in international and intercontinental migration, is generating new ties and new identities. But the four tensions I have focused on here should be sufficient to show how, amid the changes that are constantly taking place, we continue to confront problems and issues which have long historical roots.

2

Let the Mestizos Stand Up and Be Counted

CARLOS TORANZO ROCA

However much you cost, how much you're worth, my love,
if you don't have enough, I'll pay you. . . .
If you want to dance, *morenada*, you've got to have a little cash.
—Refrain of "Cuánto Cuestas, Cuánto Vales"

It is necessary to rescue the discussion of *mestizaje* from the depositary of things forgotten, and indeed, to speak of multiple *mestizajes,* because if we are talking about mestizos, it should be in the plural, not the singular. I do not intend to embark on a theoretical discussion, or to enter very far into the jungle of statistics to come up with valid arguments; rather, I seek to bring into play intuitions and perceptions from everyday life that can help us understand the variegated world of mestizos, a world which is important in helping us understand the Bolivia of today, and indeed that of tomorrow.

The reasoning contained in this chapter and the sort of intuitions it brings to bear are based on a basic premise: that it is fruitless to talk of societies—ancient or modern—as if they were homogenous, or to try to impose some sort of monoculture when dealing with political and social development. There have been many failures throughout history in seeking to reduce society to standardizations. Western culture was unable to impose Cartesianism as the only way of thinking, and various types of socialism (now just a memory) came equally unstuck in trying to impose standardization. In Bolivia, the Movimiento Nacionalista Revolucionario (MNR), which spearheaded the national revolution of 1952, found itself unable to clothe all Bolivians in the homogenous garb of *mestizaje.* Notwithstanding dreams about cultural transformation, recent efforts have been no more successful in painting the whole of society with the brush of *indigenismo.* Such is the dynamic of culture and identity—not least in this era globalization, when the Internet and the mobile phone, not to mention migration, affect what we are and every day bring change in everything, including our identities. However, change does not obliterate the past; rather, it modifies our view of it, recreating reality, culture, and identity. These are fluid, changeable, differentiated, and are not fixed in time.

Interpreting the Data

Statistics are one key to analysis; without empirical evidence, both qualitative and quantitative, it is hard to advance very far with research. But though data are essential, they do not tell us everything. We have to balance them with perceptions if we want properly to understand the issues we study. Moreover, data are often inadequate and imprecise in countries that are underdeveloped and that lack institutional continuity (Verdesoto and Zuazo 2006). So it is up to the writer—perhaps more so the reader—to use common sense when it comes to analyzing and interpreting data. Data generate intuitions and perceptions, rather than absolute truth: not least so when we are dealing with such intricate things as ethnicity or cultural identity. Furthermore, the problem of data is accentuated by the passage of time; present-day numbers do not necessarily mean exactly what they did a hundred years ago. It is one thing to talk of white, mestizo, and indigenous peoples in 1900, and quite another today.

The study of Bolivian census data therefore produces many anomalies. According to the 1900 population census, 51 percent of Bolivians were indigenous, 27 percent mestizo, and 13 percent white.[1] The 1950 census stated that 63 percent were indigenous and 37 percent mestizo. What stands out here is that there was no "white" category in the 1950 census, which prevented those who might have thought of themselves as white from self-identifying as such. The 1900 and 1950 censuses are, therefore, not strictly comparable. However, they provide referential data, and in this regard it is interesting to ask why the percentage of indigenous people and mestizos was higher in 1950 than in 1900.

The 1992 census reported that only 8.1 percent of the population (over the age of six) was monolingual in Quechua, and 3.2 percent in Aymara. Here it is clear that the Spanish-speaking population had increased, whether monolingual or bilingual. This suggests a cultural shift with respect to people's identities. However, it is important to distinguish between the acquisition of the Spanish language from the loss of indigenous identity. Instead, the trend suggests that people's perception of their identity was becoming rather more complex.

The Human Security Survey, conducted in 1996 by the Bolivian office of the UNDP (United Nations Development Program), in contrast, picks up on ethnic self-perceptions among Bolivians. Of the respondents, 16 percent identified as indigenous, 67 percent as mestizo, and 17 percent as white (Calderón and Toranzo 1996). Although these figures are not strictly comparable with the census data, they challenge our intuitions. It is perhaps odd that anyone should perceive themselves as being white in a country such as Bolivia, after centuries of ethnic mixing and *mestizaje*. A more accurate description of the majority of the population might be "coffee colored." However, it is interesting that researchers at least give the people they are interviewing the option of describing themselves as white.

Other surveys also penetrate into the world of ethnic self-perception. The 1998 Latin American Public Opinion (LAPOP), carried out by Vanderbilt University, identified 9.8 percent of the people it surveyed as indigenous or *originarios*, 62.6 percent as mestizo, and 23.3 percent as white. A UNDP survey two years later, based on slightly different data, estimated the proportion of mestizos and whites to be roughly of the same order (67 percent and 17 percent, respectively).

The 2004 LAPOP survey revealed that indigenous peoples or *originarios* made up 15.6 percent of the population, mestizos 60.6 percent, and whites 19.4 percent. The figure for mestizos is thus not significantly different from six years earlier and represents a large part of the population. More noteworthy here is that those who considered themselves indigenous rose from 9.8 percent to 15.6 percent, apparently reflecting the resurgence in *indigenista* discourse in these years, ones in which both the neoliberal paradigm and the traditional party system were beset by crisis.

In its 2006 figures, LAPOP suggested that indigenous peoples and *originarios* were 19.3 percent, mestizos 64.8 percent, and whites 11 percent. Not only do mestizos account for nearly two-thirds of the population, but the figure here is higher than in 2004, despite of the boom of *indigenismo* that accompanied the inauguration of the Evo Morales government in January 2006. Nevertheless, the numbers identifying themselves as indigenous also exhibit an increase over 2004, with the only category to shrink in size being whites. Even middle-class intellectuals and professionals began assume an indigenous identity.

Here, it is worthwhile returning to the 2001 census for persons aged 15 or above. In the census, people were asked if they felt they belonged to any of the following *originario* peoples: Quechua, Aymara, Guaraní, Chiquitano, Mojeño, "other," or to none at all. This census is clearly different and not comparable to previous ones, as the census form did not offer the choice of identifying as mestizo. As a result, 62 percent considered themselves to belong to one or another indigenous group.[2] The meaning of this 62 percentage figure is ambiguous. Not all data should be treated as completely accurate, and just as there were failings in the 1900, 1959, 1976, and 1992 censuses, there is no reason to assume that the 2001 census is completely accurate, especially when it omitted something so much a part of Bolivian reality as the process of *mestizaje* that has taken place over the centuries. Many Bolivians—perhaps the majority—feel themselves to be part of this ethnic and cultural mix.

The same census reveals the significant fact that only 11 percent of the total population was monolingual in an indigenous language. Subtracting this from the 62 percent who declared themselves indigenous, we conclude that 51 percent of population identified as indigenous and yet are either monolingual or bilingual in Spanish. Once again, it is not that we want to argue that the fact that people speak Spanish means that they are no longer indigenous; only that our intuition would lead us to think that speaking Spanish has many connotations that have a bearing on ethnicity. It involves a change in customs and culture. In these circumstances, being indigenous is no longer a categorical distinction; it becomes a matter of combining things in ways that renders reality more complex and differentiated. People feel and live this complexity, and it affects their self-perception. The 2001 census established that 62.4 percent of the population was urban and 37.6 percent rural. Again, we would not argue that living in an urban environment is synomymous with being white or mestizo, and it is clearly the case that most of the urban population is of popular extraction. To suggest that urban migrants become "white" is a misreading, but individuals should be allowed to so self-identify in the census if they wish to. This could not be done in 2001 in the case of mestizos.

The fact that 44.8 percent of Bolivians have migrated at some point is also relevant. The primary patterns are rural-urban and international migration, but there are also many instances of rural-rural migration. Is it not probable that people's culture, habits, language, customs, and self-perceptions undergo a change as they migrate from their place of origin, creating a more diverse and variegated society? Do not those who migrate pick up traits of *mestizaje*? Are they still as indigenous or *originario* as they were centuries ago? Do they retain the "long memory" in the same way when this no longer strikes a chord with everyday experience?

Those who argue that 62 percent of Bolivians are indigenous find themselves relativizing some of their own assumptions, since they admit that although in the 2001 census 74 percent of those living in El Alto said they were Aymara (because of the lack of an option to say they are mestizo), only 48 percent could actually speak Aymara. An opinion survey carried out by the Fundación UNIR Bolivia in 2006 in the various departmental capitals and El Alto showed that 56 percent of those who identified themselves as Aymara also perceived themselves to be mestizo. The equivalent figure for Quechuas is 76 percent; for Chiquitanos it is 79 percent.

Statistics are wonderful things, because they allow us to enquire whether people feel themselves to be mestizos first and foremost and then ask them if they see themselves as Aymara, Quechua, or members of some other ethnic group. But statistics are not without their intentionality or purpose. For this reason, we urge the reader to use his or her intuition when it comes to considering many of the figures mentioned here.

Discussion of the UNIR findings tilts us toward an analysis that is more complex but that better enables us to understand what we wish to analyze by giving proper emphasis to mixture, ambivalence, complexity, and diversity. We need to offer people the freedom to identify themselves as many things at the same time, not least perceiving themselves as mestizo. It should not be just out of political correctness (at a time when *indigenismo* is in vogue) that we only mention indigenous and *originarios,* particularly when confronted by an evident truth that the situation is far more complex and variegated. There needs to be scope in the statistics for all to feel free to say that they are *cholos,* mestizos, Aymaras, and Quechuas, separately or all at once. People should not be obliged to belonging to a single ethnic identity, still less a specific culture.

The Logic of Black and White, or the Invisibility of Tones In Between

Social and political analysis in Bolivia, including the analysis of societies in the past, tends to identify and highlight contrary aspects or opposites, to tease out contradictions, to identify black and white. There is much less interest in detecting tonality, the combinations or mixtures of elements. At each point in history, we like to subscribe to what is good and denounce evil, adopting Manichaean positions. Either we decry things or become apologists for them; there is no proper effort to build conceptual bridges. Concepts tend to fall captive to militancy, and in the process they lose much of their analyti- cal utility.

In spite of the undoubted quality of much historical analysis undertaken in Bolivia, rigid concepts are often employed that bring fixity just when history involves ever-changing situations and concepts. Concepts have very different reference points over time, and they are far from frozen. To talk of *criollos* in the colonial period is not the same as to talk of them in the twenty-first century. To refer to whites and *indígenas* in the nineteenth century meant something different than to do so in the twentieth century.

Much historical analysis also fails to give proper consideration to gradu- alism, idealizing revolution in the belief that when these happen, everything should change. If a whiff of the past remains, then it is assumed that the revolution or process of change was mere reformism, or else that there are Machiavellian schemes afoot to preserve the old order. Such thinking fails to grasp the fact that not everything changes at one go; rather, historical processes—revolutions included—change what they can, but not necessarily what they want. Much of this emerges in the analysis of *mestizaje* in Bolivia, and in particular in the analysis of indigenous issues. This tendency to down- play the results of revolution leads analysts to give undue stress to things like the regeneration of colonialism and the maintenance of white dominance. All processes of political and social change therefore tend to be viewed in this distrusting way. The ideological battle between whites and *indígenas* has reached such a pitch that the intellectual standard-bearers of *indigenismo* (themselves often mestizos of humble origins) use the terminology of ethnic obliteration (*etno fagia*) to refer to experiences of institutional innovation like Popular Participation, one of the more profound political reforms of re- cent times which in fact did much to promote democratization and social inclusion in Bolivia.

Dualistic analysis (Zuazo 2006), involving a good deal of Manichaeism, has long been present in Bolivia. Some classic oppositions include: penin- sular-born Spaniards versus American-born *criollos*, whites versus *indios*, *k'aras* (literally "naked"—that is, "white") versus *t'aras* (an idealized indige- nous identity), nation versus antination, dominant classes versus dominated classes, urban versus rural, *collas* (highlanders) versus *cambas* (lowlanders), west versus east (or *media luna*) and so on.[3] Such approaches have suffused the debate over ethnicity, eliminating the shades and tonality not just from the statistics but from the analysis as well. Dualistic thinking concedes no space for coffee-colored people; it does not tolerate mixture but instead reasons only in terms of polar opposites. One of the most important conservative intellectuals of the early twentieth century, Alcides Arguedas, in "Pueblo enfermo," told us that the problem of Bolivia was one of *indios*, at the beginning of the twenty-first century the more radical *indigenistas* maintain that the problem is one of white oligarchies from the east of the country, counting as white the *cunumi* bourgeoisie from the popular sectors of Santa Cruz.

Racism is never far removed from this sort of discussion. Not only is the analysis dualistic, but it is further perverted by racist overtones. Here there have been some notable sinners. Franz Tamayo revalued *los indios,* but he had a low opinion of *cholos.*[4] Like many others, he remained wedded to the notion that the *cholo* was the worst type of mestizo. But where does the definitional frontier between *cholo* and mestizo lie today?

Following this racial line of reasoning, the sort of liberalism to emerge in the early twentieth century—which should have considered all Bolivians as citizens—did not view favorably the idea of citizens participating in the construction of politics and society. On the contrary, its inspiration was in social Darwinism, with its focus on the superiority of one race (whites) over another (indigenous peoples) and the need for the latter to be expunged. How did such liberalism view Bolivian history? Did it understand why the people rose up behind "El Cholo" Belzu thirty years earlier?[5] (Peredo 1992). What importance did it afford to the mass of artisans and popular entrepreneurs in the corn beer (chicha) and coca trades, businesses hardly run by powerful liberals or the classic bourgeoisie?

Such popular sectors were not born from one day to another under the republic but instead had lengthy historical roots. They were (with some definitional license) the mestizos of the nineteenth and early twentieth centuries. They were those who built their identities, their position in society, their culture to an important degree around their changing economic status within the process of economic development. We say "to an important degree" because these sorts of changes play an important part in the process of *mestizaje,* but they are not the only factors at work. Here we want to avoid the exaggerations of old-style Marxism which liked to explain everything in terms of economic change, and to see the evolution of social status as part of a broader spectrum of transformations. These include *mestizaje,* involving as it does changes in identity, culture, habits of life, place of residence, language, self-perceptions, and many other things that fall outside the scope of this chapter.

If social Darwinist racism was part and parcel of the liberalism of the nineteenth and early twentieth century, it cannot be said that all traces of it have vanished, whether among the elites, among mestizos and *cholos* (which are practically the same thing), or among indigenous peoples. In spite of the Chaco War and the way it brought people together from different parts of Bolivia and from different social classes, and in spite of the national revolution of 1952, anti-indigenous sentiments and ideas have lingered on among social, political, and economic elites. Sometimes these anti-indigenous positions emerged with greater force among *cholos*, which is the main reason why René Zavaleta, one of the foremost intellectuals of the second half of the twentieth century, maintained the existence of a paradox of social status in Bolivia, in which oligarchic and lordly patterns of behavior are not only regenerated among the elites, but indeed (which is perhaps worse) among those who are not oligarchs or landlords. With more than just a hint of racism, this is one of the negative aspects of everyday life in Bolivia.

Furthermore, although many theoreticians may be reluctant to admit it, racism is not a monopoly of those who wield power, insofar as the indigenous or *originario* population, and many of their intellectuals, also practice their own sort of social Darwinism—believing, for example, in the superiority of the Aymara over all others. At a time when *indigenismo* is so much in vogue, many applaud the idea of imposing Aymara culture, since it has become the accepted route to social and political inclusion, failing, however, to acknowledge the monoculturalism that this implies. The talk is no longer talk of cultural multiplicity or a diversity of *originario* peoples, but of an imposed Aymara hegemony, a shift from multiculturalism to monoculturalism under the pretext of defending *indigenismo.*

Just as the liberals of the early twentieth century failed to grasp the reality they lived in—failing to see the mestizo of that time, so absorbed were they by the opposition of white and *indio*—so too today one has the impression that the mestizo is equally in danger of being left out of the equation. Such mestizos are not oligarchic elites or professionals with degrees from foreign universities. They are simply *cholos* of all sorts: street sellers, informal workers, members of the *cholo* bourgeoisie or *cunumis,* the self-employed, truck drivers, contraband dealers, public employees, taxi drivers, metal workers, carpenters, ice-cream sellers, and (perhaps surprisingly) many coca farmers.

In the wake of the process of economic democratization initiated in 1952, these mestizos are the popular middle class of our time (UNDP 2005). If we do not open our eyes to this multiplicity, we cannot begin to grasp the sort of social change that has taken place in Bolivia over the seventy-five years since the Chaco War, or even the fifty-five years since the national revolution.

National Revolution, Social Democratization, and *Mestizaje*

If the liberalism of the early twentieth century was social Darwinist and these ideas underpinned social construction at the time, it was no less true that in the 1930s, at the time of the Chaco War (1932–1935), nationalist ideology and various different sorts of Marxism became entrenched. These new currents were highly critical of liberal thought and the preexisting oligarchic state. The war with Paraguay, more than just an armed conflict that Bolivia lost (although oddly Bolivia did not lose the hydrocarbon resources that the oil companies that backed Paraguay purportedly wanted), proved pivotal. The conflict proved to be a social melting pot that brought together Bolivians of different ethnicities and social backgrounds from rural and urban areas, from east and west. It encapsulated the notion of *mezclaje* and helped forge new identities. It was in the burning sands of the Chaco, where *cambas, collas,* and *chapacos* (Tarijeños) all engaged with one another, that the idea of the nation emerged. If, when they arrived on the battlefield, the peasants shouted "Long Live General Bolivia," three years on, when the war had ended, they had a rather different impression of Bolivia as a nation to be built. But while peasant troops defended their country, many landlords simply took over their land without the least thought for the nation, that nation which those who fought in the Chaco had started to think about.

By the time the war ended, not only had those who had taken part changed, but new forms of government were beginning to emerge in the form of nationalist military regimes. Demonstrating its nationalist credentials, the government of Colonel David Toro nationalized the oil industry in 1937, only two years after the war ended. Nationalism, unlike oligarchic liberalism, took a high profile. Many indigenous peasants, particularly those from the valley of Cochabamba, began to occupy the land. Others tried to throw out the landlords. The refrain of Tristan Marof was heard with increasing frequency: *"tierras al indio y minas al estado"* (land to the Indian, mines to the state). At the same time, a civil nationalism made itself felt, with the MNR at its core. Early on, from 1943 to 1946, the MNR allied itself with the nationalist military leader Gualberto Villaroel. His dictum was that he was not an enemy of the rich, but more a friend to the poor.

So while military nationalism was born under Toro, social constitutionalism took root under Villaroel. Villaroel took concrete measures to benefit the workers. It was at this time that a Labor Inspectorate (Inspector General del Trabajo) came into being, the precursor of the Ministry of Labor. More important perhaps, the First Indigenous Congress took place under Villaroel. This was not just a state initiative to launch an inquiry into the problems of indigenous peoples, but rather a response to their mobilization. As is usually the case in Bolivia, the state tends to listen only when forced to do so by the clamor of mass mobilization. It was also at this time that the Bolivian Miners' Federation (the Federación Sindical de Trabajadores Mineros de Bolivia, FSTMB) came into being. The FSTMB became the nucleus of union activity in Bolivia, but a union activity with a revolutionary credo that saw itself as a force for political change and not just a tool for the pursuit of economic demands. It played a key role in the social mobilization of the 1940s, as well as in constructing the revolutionary state in 1952. Much later on, at the end of the twentieth century and the beginning of the twenty-first, it still provided a model for organizing the coca workers' federations and in building the Movimiento al Socialismo (MAS), which brought Evo Morales to power in 2005–2006.

The idea of the nation was thus born out of the Chaco War. Between 1935 and 1952, amid nationalist military governments and conservative countercoups, the idea of eliminating the old oligarchic state took root. This was achieved with the 1952 revolution, with the MNR at its head and in alliance with popular middle-class groups, intellectuals, mine and factory workers, and peasants. It thus involved a good part of the social mosaic of the nation. As does any revolution, 1952 brought about some profound changes: the introduction of universal suffrage, the reform of the educational system, the nationalization of the mines, and (especially important for our purposes) agrarian reform. The last of these was particularly significant for its impact on highland Bolivia and the inter-Andean valleys, but it left large-scale property intact in the eastern lowlands. The introduction of citizenship, which the MNR strived to promote, led to changes of no less significance: the development of a class of small-scale peasant smallholders made up not of *indios* or the ex-peons of the landed estates but of campesinos, a class label that the MNR grafted onto this social group. The MNR, indeed, sought to bury the notion of *indios,* seeing this term as a reflection of centuries-old social discrimination.

This was a notable step forward at the time. However, thirty years later, it had become common to look at these social changes through much more skeptical eyes. Many *indigenistas* claimed that the MNR was guilty of trying to deprive the campesino (by that time referred to as *indígenas* or *originarios*) of their identity, their culture, and their traditions, with a view to reconstituting neocolonialism. For them, the revolution had failed to introduce more far-reaching changes or to generate the true revolution that the country had been waiting for by banishing colonialism and reviving the traditional institutions and identities of its *originario* peoples.

Such arguments notwithstanding, the introduction of universal suffrage in 1952 helped democratize politics, although the full effects were only felt in the 1990s and in the first few years of the new century. The fact that Evo Morales won the presidency by means of the popular vote was indicative. At the same time, the agrarian reform eliminated the landowning class (*gamonales*) in the west of the country and the central valleys, although it became evident that a new landowning class was establishing itself in the eastern half. Likewise, the educational reforms helped provide access to education for children in both rural and urban sectors, even though some analysts have argued that this was a schooling that deprived them of their identities, customs, institutions, and language. Finally, by ridding Bolivia of the "tin barons," the nationalization of the mines helped bring an end to the oligarchic state, although this is not to say that important new business interests were not to arise within the mining industry.

The 1952 revolution not only brought social democratization; it also made possible an economic democratization by opening up scope for other social sectors to become economic actors with the potential for accumulation. As we have seen, there had been sectors devoted to marketing coca or producing and selling *chicha* back in colonial and early republican times (Rodríguez and Solares 1990). There had also been artisans who had carried out a range of economic activities. However, the 1952 revolution opened up a much wider range of economic possibilities to these and other popular sectors. They took advantage of these openings, demonstrating a nose for the market and developing a business acumen, especially in commerce and certain productive areas. Symptomatic was the growth of contraband in the 1950s and 1960s, the development in interprovincial, interdepartmental, and urban transport, the metalworking industry and jewelry trades, the meat trade, the wholesale grocery business, the sale of domestic electrical appliances, and other areas of marketing (Barragán 2006a).

All this activity, both in the west and east of the country, gave rise to prosperous *cholo* and *cunumi* bourgeoisies. To what extent are these new business owners indigenous? They would seem to be more part of a new *mestizaje;* although they may be of indigenous or campesino origin, their everyday existence makes them a symbiosis or mixture of many elements. This does not necessarily mean that they cease to be what they were before, but their everyday lives are changed, enriched, and rendered more complex. This is what mixture and *mestizaje* is all about. While the MNR promoted industrialization, what it actually produced was nonindustrial urbanization with a large measure of informality. Two-thirds of the economically active population is informal, including the self-employed, small-scale sellers, shopkeepers, ice-cream sellers, taxi drivers, bus drivers, newspaper sellers, barbers, tailors, plumbers, bricklayers, and many others besides. Such sectors feel themselves to be many different things at the same time, at once *originarios* but also as Bolivians and mestizos. Yet they feel themselves to be only a part of the great multiplicity of mestizos that exist, not some sort of universal mestizo (which does not exist). It is one thing to be a mestizo in the Siete Calles (the market district) of Santa Cruz, something else in the affluent neighborhood of Equipetrol, or in Montero to the north of that same city. Likewise it is distinct in Quillacollo (to the west of the city of Cochabamba), in El Alto, in La Paz's Pérez Velasco commercial district), or in its prosperous Zona Sur neighborhood. Each is different, a reality that is a far cry from the dreams of social standardization of the MNR and of the 1952 revolution.

Mestizos do not just consist of the *cholo* bourgeoisie; the category includes other broader sectors, like those mentioned above, that comprise the popular middle classes, sectors which sociology finds it hard to pin down as part of Bolivia's variegated middle class because they do not wear collar and tie. Whereas such apparel may not be their common currency, the fiesta most certainly is. The accumulation of popular culture is something that has matured over centuries, although it has gained force since 1952. The popular middle-class *cholos* with economic resources, wealthy but popular mestizos, are not the same as those mestizos who form part of the elite and think of themselves as white. Popular mestizos form a sizeable proportion of the national economy. Though for years they would dance to celebrate the Señor del Gran Poder in the popular neighborhood of Rosario in La Paz, today they

take over the whole city center. This is not just an expression of economic accumulation, but a cultural force of those who are not indigenous in the strict
sense of the word but rather the bearers of multiple identities that reflect a
popular urban culture. Popular culture, or the national popular culture promoted by the legacy of the 1952 revolution, is present in the cultural make-up
of many mestizo sectors. They may no longer support the MNR, but they feel
adherence to national popular culture, which may mean that they end up
rejecting their campesino or indigenous heritage (Mayorga 1993).

Max Fernández exemplifies this pragmatism and its political expression.
Fernández, a successful businessman from the *cholo* bourgeoisie, not only
rose to ownership of the country's largest brewery, but founded a party, the
Unión Cívica Solidaridad (UCS), which formed part of a number of governments in the 1980s and 1990s. It offered proof of how the political system
opened itself up to other social actors during the period of democratization
that began in 1982 with the government of the Unidad Democrática y Popular
(UDP) under the presidency of Hernán Siles Zuazo (Mayorga 1997). Fernández was not alone in this respect. "Compadre" Carlos Palenque rose to fame
on the popularity of his radio program, and his party, Conciencia de Patria
(Condepa), also formed a part of some government coalitions. Palenque appealed to the hearts of migrants such as himself in the city of La Paz who,
though not wealthy themselves, were engaging in processes of economic
accumulation and rendering the process of *mestizaje* ever more complex
(Toranzo 1992).

These new social actors, with their representation in the political sphere,
provide examples of the process of social democratization at work, and of the
ways in which the political and party systems were opening themselves up
to the popular sectors. Yet, in spite of this political modernization, it cannot
be denied that the culture of discrimination remained largely intact. In this
sense, the nature of the discrimination that had existed during the colonial
period was quite different from that of the republic, and something quite
different yet again from what existed at the end of the twentieth century, or
which has endured into the twenty-first century under Evo Morales. Bolivia
is not free of discrimination, either of the anti-indigenous type or the anti-
popular attitudes of many elites, some of them now broken economically and
in decline. Do these elites open up their social clubs or their business federations to members of the *cholo* bourgeoisie? That they do not suggests that in
the absence of contact between such sectors, it is difficult to speak of a shared
national project.

What we need to be aware of in Bolivia today is that there are other elites, elites from the popular economy. We should not fall into the trap of just referring to "white" (or rather the coffee-colored) elites of the traditional oligarchy. The elite now extends to other groups and sectors: to the nouveaux riches of popular extraction (whether urban or rural), to the *cholo* bourgeoisie, and to new political elites from humbler backgrounds, whether urban or rural, or from party and union backgrounds. We need to take into account those who now control the state, both at the central and local levels. This is not the *ayllu* or some such indigenous phenomenon; it is a mixture of every type—cultural, political, economic, racial, linguistic—a mixture of traditional custom and new dreams for the future. All this leads us to conclude that politics, economics, the power structure, and identities are much more mixed, more mestizo, than used to be the case, even though this *mestizaje* at times buys into the *indigenista* discourse.

Representative Democracy Opens Up Space for *Mestizaje*

In 1982, not only was democracy—previously snuffed out by dictatorship—reestablished, but in a representative form that had not existed before. Whereas 1952 opened up channels for new actors to participate in the economy, 1982 opened up new spaces for political participation. Indeed, it was at this point that universal suffrage became a means by which people from popular sectors—campesinos, poor urban populations, indigenous peoples—found the way open to them to win representational posts.

This democratization involved many institutional reforms; it was not a minor matter that the constitution itself was reformed or that the country officially defined itself as "pluri-multi": pluriethnic and multicultural (Toranzo 2006a). It was significant that an educational reform was initiated, based on a system that was bilingual and intercultural. Nor should the so-called INRA Law (Instituto Nacional de Reforma Agraria) be ignored: it opened up space for indigenous landholding through the *Tierras Comunitarias de Orígen* (TCOs). But there can be little doubt that the most far-reaching reform was Popular Participation (Participación Popular), not only in its municipalization of Bolivia or its geographic redistribution of state spending, but its prorural outlook and the legal recognition it afforded to preexisting forms of social organization: neighborhood, district, trade union, peasant, and indigenous. The significance of a law cannot be measured by the mere fact that, through excessive voluntarism, it sought to invent reality; rather, because it recognized reality, what already existed, it was able to move from that reality forward toward a new future.

The MAS, and Evo Morales himself, was born—politically speaking—in the municipalities of the Cochabamba tropics; it was there that what became the MAS began to play a role in public policy, running the various municipalities it controlled. It was there that Morales made his mark as a uninominal (constituency-based) deputy. It was from a municipal base that he and his party projected their demands and actions into national politics. It is no exaggeration to say that what Bolivia is experiencing today, with Morales and the MAS in power, is a direct result of the reforms introduced by the 1952 revolution and the democratic reforms initiated in 1982. It was these that provided space for the Katarista movements that thirty years ago spoke of cultural diversity, for union movements that sought greater economic democratization, and—believe it or not—for political parties that opened up the political system and carried out institutional reforms often in response to social pressure from below but also as a result of their own instinct for self-preservation.[6] Nothing comes completely out of the blue; everything comes about through drawn-out processes in which there are revolutions, steps forward and also steps backward. What stands out in the Bolivian case is the length of the process of democratization, a process that began back in the Chaco War but whose full results are only now on offer today.

The fact that this period of democratization revised the constitution so as to recognize the state as pluriethnic and multicultural was an important step forward. Now, it would seem, the challenge is to build interculturalism, not a monoculturalism that turns its back on diversity. We need to assimilate the mosaic of mixtures that exists in today's Bolivia. Interculturalism cannot be constructed on the basis of a single culture, but on respect and recognition of otherness. Even if in the past indigenous peoples faced discrimination, this cannot be a pretext for removing today's mestizos from the scene or discriminating against them. Today's challenge is to ensure that all are given space and all are respected. If the 1952 revolution tried to impose a cultural model that was homogenously mestizo, the present and the future needs to stand up for mixture, a *mestizaje* that does not seek to ignore the past but recognizes change, mutation, and the building of plural identities.

The Bolivian citizen who lives in the United States or in Spain is not indigenous simply by virtue of his or her desire to *ch'allar*—to offer libations to the Pachamama, the Mother Earth. The ILO defines as indigenous those people who come from a community that is *originario* or who conserve some *originario* institutions; clearly the *ch'alla* is such an institution. But this does not turn the Bolivian living in Madrid or in Argentina into an *originario*. The Bolivian who lives in Bolivia, in the United States, in Argentina, in Spain or wherever, is a mixture of many cultures. Likewise, in Alasitas (a festival where attendees buy miniature versions of the things they hope to receive from the Ek'eko, the spirit of abundance), people buy euros and dollars, but by so doing they do not become imperialists. They do so simply because they recognize the logic of the market and their part in the process of globalization that moves relentlessly ahead. It is not for this reason that, as mestizos, and in spite of globalization, they resort to the *ch'alla* of the diminutive bank notes they acquire, but then as proof of syncretism have them blessed by the Catholic Church. By visiting McDonalds we do not forget our past, but nor should we turn ourselves into *originarios* in order to eulogize that past. What we need to construct is a better future, one that recognizes our diversity, the mixture of different types of *cholo*, the multiple *mestizajes* that make Bolivia what it is.

Oversimplifying Identities

The Debate over What Is *Indigena* and What Is Mestizo

DIEGO ZAVALETA REYLES

The Jew is a man, whom other men look upon as a jew . . .
JEAN-PAUL SARTRE, Réflexions sur la question juive (1946)

The arguments presented by Xavier Albó and Carlos Toranzo provide some valuable insights about what ethnicity is (or is not) in Bolivia and form part of a lengthy debate over whether the country is predominantly indigenous or mestizo. This debate has assumed greater resonance in recent years in light of both political developments and the results of the 2001 census and other attempts to measure the country's ethnic make-up. This, however, is a false debate, because it assumes the centrality of a particular identity—ethnicity—in a country where multiple identities are salient. Furthermore, the debate obscures the complex ways in which ethnic identities are constructed in Bolivia in conjunction with other ways of identifying oneself, others and society as a whole: for example, class, region, and ideology.

The political intentionality behind this debate—locating basic identities in ethnicity and politicizing it to construct a state that reflects this—is based on some imprecise suppositions. More worryingly perhaps, the insistence on the centrality of this type of identity and the quest for primacy among some ethnic groups is the driving force behind the politicization of ethnicity in ways not seen before, with all the virtues and problems that this may entail. If ethnic identities are to become politicized, it is important to understand the complex forms they take and the true meaning they have for people. Even more important than this is to understand what are the elements that unite us as a society, not just those that differentiate us.

The Ambiguity of the Data on Ethnicity

The following table summarizes the results of the various surveys, mentioned in the previous two chapters, that have sought to measure the ethnic make-up of Bolivia.

The results, as the table makes clear, are highly variable, depending on the categories used. Note the difference between the 2001 census, in which 62 percent of those surveyed defined themselves as indigenous, and the LAPOP survey, in which only 19 percent did so when given the option to select mestizo instead, and between the LAPOP and CRISE surveys, the latter of which afforded the option of identifying according to specific indigenous ethnicities. Such variation has given rise to a fierce debate. On the one hand, the 2001 census findings have been widely used to show the importance of indigenous peoples and are often cited as a verified fact to justify a public policy agenda to advance their rights. On the other, the results of the surveys that offered a

Table 3.1. Survey measures of ethnic identities

	1990 Census	1950 Census	2001 Census	LAPOP[1]	PNG, UNDP/ ILDIS[2]	CRISE[3]
Indigenous (generic)	51%	63%	—	19%	16%	—
Indigenous (specific: Aymara, Quechua, Guaraní, or other)	—	—	62%	—	—	57%
Mestizo	27%	37%	—	—	67%	25%
Mestizo or *cholo*	—	—	—	65%	—	—
White	13%	—	—	11%	17%	2%
Indigenous/mestizo[4]	—	—	—	—	—	6%
None or other	—	—	—	4%	—	10%

Source: Prepared using data from Mesa (2006), Albó (chap. 1, this volume), Toranzo (chap. 2, this volume), Seligson et al. (2006), and CRISE (2006).

[1] Latin American Public Opinion Project, Vanderbilt University
[2] Programa Nacional de Gobernabilidad, United Nations Development Program (Bolivia), Instituto Latinoamericano de Investigación Social.
[3] Centre for Research on Inequality, Human Security and Ethnicity, Oxford University.
[4] The LAPOP survey question refers to Aymara and mestizo, Quechua and mestizo, Guaraní and mestizo, other indigenous people and mestizo.

mestizo category and produced radically different results have been cited to argue that the question used by the 2001 census was poorly framed, that the predominant identity in Bolivia is instead mestizo, and that the importance of indigenous identity has been exaggerated. Defenders of the census findings have responded that the use of generic categories (indigenous or *originario*), as opposed to the names of specific ethnic groups, along with the stigma attached to indigenous identity, are the main reasons for the variations in the results, but that the basic census finding (that Bolivia is predominantly an indigenous country) remains valid. Furthermore, this variation shows that indigenous people have no problem in also using the less-stigmatized label of mestizo alongside their indigenous identity, without this entailing the need to hide their identity as members of an indigenous group (Albó, chap. 1).

These variable results reflect the use of problematic categories, both with respect to the introduction of the mestizo category, as well as in the variation between the use of the generic "indigenous or *originario*" category and the use of specific names of indigenous peoples. Much could be said about the methodologies and interpretation of the data, but here the focus will be on some of the arguments commonly used to highlight the problematic nature of this exercise.

The first refers to the use of the data as if it referred to homogenous groups. This is distinctly misleading. Grouping together into a single "indigenous" category such disparate population segments—for example, different types of people living in rural areas (such as a mineworker or the member of an *ayllu*); inhabitants of big cities and those living in rural areas; the inhabitants of the same city but with different lifestyles, numbers of years residence, or economic activities; or those who identify themselves as "indigenous" in El Alto and their equivalent in Santa Cruz—seems questionable.[1] Without going any further, the evolution of ethnic categories in Santa Cruz is so distinct from those in the Andean world (due, for example, to migration and the minority status of the lowland department's indigenous groups) that we should probably seek to highlight the different ways in which ethnic identities evolve. The situation in Santa Cruz therefore may be more akin to ideas about the U.S. melting pot than to the typical analysis of Andean ethnicity. Exactly the same might be said of the mestizo category, as Toranzo points out. Such heterogeneity is underestimated by the use of generic categories.

However, the fact that people do define themselves as indigenous (or mestizo) is not something that should be underrated: people do not usually identify with something completely foreign to them. Among the people who identify themselves as Aymara, it is possible that there is relatively little in common between someone born and raised in La Paz and someone living in a small rural community in Oruro. But it is equally possible that in spite of their differences, they may feel a degree of kinship and fraternity not shared with other groups. But even supposing the data pick up on this degree of communality, it is not clear how we should typify such bonds, nor how we should judge their strength. Nor is it certain that we should suppose—as is all too often the case—that such bonds are rooted in traditional ties between *originario* peoples, and not values subject to change and evolution. It is not a given, for example, that an Aymara who has lived in the city for many years and who exports furniture will set great store by principles of communitarian justice and reciprocity that are the cornerstone of *ayllu* life in the rural Altiplano.

The second point refers to the debate over whether there is a linear progression toward a mestizo identity, or whether individuals can identify themselves as indigenous and mestizo at the same time. Both arguments are problematic. Proponents of the first view approach the question of *mestizaje* as if change over time of an indigenous identity is proof of the loss of that identity, as if all such change led an individual inexorably to becoming a mestizo. But there are no universal yardsticks to use in judging a shift in identity in order to declare that someone has become a mestizo. Is it the case that someone can only be identified as indigenous if he or she eats typically indigenous food, dresses in traditional garb, or speaks an indigenous language? On the other hand, the argument that people can be indigenous and mestizo at the same time is scarcely satisfactory. If a person identifies as mestizo, under what circumstances do we consider such a person to be indigenous and count him or her as such? Why should we assume that the indigenous identity of such a person predominates over the mestizo? If we do not assume the priority of the indigenous element of identity, it seems we are adopting a typical definition of *mestizaje* that recognizes that elements of indigenous identity may persist alongside one that is criollo, white, or whatever we want to call it. In this case, what precisely does it mean for an individual to identify him or herself as indigenous or mestizo? It is not enough to suggest that such changes are just a consequence of the stigma of being indigenous or *originario*, particularly since most of these figures relate to a time when being indigenous or *originario* had become a source of pride among many individuals, reducing the influence of stigmatization in explaining such very different figures.

The loss of indigenous language is often used as definitive proof of *mestizaje*. This is a simplification. It is true that language is usually a very significant factor in defining ethnicity. Nevertheless, there are plenty of examples of cases where language is not a relevant component of ethnic identity. Every Scot, for example, speaks the language of their conqueror (English), and relatively few speak Scottish, yet this does not mean that the Scottish identity no longer exists. The Basques have undergone the loss and then the recovery of their language, as have the Irish. Yet, this does not mean that for a time these groups lost the feeling of belonging to a specific and different group. In many places around the world, ethnic groups are defined solely by their religion, and not by language or cultural difference. The fact that an Aymara does not speak Aymara does not mean, ipso facto, he or she is a mestizo, or any less an Aymara.

The variations in the available data underline the fact that measuring ethnic identity in Bolivia is highly complex, and it suggests that it is perhaps wrong to afford it the centrality it has acquired in recent times. It is also clear that such measurements refer to categories that are problematic. But this is not to deny the salience of ethnicity in Bolivia. The important thing about ethnicity—as many writers have shown—is that people believe in it.[2] There can be no doubt that there are many people believe that what it is to be Aymara, Quechua, Guaraní, or mestizo properly describes them and reflects what they consider themselves to be. Rather than being read as such, the data need to be thought about as part of a complex process of understanding one's own identity, that of others, and of society as a whole.

A Multiplicity of Identities

The main problem in this debate is that it assumes the centrality and salience of ethnic identities while paying insufficient attention to the fact that every human is made up of a multiplicity of relevant identities.[3] The CRISE survey, for example, added two further questions to the issue of self-belonging.[4] The first invited the interviewee to identify him or herself by means of a range of identities frequently used in Bolivia (such as *colla, paceño, camba, campesino,* trade unionists), plus an open-ended question. The second asked the interviewee to reveal his or her preference between using either an ethnic or cultural identity or some other type of commonly used identities. The result was that a slightly larger percentage of interviewees preferred the alternative of using another type of identity (45 percent) rather than an ethnic or racial one (preferred by 40 percent), with 13 percent preferring to use both at the same time. Even more important were the findings that showed the weight that people gave to their ethnic characteristics when it came to describing themselves was not significantly greater than other considerations, such as religion, ideology, place of birth, place of residence, or nationality.

Amartya Sen argues that human beings "belong to many different groups, in one way or another, and each of these collectivities can give a person a potentially important identity. We may have to decide whether a particular group to which we belong is—or is not—important for us. Two different, though interrelated, exercises are involved here: (1) deciding on what our relevant identities are, and (2) weighting the relative importance of these different identities. Both tasks demand reasoning and choice." However, "in the variation of the relative importance of identities, there may be significant external influences as well: not everything turns specifically of the nature of reasoning and choice. For one thing, the importance of a particular identity will depend on the *social context*" (Sen 2006, 24–25, emphasis added). The multiplicity of identities and the importance of understanding these in specific contexts are particularly relevant in a society as diverse as Bolivia's. This sort of society produces a variety of highly complex collective imaginaries, and as a result different identities may be relevant at any particular point in time. To identify oneself as a member of an *originario* people, as an inhabitant of a city or region, as a member of an organization, or as a trade unionist is a reality that is common enough in Bolivia.

A number of elements reinforce the relevance of multiple identities, of which three are highlighted here. The first is the significant effects that collective action may have for the relevance of specific identities (e.g., MacAdam, Tarrow, and Tilly 2001; Tilly and Tilly 1981). This is a key element in a country with a long tradition of social mobilization. Collective action presupposes a degree of group organization. The vitality of this in Bolivia is reflected by the multiplicity of associations, federations, neighborhood committees (*juntas vecinales*), trade unions, and so on, a characteristic further strengthened by the cultural importance afforded to collectivism. These organizations provide a potent sense of belonging and generate new identities (such as the members of mining cooperatives or the coca farmers).

The second aspect relates to substantial patterns of internal migration. These have forced people to accustom themselves to new realities, switching from peasant communities, unions, and agricultural cooperatives to new forms of organization such as neighborhood committees, federations, and labor unions. But in many instances they maintain their ties with previous forms of collectivism, building new identities in which to find a sense of belonging.

A third element relates to the historical importance of economic activities in defining the way in which ethnic identities and categories in Bolivia are forged. The establishment of the colonial system, for example, quickly established the term *indio* as a tax category, which produced new hierarchies within the indigenous population, such as *naturales* or *originarios, forasteros* (indigenous persons residing outside their communities of origin and thus not subject to labor levies), and *yanaconas* (indigenous persons without access to land), linked principally to the *mita* system that drafted labor for the mines, as well as to landholding. This had a strong impact on the social structure of indigenous populations.

Economic factors were also important in shaping the process of *mestizaje.* On the one hand, strategies of tax evasion were coupled with the natural miscegenation between groups (see also Bouysse-Cassagne 1996). On the other, as Barragán has shown, the consequence of social mobility, *mestizaje,* was intimately connected to participation in markets, and in particular the appropriation by indigenous peoples of such occupations as operating markets, producing handicrafts, and working in domestic service. "Specialization and *mestizaje* were, therefore, two sides of the same coin" (Barragán 1992, 98). Toranzo, (2006) meanwhile, has explored the rise of what he calls the *"cholo* bourgeoisie," a consequence of new segments of the economy being opened up by the national revolution in 1952, especially in domestic commerce, interprovincial transport, and contraband (Toranzo 2006, and chap. 2; see also Ayo 2007).

All this has given rise to a highly complex edifice of ethnic identities. On the one hand, ethnic identity doubtless has considerable importance in the ways in which Bolivians understand themselves. On the other, different forms of identity remain highly relevant, a product of the country's social make-up and the way this has changed over time. This means that peoples' central identities—based on region, city, class, or ideology—have all been constructed in one way or another on the basis of ethnicity (and vice versa).[5]

Some Further Difficulties in the Debate about Ethnicity

To those already mentioned above, two further elements need to be added: the complex and often contradictory social relations between groups and the continuing confused discourse about ethnicity in the country. Social relations between ethnic groups in Bolivia are highly complex—influenced by, among other things, the proximity between them—which means the salience of ethnic identities is dependent on context. By proximity I mean the nearness between different groups: physically, culturally, and in terms of the exchanges of everyday life.

Physical proximity has shaped interethnic relations since colonial times. Both the building of new cities and the ratio of indigenous inhabitants to new arrivals produced forms of coexistence that proved more fluid than in other parts of the Spanish Empire, creating particular forms of interethnic relationships (Barragán 1992; Zavaleta Mercado 1986). This physical proximity has not changed in any fundamental way since that time. The proportion of indigenous people to the rest of the population remains high. At the same time, whether because of the weakness of the state in imposing policies of *mestizaje* outright or because attitudes were more tolerant for a number of reasons (geographical proximity, policies of social equalization applied by the revolutionary governments post-1952, or the poverty of Bolivian elites, for example), Bolivia exhibits lower levels of cultural inequalities than one would expect given its institutional inequalities.[6] The national state and other levels of government allow, promote, and support a range of parallel institutional systems (such as communitarian justice), festivals (such as the *entrada* of the Gran Poder or Alasitas), traditions (such as the Tinku), and other cultural events which reflect the culture of different ethnic groups. The mixture of geographical and cultural proximity has resulted in a de facto multiculturalism that has a powerful impact on how people understand themselves, others, and society as a whole.

This is not to say, though, that the state or members of particular groups do not indulge in ethnic discrimination in a variety of ways. Here, I simply wish to point out that in such a multicultural environment, social relations between different ethnic groups have developed in complex, fluid, and often contradictory ways, albeit within a generally discriminatory framework. Studies of particular aspects of diet, for example, show that there is no direct relationship between consumption patterns across social divisions analyzed in terms of ethnicity, class, or region; rather, diet is primarily determined by the particular sociocultural context (Orlove and Schmidt 1995). Studies on relationships between domestic maids and their employers provide important evidence as to the complex relations of domination and fraternity between them and the diversity of ways of perceiving oneself and others, as well as an understanding of the interethnic dynamics built on the sort of relations established (Gill 1994). Ethnic identity, therefore, may by highly salient in certain contexts, but it is not always the key determinant of social relations.

The creation and development of ethnic categories and the constant tension that exists between these and reality, as well as the stigma of being indigenous and the prevalence of racial discrimination, have produced important differences in discourse and attitudes toward ethnicity among Bolivians when one compares the public and private spheres. In public life, individuals may conform to established statuses and norms but transgress them in the private sphere, or vice versa. Furthermore, individuals may adjust their behavior and opinions toward other groups under the influence of social conventions. For example, racist ideas can be expressed in very different ways depending on the social context. The difference between the public and private spheres may help explain why in Bolivia there is a relatively high sense of ethnic belonging, but one that has never been very relevant in the public sphere in any sustained form. People may value their ethnicity as a form of identification, but political life has tended to be guided by other considerations.

We must finally consider discourses about ethnicity in order to understand its relevance in the Bolivian context. We Bolivians have used a number of basic or fundamental narratives throughout our history to inform our view of the world and our actions.[7] Some of these narratives are based on demonstrable facts (there is a structure of domination and discrimination that is real enough) or on facts that were real at one point. Other narratives, however, have generated ideas widely considered to be true, but that are based on wholly misplaced interpretations of reality. This has given rise to a variety of discourses on matters which ordinary people can relate to (such as racial concepts, the use of certain types of dress, attitudes, discrimination) in differentiating between groups. Such discourses are widely taken to be true and are widely used, even in academic discussion. The use of dichotomies such as white versus indigenous, modern versus traditional, or market versus reciprocity are examples of common simplifications that cloud the analysis of ethnicity in Bolivia. Such notions often obscure the understanding of ethnicity.

Two examples serve to illustrate this problem. The first relates to a commonly understood notion of society as a single stratified pyramid, with whites at the top, mestizos in the middle, and indigenous peoples at the bottom, with a concomitant pattern of income distribution. This generalization, however, ignores the hierarchies and power relations within each group and important gender differences both between and within them. Even more importantly, it fails to take into account the strata within each group and their relations vis-à-vis strata of different groups. It is unclear, for instance, whether an Aymara Jillanku (a traditional community leader) suffers a lower social status or enjoys less power (either within a specific context or vis-à-vis the rest of society) than a mestizo of low social strata. The psychological effect of social status, especially in a society as hierarchical as Bolivia's and so accustomed to the use of symbols, is still something that has not been properly studied. However, it is not difficult to imagine that it provides powerful mechanisms that buttress pride and self-respect and reduce perceptions of inferiority to other groups. Much the same is true in the economic sphere. There are large numbers of so-called *cholos* who enjoy greater economic power than many of those traditionally classified as members of the country's elite.

These elements illustrate the debatable nature of many of the suppositions that underlie discussion over what is indigenous and what is mestizo in contemporary Bolivia. Historically, this has contributed to unresolved tensions, since it is posed in oversimplified ways. If such elements are to be politicized—as is the case at the moment—it is important to clarify the extent to which ethnicity is key to identity, the forms that such identities take, and—even more important—to understand the elements that unite society as well as those that divide it.

PART II

Regionalism has emerged with new force in the last few years, in ways which—at times—have seemed capable of tearing the country apart. Regionalism is a dynamic in most Latin American countries, often underscoring competition for resources between capital cities and peripheral centers, but in few has it been such a source of tension—and on occasions political paralysis—as in Bolivia. Regional tensions have become more acute in the last few years, reflecting the fact that regionalism has been used both by the supporters and equally by the opponents of President Evo Morales to rally sentiment either for or against the MAS (Movimiento al Socialismo). This has been particularly the case in Santa Cruz, the most prosperous and demographically expansive of the nine departments, but it has also brought to the fore regionalist pressures in other departments. As well as Tarija, Beni, and Pando (which together with Santa Cruz make up the so-called *media luna*) other departments such as Chuquisaca and Cochabamba have also seen attempts to rally antigovernment sentiment through the invocation of the spirit of regionalism. Traditional parties have found themselves marginalized within the formal political scene following the Morales landslide of 2005, their support concentrated in those departments that made up the *media luna*. It was therefore only natural that they would seek to restrain the government by invoking the perceived interests of these departments against the central government. The salience of regional politics was also enhanced by the decision of the previous Carlos Mesa administration to allow for the election of departmental prefects. Whereas these had previously been executive appointments, prefects had the potential to use their local legitimacy to become independent advocates of departmental interests, even as opponents to the central government. This therefore opened up a new political arena that had not existed previously, not least because in the 2005 prefectural elections the MAS candidates only won in three of the nine departments. In conjunction with democratically elected prefects, civic committees found their scope for action greatly enhanced, especially where prefects identified themselves strongly with the opposition. The prefect of Santa Cruz became a leading light of that department's campaign for autonomy.

However, as the chapters by Roca and Barragán show, regionalism is as old as the republic itself, growing out of the way in which the country was first constituted. Unlike most of its neighbors, Bolivia was never dominated by a hegemonic city. Although La Paz took over as capital from Sucre as a consequence of a war at the end of the nineteenth century, it too came to be rivaled in the last half of the twentieth century by Santa Cruz, a rivalry that has done much to fuel contemporary regionalist antagonisms. Even in the years that followed the 1952 revolution, the emergent new state was insufficiently powerful to impose itself on local elites, and in the case of Santa Cruz the use of force ended up simply compounding regional resentments. The spirit of regionalism was also kindled by a variety of other factors, such as ethnic resentments, unequal patterns of development, inequities in public investment, and fiscal privileges. But as the reader will see, the postrevolutionary governments of the victorious Movimiento Nacionalista Revolucionario (MNR) did their best to resist centrifugal tendencies and to maintain a unitary state. The last great defender of that tradition, the *MNRista* Gonzalo Sánchez de Lozada, introduced his Popular Participation program in part to limit the powers of departmental power groups by decentralizing to the municipal level.

The decision to convene a Constituent Assembly to refound the republic was therefore always likely to involve reopening of the old dispute over the rights and responsibilities of departmental government as opposed to those of central government. Under pressure from the departments, primarily from Santa Cruz, the issue of autonomies was bound to emerge if the assembly was to be given carte blanche to redesign the country's political institutions and the relationships between them. But the discovery of large quantities of natural gas in the late 1990s in the department of Tarija raised awkward questions as to how these resources would be used and whom they would benefit. It is perhaps ironical that Evo's reform of the hydrocarbon sector—a move that most Bolivians ended up warmly supporting—should, by greatly increasing the resources at the disposal of the state, help to further foster conflict over the distribution of the rents arising therefrom.

The debate over autonomies, which loomed large during the first two years of Evo's presidency, raised important questions as to the future rights and responsibilities of departmental administration, as well as to issues of participation within a more decentralized structure of power. For the civic committees, especially the Comité Pro Santa Cruz, departmental autonomy seemed to involve a sort of federalist solution in which departments would win greater decision-making powers with respect to their local jurisdiction and receive more of the benefits of the particular types of output they produced. The de facto "statutes of autonomy" announced in December 2007, represented an extreme form of federalism. For the MAS government, departmental autonomy could represent a way to curtail the rights and privileges of local elites if it meant transferring greater power to urban and indigenous communities, particularly in spheres such as control over resources within their territories and recognition of their cultural, legal, and linguistic rights. Such a proposal was anathema to those, like the Comité Pro Santa Cruz, who regarded indigenous empowerment with the utmost suspicion. The government rejected the "statutes of autonomy," arguing that they were not only illegal but ran wholly contradictory to the new constitutional text.

Regionalist sentiments are clearly tinged by perceptions of how some have advanced at the expense of others. Different conclusions can be derived from differing readings of the past. In his chapter, José Luis Roca, a Santa Cruz native who has studied and written more than anyone on the history of economic development in the eastern lowlands of Bolivia, blames what he calls "a central power obsessed with the 'unity' of the country" for the fact that regionalism expresses itself so forcefully as a sort of pressure group on the central government. He sees regionalism as the main contradiction afflicting Bolivia and resolving this contradiction as the sine qua non for harmonious institutional development in the future. He is highly critical of the post-1952 MNR governments and fearful that the "racist" interpretation of the east-west divide will further exacerbate regional tensions. For her part, Rossana Barragán takes a rather different view, stressing the way in which highland Bolivia effectively financed Santa Cruz during the late nineteenth and early twentieth centuries through the redistribution of mineral earnings, while more recently Santa Cruz has been reluctant to share its oil wealth in the same vein with the rest of Bolivia. This underscores the argument that the natural wealth of one department is not its "property," and that the gas riches of Tarija and Santa Cruz should be tapped in such a way that they benefit the whole country, especially the poorest parts most in need of development. She takes issue with the idea of some regions being oppressed by a powerful central government, seeing the state as having acted weakly in responding to organized pressure groups, latterly those of Santa Cruz. The implication here is that the central state should be rather more careful and efficacious in how it distributes the public resources available to it.

Regionalism Revisited

JOSÉ LUIS ROCA

In the present analysis, regionalism is understood to be the power wielded by regions within a given country and is expressed in terms of conducts, attitudes, and specific forms of action. In Bolivia, regions vie with one another; they constantly seek to exert influence over the state and question the acts of a central administration seen as authoritarian and centralizing. Regionalism is clearly visible throughout Bolivia's history, creating artificial problems while obscuring real ones and generating animosities between people living in different parts of the country. Regionalism also creates obstacles to the efficient administration of the state, resulting in decisions that are frequently injurious and counterproductive to the country as a whole. It operates under the tutelage of an elitist ideology that sees itself as the vanguard of a heterogeneous social mass.[1] For our purposes, then, regionalism is not regional development or the history of a country's regions. Nor is it the efforts of neighboring regions belonging to different countries to make common cause in confronting the challenges of modernity, globalization, or development in ways different from the states they belong to. Such issues are relevant and interesting, but they deserve to be analyzed separately using concepts other than those used here.

Bolivia is fragmented into regions whose outlook is one of constant complaint and criticism of the central government for its inability to steer the country toward progress and increased social well-being. Regions demand what they see as fair treatment in the distribution of fiscal revenues and public sector expenditures. This is exemplified by the historical grievances of Santa Cruz, which saw its interests ignored by the central government and as a result suffered poverty and neglect until the middle of the twentieth century. Given the boom experienced by Santa Cruz since the 1970s, the Andean departments argue that this department has attracted all the attention of the state, to the detriment of the rest of the country. In Bolivia, the term *region* is synonymous with *department*, the nine constituent units formed at the founding of the republic. Region can also be taken to mean the provinces that make up each department, many of which do not necessarily identify themselves with the departments they comprise. These provinces view departmental authority as another version of central government, with the same sorts of deficiencies and acquisitive instincts. The more than three hundred municipalities created since the mid-1990s also feel they have their own particular identities and rights, notwithstanding the formal ties that bind them to the departments of which they are a part.

Historically, the departments have had more power that the national government as a whole; this permanent centrifugal tendency has contributed much to the country's notorious and chronic instability. But rather than recognizing this and seeking to negotiate some sort of social pact that would ameliorate it, both the military caudillos of the nineteenth century and the oligarchic parties that superseded them sought to strengthen themselves by subduing the departments. This is the same policy being followed by the left-wing and indigenous government of Evo Morales, which has found itself in a state of constant tension with the departments. The most frequent method traditionally used to weaken the departments has been to repress all instances of indiscipline toward the central government. It has been against the departments in particular that the dictatorships (which have cast a long shadow over Bolivian history) have vented their rage.

At other junctures, unable to offset the power of the regions, proponents of centralism have sought to redraw the map of the republic by creating new departments or redefining the existing ones. Some still feel that Bolivia needs to divide itself up into more departments and that the boundaries of the existing ones ought to be redrawn along more pragmatic lines related to their development needs. They tend to ignore or to minimize the fact that the formation of Bolivian regions owes more to history than to geography and more to cultural formation than to techno-bureaucratic considerations and policies poorly grounded in reality. For these reasons, such attempts tend to fail.

Regional demands thus threaten a central power obsessed by the unity of the country, which, deep down, is no more than a justification for a style of governance.[2] In reviewing the literature on federalism in Bolivia, we find the oft-repeated argument that a federal regime would condemn the republic to dissolution. In the 1990s, it was argued stridently that decentralization would serve only to Balkanize Bolivia, an allusion to the frightful internal wars that destroyed the former Yugoslav federation.[3]

Regions to which the right of self-government has been denied act as political pressure groups in the same way as labor unions, business organizations, or indigenous communities do—albeit with much greater force than these can muster. They do not ask; they demand. They take little interest in what is going on around them, because the only important thing for them is meeting their own needs and requirements. Confronted in this way, national administrations make unrealistic promises to forestall negative reactions and to counteract adverse propaganda. It has become a ritual that to commemorate a civic anniversary, the president of the republic pays a visit to a departmental capital, where he announces a list of measures—a sort of birthday offering—including laws or decrees (often purely symbolic) designed to attenuate dissatisfaction. This is therefore a tussle that weakens and frustrates both the center and the periphery.

Demands are channeled upward through civic committees, which are voluntary nonpolitical institutions that bring together wide sectors of civil society and enjoy different degrees of representativeness according to the sectors in which they work. Since these committees first began to attract support in the 1950s, by far the most successful has been that of Santa Cruz. Its standing surged when it managed to secure for producer departments a royalty equivalent to 11 percent of the production of crude oil and natural gas. This share-out was established following more than two years of confrontation and violence between 1957 and 1959. Authority in the region was wielded alternatively by the civic committee and a dissident caudillo of the ruling party, in both cases almost independently of the government in La Paz, which for its part foolishly sought to resolve the conflict by dispatching army troops and paramilitary peasant militias to this disorderly region. There were political prisoners and exiles, armed confrontations and casualties, none of which were able to avert the eventual approval of a royalties law which remains in force to this day and benefits not only Santa Cruz but also Cochabamba, Tarija, and Chuquisaca.[4]

This shows us that regionalism is the main contradiction in Bolivian society and that while it remains unresolved the country will be unable to complete its institutional consolidation or to take effective steps to spearhead development. Moreover, there remains the issue of a repetition of the 1899 civil war to establish a new capital that includes all three powers of the state. Such a conflict provides us no guarantee that at the end of it, and no matter who wins, the centralized state will vanish. At the time of writing, hopes of achieving institutional consolidation remained in suspense, since the Constituent Assembly of 2007 had proved unable to achieve consensus on the question of local autonomies. Such a regime of departmental autonomies would raise regional self-esteem and create a new internal balance within the country that had not existed previously. Achievement of an agreement on the mass of detail and shades of meaning that a system of autonomies would imply would untie the Gordian knot that has helped hold the republic captive from the very date it formally came into being.

The other side of the coin is that regionalism has helped create a country that is both plural and diverse, enriched by strong and authentic expressions of localized culture. During the years when the regional development corporations operated (1975–1995), technical and professional expertise emerged; each corporation was concerned with understanding the specificity of its region and working to improve conditions within it. Given the sheer size of Bolivia's regions and their varied geography and cultures, they constitute a microcosm of the country as a whole; such regional initiatives contributed to a better understanding of the whole and generated a greater commitment toward it.

Historically, the strength of Bolivia's departments has been one of the most effective dissuasive forces against antidemocratic *caudillismo*. If we examine the ruptures (including revolts, military coups, and popular insurrections) that have brought dictatorships to an end, we can see how these all originated in regional insurrections that then expanded to the rest of the country. The great aspiration of many an autocrat has been to undermine the departments or ignore them in decision making. Two examples from different epochs spring to mind. President José María Linares, only a few months after taking office in 1857, signed a decree on December 25 that reconstituted Bolivia's nine departments into thirty-two "political commands"; a year later (through another decree), he set himself up as dictator.[5] (He was overthrown before this territorial reorganization took root.) The other case, similar in its conception and purpose, took place in 1993, when President Jaime Paz Zamora and his successor Gonzalo Sánchez de Lozada made a deal to frustrate a draft decentralization bill that enjoyed widespread support in the country and was on the verge of being approved by Congress. In its place, a substitute measure, known as "Popular Participation," was passed. This law created 311 municipalities, each enjoying a direct relationship with the central government that bypassed the departmental capitals and prefects.[6] Though still in force today, this model has lost much of its former importance, because new ideas and developments have reestablished of the primacy of departments, particularly the direct election of prefects and the rise in popular support for departmental autonomies.[7]

The Bolivian's Sense of Identity

If one was to ask what are the characteristics of the Spanish language in Bolivia, what the music is like, or the local food, the answer would be that they are one thing in Santa Cruz and the Beni, and something different in Chuquisaca or La Paz. To discover the identity of the Bolivian, you need to analyze it in small packages, just as Alcides Arguedas did in "Pueblo enfermo" (1909). He referred to the imagination of the people of Cochabamba and the obstinacy of the Aymaras of La Paz, but he did not manage to draw a psychological profile of the average Bolivian as such.[8] In truth, this person does not exist unless one relates him to the regional variants.

Although true of many other parts of the world, the specificity of Bolivia is overwhelming. In spite of being a unitary republic, each department has its own proportional representation in the Chamber of Deputies, with three senators irrespective of population. In the Supreme Court, judges also represent departments. Each department has its own anthem, flag, and coat of arms; each has a date (a public holiday in each case) on which some local hero is commemorated. Sucre and La Paz have kept up their age-old rivalry as to which of the two cities was the first to rebel against the king of Spain; each believe it was them, given that both declarations took place in 1809, one year earlier than the rest of Latin America. The dispute over this primogeniture was so long lasting and persistent that it became the trigger for the 1899 civil war, in which the interests of large-scale *paceño* mining and commerce imposed themselves on Sucre and from that time on came to dominate the rest of the country.

Oruro, for its part, celebrates its anniversary on November 10, due to the fact that it was on this day in 1781 that an uprising broke out among locally born *criollos* against the abuses of the Bourbon reforms, but in particular against the Spanish-born elite (or *"chapetones"*) who monopolized all the posts in the colonial administration of Charcas. Finally, the two newest departments—Beni and Pando—commemorate the date on which they were established as such. The common denominator of all these various disparate criteria is the affirmation of a regional sentiment, a sense of belonging to one's native soil, a pride in being part of a human grouping where (in spite of deep social and economic differences) people feel part of an imagined community in line with Anderson's classic formulation (1991).

It is perhaps paradoxical that all this takes place in a context where an article of faith for those who control the levers of power is to restrain tendencies toward federalism or decentralization, whether civilians, military leaders, oligarchs, or revolutionaries. Suffice it to recall that in 1899, La Paz triumphed under the banner of federalism. But far from changing the type of government once the war ended, President José Manuel Pando further reinforced the system of unitary government. In the same vein, a decree of 1931, signed by the military government of President Carlos Blanco Galindo, incorporated into the constitution a much more decentralized system of government (previously approved by referendum), which was then ignored by the civilian government of Daniel Salamanca that followed it. And in 1993, as we saw above, after the national senate had given unanimous approval to a bill that introduced departmental governments and created an assembly of departmental representatives, the scheme was nipped in the bud by the Paz Zamora government.

The strong personality of Bolivia's regions is derived from the fact it is the only country in Latin America where the political/administrative structure designed by the Bourbon kings in the eighteenth century remains intact. The republic was organized on the model announced in 1782 in the Ordinance on Intendancies of the viceroyalty of Río de la Plata. The intendancies were based on the previously defined *corregimientos* that formed part of the Audiencia of Charcas. It is for this reason that from very early on the intendancies became conscious of the territorial spaces they occupied, as well as of their prerogatives. This is clear, for example, in Pedro Vicente Cañete y Domínguez's *History of Potosí* (1952). Written around 1787, this monumental and learned work portrays Potosí as if it were a state in its own right, and the author gives detailed descriptions of its five internal regions or *partidos:* Porco, Lípez, Chichas, Atacama, and Tarija. The book focuses on Potosí's natural resources and (as might be expected) the mineral wealth of the famed Cerro de Potosí, the role played by its indigenous population, its parishes, its Pacific ports, its ecclesiastical jurisdictions and tribunals, and the commercial relations it had with neighboring regions. Cañete defends the rights of Potosí not just to the Atacama but to Tarapacá as well, demonstrating the attractions of commerce between this province and Potosí.

A somewhat similar account of Santa Cruz and Cochabamba is to be found in the *Descripción geográfica y estadística de la Provincia de Santa Cruz de la Sierra*. Written in 1793 by the governor/intendant Francisco de Viedma, this volume contains a report on the peoples, parishes, and missionary settlements of what today are two departments but at the time formed a single jurisdiction, with its capital in Cochabamba (Pedro de Angelis 1836–37). Only a few months after the outbreak of the May 1810 rebellion against Spanish rule in Buenos Aires, Cochabamba proclaimed its support for the cause. Since that time, September 14 has been the date of the civic fiesta in Cochabamba. Santa Cruz was a *subdelegación* of the intendancy of the same name. The rebels in Cochabamba ordered the removal of the royal authorities without a shot being fired. When the system of intendancies was abolished at the beginning of the War of Independence, Santa Cruz managed to get General Manuel Belgrano (head of the second Argentine expedition to Upper Peru) to restore its self-governing status, thereby ending its dependence on Cochabamba.

The intendancies were extensive territories under the jurisdiction of the viceroyalty, although the Spanish crown devolved a wide range of functions to the official that ruled them so as to counterbalance the power of the viceroy, as well as that of the previously powerful Audiencia of Charcas.[9] Despite the fact that half a century passed between the adoption of the intendancy system and the advent of the republic, the strength of the units survived intact; so much so that one of them—Paraguay—refused to form part of the United Provinces, the entity that succeeded the viceroyalty of Río de la Plata, and ended up opting to become a republic in its own right.[10] As for the intendancies of Charcas, these initially adhered to Buenos Aires but during the course of the War of Independence decided to form a separate political entity, overriding the objections of the Liberator Simón Bolívar.[11]

The 1825 assembly that gave birth to Bolivia as a nation brought together a number of provinces that already enjoyed a degree of self-government; together they signed a republican pact which helped in the adoption of a federal system—or a sort of confederation, akin to the thirteen colonies of the United States. But this idea was repugnant to Bolívar and the *criollo* elite of Charcas and was rejected out of hand. Bolivar had undertaken his first campaigns in New Granada, where he had witnessed a devastating civil war provoked by the federalists between 1812 and 1814. For their part, the Charcas elite considered themselves the owners of the power inherited from the *audiencia.* They therefore also rejected the notion of federalism. The representatives present in the assembly that founded the republic declared, "A federal government is not in accord with the will of the peoples, in the belief that this would not be the most secure source of happiness for a lasting peace and social union . . . this government is concentrated, general, and singular for the whole republic and its departments" (República de Bolivia 1926, 57).

Notwithstanding, this "concentrated, general, and singular" government would do nothing but encourage rivalries and conflict between the provinces; one might rather say that it was dispersed, particular, and various, just as the intendancies were. This helps explain the chronic political and institutional instability of Bolivia in the nineteenth century and its consequences: further instability, scant development, territorial mutilation, and a deep skepticism as to the future.

The Struggle for Hegemony

Historical experience suggests that power in a country is exercised from a hegemonic territorial center which comes to occupy this position as a consequence of successive power struggles. This is what happened at the birth of the various European nation-states. In Latin America, the hegemonic region was one and the same as those that had existed during the colonial period when they were the capitals of viceroyalties, captaincy generals, intendancies, or *audiencias.* In some instances, as in the case of Argentina, the power of the capital, Buenos Aires, was fiercely challenged by the provinces, leading to a lengthy succession of civil wars that lasted up until the middle of the nineteenth century, at which point the port of Buenos Aires finally managed to impose itself upon the regions of the interior. The hegemonic center thus exercises a sort of centripetal attraction where the activity and energies of a country tend to converge.

The Bolivian case is sui generis. This is because the dominant region has shifted from one place to another. In spite of the fact that Chuquisaca had been the seat of the *audiencia,* it was unable to consolidate its power. For this reason the capital became itinerant and nomad. During the course of the nineteenth century, the legislature met in four different cities (Sucre, La Paz, Oruro, and Cochabamba), and the executive oscillated between Sucre and La Paz. This situation was graphically highlighted by a decree by General Manuel Isidoro Belzu (1848–1855), which declared that the capital of the republic was the place where the president happened to be. In private, he identified it as being "the back of my horse."

Bolivia's position in the center of South America, astride the cordillera of the Andes and looking at once to the Pacific and to the Río de la Plata, meant that from its very foundation in 1825 it was beset by the rivalry of two regions, Sucre and La Paz, each of roughly equivalent strength. But Sucre proved inadequate as a capital, owing to its lack of economic resources, its isolation from the rest of the country, and the enormous distances that separated it from both the Pacific and the Atlantic oceans. La Paz looked toward Peru, as it had for most of the colonial period until Charcas was transferred to Buenos Aires in 1776.[12]

The Peruvian-Bolivian Confederation, resisted by both nations, was the result of this. It was backed only by its author, Andrés de Santa Cruz, whose defeat became the prelude for a more serious and tragic loss: that of Bolivia's coastline to Chile in the War of the Pacific of 1879. Paradoxically, it was this catastrophe that led to the revival (albeit ephemeral) in the power of Sucre and the south. A railway was built from there to Antofagasta, encouraging the rapid development in silver mining and bringing a short-lived prosperity to the south. But when a definitive peace treaty was signed in 1904, it was decided to build a railway from Arica to La Paz, which ended up competing with the Antofagasta line. Favoring the interests of La Paz, it changed the direction of commercial flows northward, away from Sucre.

The conflict between La Paz and Sucre was resolved to the benefit of the former following the brief but bloody civil war in 1899. However, the victorious *paceños* committed the fatal error of not formally transferring the capital to La Paz, thus creating an ambivalence that remains to the present day. In spite of its dominion over the rest of the country, La Paz enjoys the rather modest title of "seat of government" while one of the powers of the state (the judiciary) still resides in the nominal "capital" of the republic, Sucre.[13]

With this antagonism resolved, a new source of conflict arose as of the middle of the twentieth century between Santa Cruz and La Paz. This owed its origins to the rapid development of agriculture, agribusiness, and hydrocarbons in Santa Cruz and the simultaneous decline of tin and other mining exports that had previously helped sustain the *paceño* economy. The 1952 revolution led to the physical integration of Santa Cruz. A strategic highway linking Santa Cruz and the highlands was built, and the state began to invest in *cruceño* agriculture. Thus it was that Santa Cruz arose as a counterpoint to the power of La Paz. Curiously, La Paz was considered the north of the country in the nineteenth century, as opposed to its southern rival in Chuquisaca; from the middle of the twentieth century onward it began to be seen as the capital of the west, known today as the Andean macroregion. Tarija, in the extreme south, has tended to identify itself in recent times with the east, forming what has come to be known as the "half moon" (*media luna*).[14]

This latest regional alignment owes much to the recent boom in the production of natural gas in Bolivia. Tarija, as the main producer of this highly valued hydrocarbon, has advocated liberal rules on foreign investment, in line with the dominant outlook of Santa Cruz.[15] This has encouraged the emergence of a development ideology that has sought to bring the era of centralism to an end, replacing it with a regime more beneficial to the producer regions.

Racial and cultural factors have come to play an important part in the conflict between west and east. In the former, Aymara and Quechua peoples predominate, while in the latter peoples of European origin and those of mixed race (mestizo) are a majority. In the *oriente*, there is an indigenous minority of Guaraní and other smaller ethnic groups who do not harbor serious grievances toward the urban elites, whereas in the west of the country indigenous peoples feel themselves adversaries of the nonindigenous. Such conflicts have given rise to the existence of "two Bolivias," each with a different vision of the world and of the country's destiny. So while in the eastern *media luna* there is broad support for neocapitalist development and market economics, in the west people invoke the ancestral rights of indigenous groups, whose customs and values are strongly influenced by traditionalism—to the point that some advocate the return to pre-Hispanic societal modes across Bolivia.[16]

An ideology that is left-wing, *indigenista*, and statist now prevails in a space that until fairly recently was dominated by the *paceña* oligarchy. The electoral landslide of the Movimiento al Socialismo (MAS), led by Evo Morales, imbued the regionalism of western Bolivia with these characteristics, putting a new twist on the battle for hegemony between the regions. The *paceño* elite, meanwhile, are slowly adapting to the new situation.

Changes in Regional Thinking about Centralism

During the years of the national revolution (1952–1964), when politics were dominated by the Movimiento Nacionalista Revolucionario (MNR), a strong central state prevailed that did nothing to encourage or address regionalist particularism. Government was conducted in a top-down fashion from the

Plaza Murillo, home to both the presidential palace and the legislature. All mayors and prefects were appointed by the president. Even in the remotest corners of the county, the nomination of public officials emanated from one ministry or another, or from state-owned companies, all based in La Paz. Even though municipal autonomy was consecrated in the 1938 constitution, it was not until 1983 that mayors were actually voted in by popular suffrage. The national finances were concentrated in the hands of the treasury, from which resources were distributed to the departmental capitals; subprefectures and provincial municipalities received no more than the wages of their employees. Their operational funds had to come from a variety of sources, such as levies on local gambling, taxation on cattle, and patent fees for public entertainment.

The 1952–1964 period was one of harsh political repression; dissidence was not tolerated, unless subject to prior negotiation. At that time, the only regional voice to make itself heard was Santa Cruz. This department complained about its marginalization, lacking as it did such basic public services as electricity, drinking water, and sewers. The city and region of Santa Cruz had been progressively impoverished from the middle of the previous century onward because of the damage done to its agriculture by foreign competition in supplying the markets of the Altiplano. Its civic committee, the Comité Pro Santa Cruz (founded in 1950), managed to mobilize all social sectors in protest against the central government. There were serious disturbances in support of the demand for the 11 percent royalties on oil production, just at the time when a far-right opposition party was conspiring against the government. It was in these circumstances that the government accused Santa Cruz of being separatist, repeating what had been said in the 1920s at the end of the liberal regime, when parties emerged calling themselves "*orientalista*" and "*regionalista*."

The period of military government from 1964 to 1982 brought with it greater regional participation in the way the country was run. Lacking any party support and pitted against the labor unions, the military in government sought to drum up backing from the peasantry and the regions. With the former, they entered into a pact known as the Military Campesino Pact. Although a written text of this agreement has never been located, it worked in practice by securing the continuance of land distribution under the 1953 agrarian reform and giving assurances to the peasants that their land titles would not be reversed. Not only did the military comply with the terms of the pact, but it used foreign assistance funds to develop colonization schemes to encourage the migration of poverty-stricken peasants from the Altiplano to the fertile lands of the *oriente*. The alliance with the regions was also a success. Its most creative phase was under the military government of Hugo Banzer (1971–1978), when regional development corporations were set up in the nine departments, funded by oil and other natural resources royalties or by treasury transfers. Santa Cruz thus managed to provide itself with the public works and essential services it had demanded for so long, ushering in a period of exceptional prosperity.

With the reestablishment of democracy in 1982, public attention turned toward how to reform governmental administration. At least a dozen legislative bills were introduced to decentralize the system of government, each bearing the seal of regionalist interests. In the years that followed, pressure to end centralization built up around the activities of civic committees, organized by that time in each and every department. As we have seen, by 1993 a decentralization law had been drafted and was ready to be submitted to Congress. Though carefully worked out with the consent of the regions, unions, political parties, parliamentary groupings, and indeed the civic committees, it ended up being unceremoniously dropped.

The fourth term of President Víctor Paz Estenssoro (1985–1989) froze out any attempt to decentralize the country. The venerable leader of *movimientismo* remained firm in his opposition to any sort of devolution, convinced of the old argument that it would precipitate Bolivia's unraveling as a country. The dominant figure between the early part of 1993 and the end of 2003 was undoubtedly Gonzalo Sánchez de Lozada, overshadowing Hugo Banzer's second administration (1997–2001) and that of Jorge Quiroga, who briefly succeeded Banzer in 2001. Banzer and Quiroga did little but continue the policies that Sánchez de Lozada initiated, including the maintenance of a strong and authoritarian central government. This was supported by the *cruceño* elite, who, during this decade, simply forgot about any ideals of decentralization.

It was only during the last three years of the twentieth century that the popular and indigenous insurrection against the old regime gathered force. The year 2000 saw violent protests and social mobilization in Cochabamba against a foreign company that had been granted a concession to provide water and sewer services. The company began by imposing an exorbitant increase in the tariffs it charged, ostensibly designed to cover the investment costs that it had agreed to with the government. The clashes to which this gave rise—and there were many casualties and wounded—came to be known as the "water war."

Events in Cochabamba had their repercussions in the Altiplano, where Felipe Quispe, a charismatic and fundamentalist *indigenista,* organized lengthy and widespread road blockades across the region. Meanwhile, Evo Morales and the *cocaleros* carried out similar moves in the Chapare. Quispe proclaimed the existence of an "Aymara nation," a sort of reconstruction of the old Incaic Kollasuyo.[17] The response from Santa Cruz was not long in coming, where the "Camba nation" was proclaimed shortly afterward.[18] This was a movement orchestrated and led by the *cruceño* elite but which also attracted wider popular and indigenous support in opposition to the supposed advance of the *collas.*[19]

Thus it was that, fifty years after it began, the rivalry between Santa Cruz and La Paz had acquired a distinctly racial connotation which reached new heights following the fall of Sánchez de Lozada in October 2003, just over a year after he had assumed the presidency for the second time. His successor, Carlos Mesa, sought to take advantage of the *indigenista* wave. His support for a number of *indigenista* initiatives did little but stir up stronger reactions in Santa Cruz. Never before had the *camba-colla* confrontation become so explicit and raucous than during the Mesa administration. It lasted only twenty months, but during this time the social and indigenous movements became ever more aggressive in tone.

In fact, this was not the first time that regional issues had become intermixed with racial antagonisms. Something similar had taken place during the 1899 civil war, when the Aymara population mobilized to fight on the side of the *paceño* liberals against the elite of Chuquisaca. The latter suffered a series of defeats at the hands of indigenous groups in a conflict embittered by such large-scale massacres as that of Ayo Ayo.[20] At this time, indigenous bands were also protagonists in killings in the locality of Mohosa, where the victims were *paceño* troops supposedly on the same side as the Aymaras.[21]

After the fall of Mesa in 2005, his successor, Eduardo Rodríguez Veltzé (previously president of the Supreme Court) called for fresh general elections. To do so, however, it was necessary to reassign the number of deputies per department in line with demographic changes since the previous election. Disagreements over the number of representatives for each department revealed once again that commitment to region was a more powerful force than support for the positions of political parties.

Election of Prefects and Departmental Autonomies

To calm this climate of agitation in the regions, Mesa had issued a decree in January 2005 by which prefects were to be elected directly in each department. This measure constitutes an historical landmark: on the one hand, it took the lead in breaking with centralism; on the other, it sought to avert any criticism that this form of election was unconstitutional. In order not to violate this principle, it was established that the election represented just a "selection" of a prefect and that the president would ratify the winner by nominating him (or her) to the job, thereby respecting the verdict expressed through the ballot box.

After a ten-year period in which Santa Cruz had exerted little or no pressure to decentralize, the idea of departmental autonomy was born in 2004, inspired partly by the Spanish experience. Yet, popular organizations in the western half of Bolivia rejected this proposition; instead, they proposed the notion of "indigenous autonomies." How these would work, however, remained unclear. Meanwhile, in Santa Cruz there were massive demonstrations in support of departmental autonomies and the collection of signatures to hold a referendum to ratify them. The debate was a passionate one. The media in La Paz and Santa Cruz vied to see which could provoke the other most, creating an atmosphere of imminent conflict of ever greater proportions. This situation lasted for a year and a half, during which Mesa was forced to resign, having previously fanned the flames by making decisions considered one-sided. Then in February 2006, the Congress passed a law to convene a constituent assembly and hold a simultaneous referendum with the following single question:

> Within the framework of national unity, do you agree to giving the Constituent Assembly the binding mandate to establish a regime of departmental autonomy, to be applied directly after the promulgation of the new constitution in the departments where this referendum produces a majority, in such a way that the authorities are directly elected by the citizens and receive from the national state those executive powers, normative and administrative attributes, and economic and financial resources assigned to them by the new constitution and the laws?

Nationally, the result was 56 percent against the referendum and 44 in favor. The departmental breakdown, however, revealed the deep fissure between east and west. The "yes" vote prevailed by 70 percent or more in four departments (those of the *media luna*), whereas 65 percent voted "no" in the remaining five, which are more populated and indigenous. The Morales government openly campaigned for the "no" option and claimed victory. Even though there is no insuperable difficulty in having some departments with autonomous regimes while others opt for the status quo or some other form of decentralization—this is how things work in Spain—the results of the referendum only further embittered regional rivalries. The perception common in the west is that putative departmental autonomies reflect the interests of Santa Cruz more than those of the country as a whole. For its part, the *cruceño* view is that the autonomies regime should necessarily be included in the new constitution. As a way of frustrating the autonomies demanded by the departments, the MAS representatives in the Constituent Assembly muddied the waters by putting into the draft text two other types of autonomy: indigenous and regional (the latter in addition to existing departments and municipalities). This seemed geared toward reducing the power already in the hands of the departments.

Notwithstanding this, it is interesting to note that in some departments where the "no" vote won overall, the departmental capitals nevertheless inclined toward voting "yes." This may suggest that the regime of autonomies encounters greater opposition in indigenous rural areas, revealing a significant level of disagreement between these and urban nonindigenous voters.

Regionalism and Landownership

A new and explosive controversy has arisen in recent years over landownership. The prevailing view in the west is that the elite of the *oriente* have unjustly and illegally amassed large extensions of land which lay idle for speculative reasons. It is argued that such lands should be redistributed among the indigenous populations of the west, who lack adequate land. The response from the *oriente* has been to deny that land hoarding exists, since the size of agricultural holdings is a function of the sort of modern, business agriculture and extensive cattle ranching practiced; to be economically efficient, large units of pasture are required. To this argument the following addendum is tacked: the techniques of farming use demand that land be left fallow for a certain number of years, which does not mean that the land has been abandoned. Finally, there is the argument that within a unit of landholding, the amount of land cultivated varies according to market trends, and that this may mean that substantial areas of land have to stay idle for a while. Landowners also point out that land that did not form part of former haciendas was either assigned under the 1953 agrarian reform or legally acquired through purchase.

In view of the strength of the emotional, regionalist, and racist connotations, land concentration is a problem that cannot easily be resolved through technical reasoning. Not only is the debate about the fairness of land distribution but also the supposedly abusive stance taken by the smaller population of the east toward the more numerous indigenous populations of the west. This has given rise to the fact that the agrarian laws of the 1950s became wholly discredited and were supplemented by a new legislation, the INRA law, in 1995. This established a rigorous system of control over land left idle, the so-called unproductive estates, through a system of land title revision (*saneamiento*) that would determine whether land should remain in the hands of its current owners or revert to the state for subsequent redistribution. The system of revision is complex, expensive, and slow. Completing it, it is reckoned, may take another twenty years. Meanwhile, regionalist arguments over land continue, with all the distortions that they attract, and the potential for clashes over landownership remains as potent and dangerous as ever.[22]

Were it not for the antagonism between *collas* and *cambas*—or east and west (which now amounts to the same thing)—there would be no conflict. With a territory of over a million square kilometers and a population of nine million, the index of land occupation in Bolivia is a mere 1.4 persons per square kilometer. This compares with 40 persons in Brazil and 200 in Central American countries. At the same time, the assumption that all the inhabitants of a country should have access to the land may be justified in predominantly agrarian societies, where people derive their income more from subsistence farming than any other form of employment. However, in Bolivia, the percentage of the rural population has been in progressive decline over the last half century. Today the country is about 35 percent rural and 65 percent urban. The pressures on landholding therefore have regionalist and political connotations rather than ones of economics or survival.[23] This is particularly so if the prevalent free market system is taken into account; this enables those living in the Altiplano to choose—because it is more economical to do so—to import food products rather than cultivate them themselves, or to involve themselves in commerce rather than tilling the land.

What Lies Ahead?

Regionalism has acquired a racial dimension in recent years that makes it especially dangerous, and the struggle between east and west has revealed itself in multiple ways. A manifestation of this has been the debate over whether the Constituent Assembly—in which the MAS was in a majority and most of its delegates were of indigenous origin—should be *originaria*. This would mean that the powers of the assembly were not subject to formal limitations, insofar as it can introduce whatever changes that it considers necessary, conferring on itself the authority to start from scratch with institutional change. This proposal ran into an unflinching opposition among the rest of the parties, who argued for the need to conform to the basic principles contained in the existing constitution. They were supported in this by the leaders of the regional civic committees, alert to the defense of rights they considered in danger of being violated.

The other burning issue is the adoption—or not—of departmental autonomies. The MAS argued that because the majority of voters showed that they were against autonomies, these could not be incorporated into the constitution, irrespective of the verdict of the referendum. For their part, the departments of the *media luna* and the opposition parties argued that the regime of autonomies should apply—at the very least—to those departments that voted "yes." While this may happen, various indigenous organizations that support the MAS rallied against the landowners of Santa Cruz, whom they characterized as *latifundistas* and exploiters. In this setting, animosities among ordinary people for those living on the other side of the Andean divide grew and multiplied.

This, then, is not a classic democratic confrontation between government and opposition. Much more worryingly, it involves rivalries between two regions which—each in its own way—are fighting for supremacy to run the country or to preserve what they have possessed for over a century.

A peaceful, consensual, and definitive solution to this was the task allotted to the Constituent Assembly, which first met in Sucre in 2006 with a view to rewriting the constitution by August 2007. That date came and went, however, and the Congress extended its sessions up until December 2007. With this new deadline approaching, new obstacles emerged, such as the insistence on a two-thirds majority for approving the new constitutional text and the dispute over Sucre as full capital of the republic. This prompted the ruling party to push through approval of a draft that had been rejected by the opposition parties and by six departments (represented by their prefects and civic committees). So it was that 2008 began with positions polarized. Doubts remained as to whether a system of autonomous departments and municipalities or some other system of real decentralization would be achieved. In May 2008, a referendum was organized by the civic committee of Santa Cruz to approve the "statutes of autonomy," a text that ran quite contrary to the system of autonomies countenanced by the Constituent Assembly. A substantial majority of those who took part voted in approval. In the opinion of this author, greater autonomy would raise the self-esteem of Bolivia's regions, creating a new political balance within the country and dispensing with a model where one hegemonic region exists as the generating source and distributor of power. But as always, the future of Bolivia is a question mark.

Oppressed or Privileged Regions?

Some Historical Reflections on the Use of State Resources

ROSSANA BARRAGÁN *with the assistance of José Péres Cajías*

Somewhat provocatively, José Luis Roca has written that the history of Bolivia was a struggle between regions and not classes (Roca 1999, 39). Recent history, however, shows that political and social dynamics are not just regional, and that regionalism can encompass ethnic oppositions, class conflict, and political projects of different orders. It is an opposition of east and west, *collas* (from the Altiplano) and *cambas* (from the lowlands), indigenous peoples, whites and mestizos, tradition and modernity, collectivism and private initiative, peoples and oligarchs.

Centralism has been described as an oppressive power, as an expression of internal colonialism that has supposedly unleashed such wrongs and injuries that the regions have suffered in equal measure with indigenous or other subaltern groups.[1] Such clean-cut, dualist explanations tend to reproduce overly simplistic histories. Here we seek to analyze this complex issue, focusing attention toward a specific and key attribute: fiscal resources, their origins, and their distribution. We suggest that it was the central government which financed the regions, while to some extent giving rise to *cruceño* regionalism at the end of the twentieth century. We argue that if there was a single state policy that was constant, sustained, and enduring, it was the policy that favored Santa Cruz, a policy that came at the cost of serious internal imbalances.

Our starting point involves an analysis of population distribution. It was never possible in Bolivia to build the sort of hegemony of a single region or city that was seen in the examples of Lima in Peru or Buenos Aires in Argentina. Rather than a center, Bolivia had axes, or *ejes*—giving rise to the term *ejemonía*.[2] That we talk of axes is in itself significant, involving as it does the primacy of large spaces and regions. In the nineteenth century, the axis ran between north and south, but neither had complete hegemony over the other; rather, there was a partial dominance that fluctuated between between

La Paz and Chuquisaca. From the beginning of the twentieth century through around 1970, the hegemony shifted toward the central, transversal axis of La Paz–Cochabamba–Santa Cruz. Within this axis, the hegemony of La Paz was latterly disputed by Santa Cruz. Over the long run, the center has always been a matter of dispute, and no single center has been able to consolidate itself.

We will use this perspective to analyze the state's income, the role of the departments in generating that income, and its distribution. These resources were never divided up equitably from a demographic point of view; those which benefited most were in the least densely populated parts of the country. However, over time there has been a trend toward a greater correlation between population and budget, a shift that needs to be seen as a transition from one set of relationships and linkages with the state to another.

Another basic feature of the budget was that it was geared primarily toward sustaining a state bureaucracy that after 1825 grew with a particular logic to it. It was not a growth imposed by a political center on different layers of territorial organization. Rather, state growth was led by demand within the different levels of political administration: departments, provinces, and cantons. Each department (or more accurately, each departmental capital) strove to become a center of the judiciary (superior courts), the church (dioceses), and the education system (having their own university). Thus was established a tension between the unitary state and what today we call devolution and decentralization, especially toward departmental capitals. This gave rise to a debate over the generation of revenues and their expenditure, a debate expressed in terms of the unitary state versus federalism. The unitary principle presupposed that the budget was a collective and common purse for the benefit of those "poor" departments that could not meet their own spending commitments.

Thus, both the strengthening of the center and of the departments happened simultaneously, grounded on the differentiation established for the raising of revenue in the last decades of the nineteenth century between the national, departmental, and municipal levels of government. The frequent disputes between these three over taxation helped consolidate them, revealing at the same time the inadequate fiscal powers of each.

When we examine the nature of state resources, we see the fragility of the central state and how it had to fight to impose itself over economic sectors and groups through endless disputes. Thus, Potosí and La Paz subsidized a number of departments that lacked the capacity to raise taxes. The center indeed, constructed and strengthened the regions. The demands made by the regions on the center, and their own *regionalismo,* can be attributed to the liberal policies and to the disputes over how to divide up the resources from the loans and debts that built up with the development of transport infrastructure (basically railways) at the end of the nineteenth century. In more recent years, royalties from oil production have also played a role in the construction and consolidation of regions. In 1872, it was established that all exports were national resources; consequently, all mining production was classified in this way, enabling subsidies to be offered to the departments of the east. With respect to oil production, however, departmental royalties not only allowed producing departments to develop but—over the medium to long term—become sources of regional imbalance and inequality.

From *Ejemonías* to Hegemonies: Economic Prevalence of the North and Fragile Relations between North and South (1825–1900)

Between 1825 and 1900, Bolivia's population rose only slightly, from 1.1 million to 1.6 million. It was a basically rural country (with only 10 percent living in cities in 1825). Until 1900, La Paz was the largest department, accounting for 35 percent of the population in 1825 and 24 percent in 1900. Notably, five departments—La Paz, Oruro, Potosí, Chuquisaca, and Cochabamba— accounted for 93 percent of the population in 1825 and 82 percent in 1900 (Barragán 2002). The population of Santa Cruz accounted for only 7 percent in 1825, and the combined population of Santa Cruz, Beni, and what would later become the department of Pando (together representing 60 percent of the country's territory) accounted for 14 percent in 1900. The western part of the country therefore accounted for the lion's share of Bolivia's population.

No department enjoyed hegemony as such; rather, there was a broad axis of north and south. This north-south axis or arc came about in large part because of patterns of trade and access to available ports. Potosí and the south enjoyed a preferential link through the ports of Cobija or La Mar on the Pacific. The north, particularly La Paz, Oruro, and Cochabamba, were linked more closely to the port of Arica. State policy played a key role in increasing trade through one or other of these ports, and as a result alternated between favoring the north and favoring the south.

The population began to increase faster after 1900, but the big change only took place in the second half of the twentieth century. Between 1900 and 2000, the population of Santa Cruz multiplied fivefold; that of the Beni, tenfold. With the growing importance of the city and department of Santa Cruz, the north-south axis became an east-west one. However, there was also a central "urban axis" around the three largest cities, which, between them, accounted for two-thirds of the population of the country (UNDP 2004, 64).

From independence and through most of the nineteenth century, Bolivia and the Bolivian state lived from the tax on indigenous peoples (Sánchez Albornoz 1978; Griesehaber 1977; Platt 1986; Huber 1991). This accounted for an average of 35 percent of its revenues between 1825 and 1880. Those departments with the largest indigenous populations (La Paz, Potosí, and Oruro) were those that contributed most to the state coffers. As of the 1880s, taxes from mining exports came to predominate, but this did not mean that revenues from more traditional taxes diminished.

Whereas the mining departments and those with large indigenous populations provided most of the revenue, spending was distributed more equitably. However, on a per capita basis, it was far less equitable. The department of Potosí (with 22 percent of the population) was the department with the largest budget in 1827 (5 percent), followed by La Paz (34 percent of the population) with 3 percent. At the other end of the scale were Chuquisaca and Santa Cruz, with very different populations (13 percent and 7 percent respectively) with 2 percent of the budget each.

In spite of what we might expect, between 1827 and 1883 there was no large increase in the spending on the central government in Sucre. While the amount enjoyed by each department did not change substantially in Cochabamba and Oruro, the amount allocated to La Paz increased.

Over the course of the nineteenth century there was a change toward more equitable fiscal distribution in terms of population. For those departments with very scanty populations, this involved an erosion of their previous economic prerogatives. Changes in the distribution of budget allocations—more specifically the installation of state administration (or "territorialization of rule" [Vandergeest and Lee Peluso 1995, 415])—is also key to understanding relations between the center and the regions. The growth in the state was not the consequence of expansion from the center but rather a reflection of the interests and demands made by political elites at the departmental level that entailed a multiplication of state structures. One example was the organization and administration of justice, which underwent an important decentralization or deconcentration during the course of the nineteenth century. The two superior courts in La Paz and Sucre were eventually replicated in almost every other department (Barragán 2002). This pattern repeated itself in

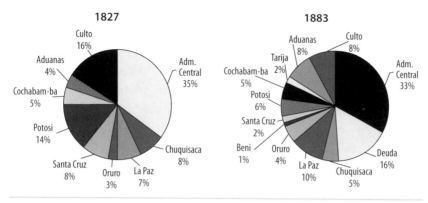

Figure 5.1. Budget allocation, comparing 1827 with 1883 (without education). In the 1827 budget, notice the relatively small difference between departments, between 3 percent and 8 percent. La Paz had 7 percent and Santa Cruz more. Potosí was the exception, since the Casa de la Moneda was established there. Tarija at the time did not appear with a separate budget, and Beni did not exist as a department. In the 1883 budget, the significance of debt payment is clear. The amount of the budget going to each department varied between 2 percent and 10 percent. Oruro and Cochabamba maintained their share of the budget, La Paz increased its share, and that of Chuquisaca and Potosí diminished. (Barragán, 2002.)

education, law and order, health, and other areas, giving rise to heated debate over revenues and (more importantly) over the nature of what was referred to as "the political association."

The creation of new state institutions at the various levels of government led to debate about the relative contribution made by each department and the type of political association to which they belonged. Representatives from departments with fewer resources—now those with most—tended to plead for a unitary system of government. The economic weight of some departments, and the size of their fiscal contribution, led them to question the way the state grew in line with of the demands of other departments.

This mismatch between the tax burden of different departments and between demands for a unitary or federal system—taking the latter to mean that each department would look after its own spending on administration, justice, education, and so on—also arose out of the discussion over how Santa Cruz should fund its budget. The idea prevailed that each department should not try to be self-sufficient, because this would be harmful to the republic as a whole, encouraging revolutions "in the name of federalism." Federalism also arose over the issue of the budget, since the department of Tarija was unable to cover its spending. A representative from Tarija responded, asking, "What is the form of government we have adopted? A federal one so that each department limits its spending to what it produces, or a unitary one in which all the nation's spending comes from the public Treasury? If we have to live with provincial meanspiritedness, let us withdraw from the Constitution."

Although Bolivia opted for a unitary rather than federal government, the system of representation was basically territorial (Barragán 2006). This was the form of representation adopted by the two assemblies that defined the creation of Bolivia. It was as though deputies represented federal states, even though the law stipulated a link between representation and population. So in 1825 Santa Cruz had one deputy per 15,000 inhabitants, followed by Cochabamba with one per 16,444. Oruro and La Paz, however, had one per 37,000 and 38,000 inhabitants, respectively. Santa Cruz and Cochabamba thus had twice the per capita representation of Oruro and La Paz, given the size of the indigenous population of the latter two. Chuquisaca and Potosí were somewhere in between these extremes, with roughly one deputy per 30,000 people. This territorial system of representation was reproduced within each department, with each province represented by one deputy for most of the nineteenth century.

This situation did not change much during the rest of the nineteenth century, and generally speaking the number of deputies increased for all departments (table 5.1). By the beginning of the twentieth century, the most overrepresented departments were Beni, Oruro, and Tarija, with one deputy per 15,000 inhabitants. Potosí had one deputy per 29,228 inhabitants, and La Paz one per 26,683. It was only at the time when patterns of migration changed the axis to one of east-west that representation became more inequitable for the east. In 1992, representation was at its most skewed in Pando (one representative per 5,439 inhabitants) whereas Santa Cruz was worst off (with one per 80,258).

In this system of political organization and representation, the capital cities were the political centers of these large spaces known as departments. The urban bias and the political hegemony of urban citizens were evident. In the 1844 elections, for instance, more than a quarter (26 percent) of voters came from the departmental capitals, even though their populations accounted for barely 10 percent of the total population.[3] However, there were important differences between departments, as well as within them. In the greatest example of disparity, nearly half the voters in Tarija and Chuquisaca (42 percent) came from their respective capitals, though these formed only

Table 5.1. Ratio of deputies to population, 1826–1992

	1826			1900			1924	1938	1992–93		
	Deps.	Pop.	Pop. per Dep.	Deps.	Pop.	Pop. per Dep.	Deps.	Deps.	Deps. (1993)	Pop. (1992)	Pop. per Dep.
La Paz	10	375,000	38,000	16	426,930	26,683	16	16	28	1,900,786	67,885
Potosí	8	245,000	31,000	11	321,510	29,228	11	12	19	645,889	33,994
Chuquisaca	5	142,000	28,000	8	200,539	25,067	8	9	13	453,756	34,904
Santa Cruz	5	75,000	15,000	7	171,592	24,513	7	10	17	1,364,389	80,258
Cochabamba	9	148,000	16,000	14	326,163	23,297	14	14	18	1,110,205	61,678
Oruro	3	115,000	38,333	6	86,081	14,347	6	7	10	340,114	34,011
Tarija[1]				5	67,887	13,577	3	7	9	291,407	32,379
Beni[2]				2	32,908[3]	16,454	5	7	9	276,174	30,686
Pando[4]								3	7	38,072	5,439
Litoral[5]				3							
Total	40	1,100,000	166,302	72	1,633,610	173,167	73	130	130	6,420,792	381,235

Source: Barragán (2006).

[1] Founded in 1831.

[2] Founded in 1842.

[3] Includes the population of the extreme north, which became the department of Pando.

[4] Founded in 1938.

[5] Litoral formed part of Potosí in 1826.

between 6 percent and 8 percent of their population. In La Paz and Oruro, the voting public of their capitals constituted 34 percent and 35 percent, respectively. Cochabamba was the city with the least electoral weight (18 percent) while Potosi was midway between Cochabamba and La Paz/Oruro.

The power and centrality of the cities also expressed itself in the figure of the departmental prefect, who resided in the capital and who appointed—in a top-down, hierarchical fashion—the governors of the provinces and the *corregidores* of the *cantones*. The prefects were omnipotent in their departments, concentrating political, economic, and administrative power. They acted as the officers of the treasury, exercising control over the local treasury and customs office, fixing tax rates, approving financial arrangements, overseeing debts, and supervising tenders. They had control over the local police authorities. They were also in charge of education and responsible for agriculture, industry, and commerce. In times of war, they were in charge of recruitment for the army, provisions, and supplies for the troops. Their powers of oversight stretched to exercising supervision over the judges and the courts.

The power of the prefects explains how every revolution or change in government arose from agreements and pacts between departmental leaders, whether prefects or those who aspired to the position, and why every government established itself on the basis of the same strategic geography—in essence a network between capital cities and the main urban centers of each department.

The Center in Check: Central and Departmental Finances (1900–1952)

The building of a central state was given a boost in 1872 with the establishment of a national treasury alongside departmental and municipal treasuries. National revenues came primarily from customs income and export duties levied on silver and other minerals. Departmental revenues were defined as all those not contemplated as national ones, and municipal revenues were established by a decree of March 16, 1864 (Anuario de Leyes 1872, 1873, 212)

It was in the latter part of the nineteenth century, too, that the state began to live off mining activity, first from silver and then later tin. However, it proved difficult for those running the state to tax an activity which was in the hands of a few but very powerful people, either the so-called "silver patriarchs" of the late nineteenth century or the "tin barons" of the first half of the twentieth century. The central state thus had difficulty in replacing the tax on indigenous peoples and came to depend on the proceeds of a variety of taxes on different activities and individuals. It is for this reason that we liken the national tax system to a "thicket" (*boscoso*) (Barragán and Péres 2006), with a tax system that was extensive rather than intensive in scope. Unable to establish blanket and/or sustainable taxes, there was a continual increase in the number of revenue sources, with none of them yielding much income. In 1900 there were 37 sources of tax income, but by 1938 the number had risen to 138, of which 91 percent—taken on their own—produced less than 1 percent of total revenue.

Economic expansion from mining thus became, without a doubt, the principal source of national income. However, these taxes did not necessarily come from the mining companies themselves, nor did they have much effect on their profits. The importance of customs income over the first three decades of the twentieth century shows how the state sought to profit from mining through import duties. Following the 1929 crisis (which hit tin exports hard and therefore national revenues) and then the Chaco War (1932–1935), the state acquired greater control over mining, and the mining companies in particular. It was able to raise the proportion of direct taxes on mining to the point where these constituted 43 percent of national tax revenues (table 5.2).[4]

As far as departmental treasuries are concerned, up until 1954 the department of La Paz generated more than one-third of the total for all departments. In 1923, it had reached 50 percent. Cochabamba also raised significant departmental revenues, while Oruro managed to raise its share considerably as of the 1950s.

However, there was no single tax system at the departmental level. Departments not only differed in the levels of revenue but also in the activities and subjects that they taxed. Indeed, even where they levied similar sorts of tax, the rates charged and the methods used to collect them varied. One of the few taxes common to all was the tax on property. This was not levied at the same rate in all departments, its impact being heavier in the west of the country. In 1903 it represented 58 percent of departmental revenues in Cochabmaba, whereas in Santa Cruz it barely reached 20 percent. In 1913, it represented 60 percent of income in the department of Oruro, but no more than 26 percent in Tarija (Barragán and Péres 2006).

So the departments had exactly the same sort of difficulties as the central government with respect to their ability to raise revenues and the legitimacy and legality with which they did so. The departmental treasuries had to fight

Table 5.2. Principal sources of treasury revenue (% of total income)

Sources of Income	1903	1913	1923	1930	1938	1949	1954
Customs	**50.08**	**47.06**	**23.48**	27.77			
Antofagasta	21.39	14.50					
Arica	5.13						
La Paz	14.26	13.59	7.98				
Oruro			7.18				
Other customs agencies	9.30	18.97	8.32				
15% charge on liquidation of taxed mercantile policies		5.53					
Customs charge on imports					12.40		3.33
Tariff charge on exports					8.21	7.73	2.71
Customs duties on imports					5.10	12.12	10.64
Additional tax on exports						26.61	4.05
Rubber, Export duties	**17.40**	**6.80**					
Mining, all export duties	**9.42**	**15.72**	**13.38**	15.24	1.15	1.52	
Silver	1.37						
Tin	6.42	14.72	12.00	14.71		1.52	
Copper	1.28						
Bismuth	0.29						
Stamped silver	0.07						
Other minerals		1.00		0.53			
Other mining taxes (added)			1.38		0.22		
Additional taxes on non-tin metals						4.66	2.03

Mining profits			5.99	6.31	1.46		
Mining patents		1.22	1.96	0.75	0.73	0.11	
Publication of mining concessions				0.03			
Flat minerals		0.02	0.06	0.02			
Mining transfers		0.14	0.06	0.02	0.07		
Tax on mining dividends					0.10	0.57	
Increase of Bs1 pound sterling tin price					0.06	0.78	
Bs. 100 s/ton charge on exported tin						0.18	
Additional charge on mining exports						0.06	
Other Income							
Railway revenues			7.18				
Legalization of consular documents				6.31			
Exchange rate differentials					31.37		
Extraordinary revenues					7.89		
Sales tax						5.68	
Tax on foreign currency sales							9.00
National tax on chicha output							6.05
National beer tax							5.84
Income from agrarian reform							4.66
Profits tax							4.48
Stamp duty							3.49
Tax on cigarettes and tobacco							3.33
% Subtotal	76.90	70.95	52.11	56.45	68.76	60.01	59.61

Source: National budgets, elaborated in Barragán and Péres (2006).

Table 5.3. Changes in departmental income, 1903–1954 (thousands of bolivianos)

	1903		1913		1923		1930		1949		1954	
	Amt.	%	Amt.	%	Amt.	%	Amt.	%	Amt.	%	Amt.	%
Chuquisaca	242	11	199	8	274	4	255	4	8,890	5	22,289	5
La Paz	726	32	949	36	3,023	50	2,917	42	47,819	28	154,188	32
Cochabamba	318	14	420	16	754	12	1,072	16	47,569	28	50,062	10
Potosí	394	17	461	18	824	14	733	11	26,747	16	127,010	26
Oruro	186	8	158	6	703	12	1,383	20	14,565	8	44,206	9
Santa Cruz	152	7	150	6	161	3	162	2	12,915	7	21,598	4
Tarija	110	5	129	5	170	3	256	4	9,171	5	33,957	7
Beni	167	7	166	6	193	3	130	2	2,610	2	16,225	3
Pando	0								2,216	1	12,133	3
Total	2,296	100	2,631	100	6,101	100	6,908	100	172,504	100	481,668	100

Source: Barragán and Pérez, 2006.

with the central state to define exactly which income streams were national and which were departmental. Such conflicts revealed the many limitations in taxing specific products or social groups; those sources that proved sustainable over time often involved double or even triple taxation. Few products and few subjects or citizens bore the burden of the tax system. One area that was particularly prone to tax was consumption of alcohol—chicha, *aguardiente,* and beer—which were subject to taxation at the national, departmental, and municipal level.[5]

Such constant complaints and arguments between different levels of taxation thus revealed the way in which the state developed in Bolivia from the nineteenth century onward. This was characterized by constant trials of strength between the national and departmental treasuries.

The Center and the Strengthening of the Regions

As well as establishing the origin and flow of revenues at national and departmental levels, it is equally important to analyze how these resources were spent and how national treasury funds were distributed among the different regions and departments (table 5.4). In fact spending was divided fairly equally between the central state and the departmental level of government from 1903 up to the early 1920s.[6] From then until 1938, the central state began to accumulate a larger proportion of resources: 69 percent in 1923, 77 percent in 1930, and 65 percent in 1938.[7] However, the magnitude of this spending is reduced if we bear in mind that it includes military expenditures and the payment on the public debt (this last previously assigned to the treasury budget). Together, these constituted the largest item of public spending throughout the first half of the twentieth century, and as of 1920, they absorbed nearly half of national spending.

But it is also important to show how the national state spent its resources in each of the various different regions and departments over the first half of the twentieth century. In 1903, the gross amounts channeled to each department suggest that there were no major differences between them and that there was no particular concentration in spending on bureaucracy or services in any particular place. If we analyze such spending by population (using the 1900 census as a base), we see that the per capita figures are small and that there are no significant differences among the western departments (Bs. 0.44 per person in Chuquisaca, Bs. 0.32 in La Paz, Bs. 0.38 in Potosí, Bs. 0.6 in Oruro, and only Bs. 0.15 in Cochabamba). In the eastern departments,

Table 5.4. National spending on central and noncentral government, 1903–1954 (millions of bolivianos)

	Spending Division	Total	%	Minus Military Spending	%	Minus Military Spending and Debt Servicing	%
1903	Central	3.3	44	2.3	46		
	Noncentral	4.3	56	2.8	54		
1913	Central	9.7	44	8.2	47		
	Noncentral	12.5	56	9.4	53		
1923	Central	25.9	69	18.2	61	3.6	24
	Noncentral	11.6	31	11.6	39	11.4	76
1930	Central	36.5	77	27.8	71	9.0	45
	Noncentral	11.1	23	11.1	29	11.1	55
1938	Central	178.7	65	91.9	49		
	Noncentral	95.5	35	95.5	51		
1949	Central	972.4	46	580.7	33		
	Noncentral	1,153.1	54	1,153.1	67		
1954	Central	9,026.5	59	7,296.7	54		
	Noncentral	6,272.4	41	6,272.4	46		

Source: National budgets, compiled in Barragán and Péres (2006).

the scant population translated into higher per capita spending, and the least economically important department is that which received the most per capita to cover the workings of its bureaucracy. The figures were Bs. 0.99 in Tarija, Bs. 0.92 in Santa Cruz, Bs. 6.81 in the Beni. Since much of the budget went to pay officials' salaries, these amounts would indicate a larger number of officials per inhabitant in these less-populated departments.

What might be interpreted as state inefficiency can be explained by the need to create a physical presence in the more remote parts of the country. A quick look at the spending figures shows that 15 percent went toward colonization services, of which more than 90 percent went to the Territorio Nacional de Colonias, which would become the department of Pando.

Ten years later, in 1913, colonization spending was distributed to missions throughout the length and breadth of the country, but with an emphasis still on the lowlands. In 1913, educational expenditure within the regions took on a more important role, accounting for one-third of the monies reaching the departments from the central government's coffers. In 1923, the most decentralized services were education, government, and communications. Schools accounted for 8 percent of national spending, police 7 percent, and postal services and telegraphy 6 percent. In 1930, the budget showed that education spending in all departments absorbed at least one-third of resources transferred to the departments. Two decades later, in 1949, the importance of educational districts had increased considerably. Spending reached 16 percent of national treasury outlays, accounting for half of the resources received in the great majority of departments.

With the passage of time, spending on departmental bureaucracies became more concentrated in La Paz. In 1923, one-third of national spending on departmental administration, and 15 percent of spending on communications went to the department of La Paz. By 1930, the department was receiving 40 percent of national spending on departmental administration and 33 percent of spending on education. Analysis of the 68 percent of national spending on the departments showed that La Paz received more resources because of the spending focus on hygiene, education, and government. This does not mean that the distribution was unjust, since the smaller depart-

Table 5.5. Spending by principal areas, 1903–1954 (% of total budget)

	1903	1913	1923	1930	1938	1949	1954
Defense	33	21	21	18	32	18	11
Debt payment			39	39	26	29	32
Education	2	11	9	9	8	18	23
Treasury	19	18	4	2	3	3	2
Government	8	17	8	5	6	8	10
Colonization	19	6	1	2	0	0	0
Development/ public works	10	11	2	1	5	1	1
Other	10	16	16	23	19	22	20

Source: National budgets, compiled in Barragán and Péres (2006).

ments also received priority attention. Looking at departmental spending items in the national budget in 1950, Tarija received Bs. 359 per inhabitant, Beni Bs. 299, La Paz Bs. 290, and Santa Cruz Bs. 286. So, even if there was a concentration of national spending in La Paz, the central state took care to attend to the needs of the regions less able to generate their own income. Oruro and Potosí, which generated significant departmental fiscal revenues, received Bs. 244 and Bs. 225 per person, respectively. Chuquisaca received only Bs. 206, and Cochabamba came last (as in 1903) with Bs. 193.

If central state resources had been distributed in line with revenue generated and population, Santa Cruz, Tarija, Beni, and then Pando would have received far less than what they did in fact. In other words, the national government subsidized the building and operation of departmental administrations and institutions (and the lion's share of services like education) for those departments unable to to finance those functions based on internal revenues.

Because only some departmental treasuries were self-sufficient, while others were highly dependent on transfers from the national treasury, the issue of financial sustainability had been explicit ever since the tax decentralization moves of 1872. The country needed a way to ensure that those with surpluses helped finance those without. It was thus that the national treasury, which received funds primarily from the three mining departments, constantly subsidized the rest from the very moment that separate departmental treasuries came into being.

In 1872, it was undoubtedly the case that the department of La Paz was the one which generated most revenue, producing 42 percent of total departmental income. Second came Potosí, with 16 percent. The surplus from La Paz represented 57 percent of the total, and Potosí 15 percent. La Paz used only 26 percent of the revenue it generated, and the remaining 74 percent was distributed between the other departments.

During the first half of the twentieth century, subsidies from the national government were essential to enable the economically smaller departments to function (see table 5.7). Deputy Roca (of Santa Cruz), for example, sustained in 1921–22 that "the subsidy that the national treasury owes to the departmental treasury of Santa Cruz is not for the payment of debt, rather to cover the deficit that appears in the budget for that department. My honorable colleagues are well aware of the situation of penury that is afflicting the country at this time, and of the particular crisis now suffered for some time by the department of Santa Cruz. It is for that reason that the depart-

Table 5.6. National revenues by department, 1872 (tens of thousands of bolivianos)

	Amount	% Collected	Excess	% Collected	% Row	Total Income	%
Chuquisaca	9.1	15	6.0	8	40	15.1	12
La Paz	14.8	24	40.9	56	73	55.7	42
Cochabamba	10.6	17	2.0	3	16	12.5	10
Potosí	10.6	18	11.0	15	51	21.6	17
Oruro	4.5	7	6.7	9	60	11.1	9
Tarija	1.0	2	1.4	2	59	2.4	1
Santa Cruz	5.5	9	2.0	3	27	7.5	5
Cobija	2.8	5	2.2	3	43	5.0	4
Beni	1.6	3	0.4	1	3	15.1	1
Total	604.8	100	722.4	100	54	1,327.2	100

Source: Redactor del año 1872, 594; percentages have been rounded.

ment in question requires immediate support from the national treasury" (Congressional Proceedings for the ordinary and extraordinary legislatures of 1921–22, 199).

The fragile and dependent nature of the *cruceña* economy was such that the "particular crisis" in question was in fact a chronic problem throughout the 1930s. Even though table 5.7 suggests that the problem appeared only as of 1949 because of the late formal creation of Pando as a department, the situation was in fact alarming throughout the north and east. The departmental treasury in the Beni was incapable of self-sufficiency and was entirely dependent on the national treasury through 1954. The same was true to a lesser extent for Tarija.

It was in this context then that executive complaints about the constant increase in flows of money to the regions and their lack of contributions became commonplace. The executive decried the continual demands and pressures exercised through parliament, pointing out that the national treasury and central state found itself forced to "invent" sources of revenue or to resort to borrowing. The Bolivian state began to contract loans, primarily for the building of railways and roads, at the beginning of the twentieth century. Disputes arose over how such borrowing should be invested. Images of aban-

Table 5.7. National treasury subsidies to departmental treasuries, 1903–1954 (bolivianos)

	Pando		Beni		Tarija		Santa Cruz		La Paz		Potosí	
	Amount	% of Dept. Income	Amount	% of Dept. Income	Amount	% of Dept. Income	Amount	% of Dept. Income	Amount	% of Dept. Income	Amount	% of Dept. Income
1903			115,000	69	26,915	24	30,000	20				
1913			91,916	55	45,000	35	37,504	25				
1923			63,110	33	41,976	24	36,913	22			30,000	4
1930			31,395	24					142,880	5		
1949	2,000,000	90	2,000,000	77								
1954	11,200,000	92	11,200,000	69	190,000	6						

Source: National budgets, compiled in Barragán and Péres (2006).

donment and overcentralization were closely linked with how that spending should be distributed and the impact of liberalization in the late nineteenth century: the construction of railway links to the Pacific and the opening up of frontiers, leading to the loss of key highland markets for commodities from Santa Cruz (Rodríguez 1993).

For this reason demands for a rail linkage multiplied in Santa Cruz, the most land-locked department of the republic. A memorandum was written in 1904, and in 1910 there were representations made to the Ministry of Government and Development, pointing out, "The public is well aware that since the Antofagasta railway reached Oruro, there has been ruinous competition from foreign goods similar to those from Santa Cruz, such as sugar, rice, and others that have been entirely displaced from the national market. Today, it is only just possible to send leather, alcohol, and coffee in much reduced amounts to Sucre and Cochabamba" (quoted in Barragán and Péres 2006).

However, after the Chaco War and in view of the oil potential of the eastern lowlands, state support to these departments—Santa Cruz in particular—translated into an important injection of capital. The flow of investment thus changed direction. As of 1942, the U.S. Bohan Mission suggested the guidelines for a policy which was to continue up until the end of the century. This included the construction of communications, the development of agriculture, and the production of hydrocarbons in the *oriente*. Among the most important investments were the building of an eastern railway network, with connections from Santa Cruz to Puerto Suárez (1948) and to Yacuiba (1954), as well as the completion of the road between Santa Cruz and Cochabamba (1954) (Ybarnegaray 1999).

But the new role of the state was not limited just to investing the resources obtained but also to undertaking legal changes to make better use of the oil-producing regions. The policy of the Bolivian state toward hydrocarbons was quite different than its policy toward mining. Mining taxes were always considered to be national revenues, and it was these that gave life to the Bolivian state in the late nineteenth century and the first half of the twentieth century. They made it possible to provide state services in the more remote, less-favored, and less-populated parts of the country. Because they were national revenues, earnings from mining did not generate significant resources for the departmental treasuries or for the producer departments.[8]

Oil revenues, however, were dealt with differently, due probably to the influence of the Bohan Mission, as well as the decision of the state to respond to regional demands. In 1938, it was decided that 11 percent of the value of oil production would go in payments to the region where it had been produced (Miranda 2005).[9] In this way, the budget resources from oil represented 22 percent of departmental revenues in 1949.[10] In Santa Cruz, oil production became a crucial component of the departmental budget. In 1949, 66 percent of all oil royalties went to Santa Cruz, representing 78 percent of that department's budgeted income. Of planned revenues in 1954, participation in oil production brought in one-fifth of the total income of the department. In 1955, 96 percent of the country's oil royalties went to Santa Cruz. The department received US$76,000 in 1954, US$355,000 in 1955, and US$622,000 in 1956 (Sandoval et al. 2003). This rose to US$3 million between 1959 and 1964, and US$400 million between 1960 and 1986 (UNDP 2004, 41).

In this chapter we have looked at the other side of the coin of departmental fiscal imparity. The west not only facilitated the workings of the state apparatus in the east for much of Bolivia's national history, but it also subsidized spending and investment (for instance on education) there. For most of the nineteenth century (through 1870 at least), the tax on indigenous peoples was the main source of state revenue. The departments with the largest indigenous populations were La Paz, Potosí, and Oruro, and these therefore sustained the country, fiscally. The 1872 reform, which introduced a distinction between national, departmental, and municipal revenues, established that all export revenue was national revenue. Mining revenues, generated exclusively in specific departments (Potosí, Oruro, and secondarily in La Paz) fell under this rubric. Such revenues brought few direct benefits to the regions concerned, particularly in Potosí.

With respect to the tax on indigenous peoples, we should bear in mind the estimates made by Drake for the 1920s (Drake 1989). He calculated that the per capita tax contribution of indigenous peoples (50 percent of the population) was Bs. 1.94, while *mestizos* (35 percent of the population) contributed Bs. 11.89 and whites (15 percent of the population) contributed Bs. 43.25. Drake stressed that, given the poverty of the first group and the poor distribution of income, tax payments represented 19 percent of indigenous incomes but only 4 percent of those of the upper class.

We have also seen how the central state was less powerful than is sometimes suggested. Rather than an ironfisted centralism, the state was weak in confronting groups like the tin barons and only relatively strong in its dealings with subaltern groups like indigenous peoples who produced alcohol, chicha, and *aguardiente*.

These difficulties for the central state also affected the departments. Their revenues and resources were, by and large, insufficient to meet even the most basic spending, and it was for this reason that they received constant subsidies from the central government. Conflicts arose between the departmental treasuries and the national treasury over their respective sovereign attributes. One deputy stated that there was a national treasury "which all departments should support," but in practice revenues were demanded by the departmental treasuries from the national one. While the departments had representatives all over the place, the national treasury had none (Proceedings for the ordinary and extraordinary legislatures of 1921–22, 8).

As of 1930, and particularly on into the 1950s, the situation changed completely because of the state policies toward oil production. This was considered a national source of income but also a departmental one due to the system of fixed-rate royalties. The contribution of royalties became a pillar of longer-term policy. Another such pillar was the constant channeling of resources toward the east. Of the total agricultural credit made available, 42 percent went to Santa Cruz between 1955 and 1964, or around US$1.3 million (Sandoval 2003, 68). Between 1964 and 1970, it was 43 percent, and between 1970 and 1975, 69 percent (UNDP 2004, 42). During the 1970s, Santa Cruz received 43 percent of the budget for regional administration, while Cordecruz, the local development corporation, received around 63 percent of tax income.[11] Finally, of the loans made by USAID (United States Agency for International Development) between 1961 and 1971, 47 percent went to Santa Cruz (or US$77.5 million) (Sandóval 2003, 69).

If there is any constant policy that unites regimes of a variety of ideological colors and characteristics, it was that which enabled the flow of investment and capital toward Santa Cruz. This was all the more remarkable in a country that has been a byword for instability. We would argue that Santa Cruz has, to some extent, received privileged treatment. Recognizing such a policy of economic support by the central state does not negate the existence of centralism; we have tried to suggest here that what needs to be done is to break down what is meant by *centralism* and *regionalism* and to be more specific in what we are talking about. We need to analyze these concepts in a way that discerns between their various ambits and levels. Here we have focused our attention on the generation and distribution of resources. This has once again become a major factor behind the demands of departmental government for self-rule and autonomies. In such circumstances, it is surely worthwhile highlighting factors from history that are frequently obscured in the fury of contemporary debate.

PART III

The chapters paired in part 3, by George Gray Molina and Franz Barrios, seek to probe into the distinctive relationship between the state and society in Bolivia, and how this has changed according to historical circumstances. A major theme here is the balance between democracy and democratic participation on the one hand, and the rule of law on the other. For some observers, the extension of popular democracy places the rule of law in jeopardy, as the previously excluded seek to use democratic rights to advance their interests; for others, the rule of law is a cloak to mask the attempt of elite groups to maintain the status quo.

In one sense, the formation of the MAS (Movimiento al Socialismo) government in 2006 represented an important turning point in the historical pattern of state-society relations in Bolivia; indeed, it was born out of a crisis in relations between social movements of various types and a society which, at least apparently, had seen its links with society atrophy over the previous two or three decades. Not only had Evo Morales emerged as the standard-bearer of one of Bolivia's most powerful social movements—the coca farmers of the Chapare—but he also represented in very visible form the country's indigenous heritage. From the outset Evo wanted to present his government as a new beginning in terms of the active involvement of social movements in the work of government. The conformation of his first cabinet brought into office many of those who had played a conspicuous role in the social movements that had challenged previous administrations.

In another sense, however, the MAS government conjured up a relationship between state and society that was by no means new. This reflected itself particularly in the dividing line between social participation and the less-politicized areas of public administration. Bolivia has seen many instances in the past when social pressures arose that overwhelmed state structures, creating situations in which social movements have sought to claim the state for themselves, often in the name of democracy. The 1952 revolution was perhaps the clearest evocation of this principle, but it has also emerged at various points since then. Indeed, for some, the "revolutionary tradition" is precisely the uprising of the downtrodden majority of the population and the rejection of rule by a small, unrepresentative elite. Perhaps the most radical evocation of this principle was the notion of "cogovernment" (*co-gobierno*) with workers' control in certain state-owned enterprises. But participation has also emerged in other ways, under governments that were far from radical. The system of municipal oversight created by Gonzalo Sánchez de Lozada in the 1990s, Popular Participation, is but one instance.

This tradition of participation has received new impetus since Evo took over the helm at the beginning of 2006, although the boundaries that define where popular participation ends and more conventional ideas of public administration begin remain ill defined. Morales's assumption of office triggered a fairly thorough changeover in the public administration. Those involved in social movements gained important positions, while many of those who had been associated with the policies of previous administrations lost their jobs. Although it was by no means the first government to preside over a major transfusion of workers in government, this time it went much further than usual, reflecting not only a radical shift in policy direction but a belief that the election victory of December 2005 gave the new government the right to institute a government of *"lo popular."* Clearly, such a changeover had a debilitating effect on the experience and capacities of those playing key roles within the public administration, but the hope was that new administrative cadres would emerge over time and that this would help consolidate the new model. It is also important to note that Morales himself gave great importance to maintaining contact with the social movements that provided the natural base of support for his government, frequently deploying the argument derived from the language of trade unionism that the grassroots (*la base*) had the right the evaluate the work of the leadership (*los dirigentes*) and to correct this when they considered that government did not adequately represent their interests.

While this evoked a certain tradition of state-society relations, there is no doubt that the nature of this relationship has changed in important ways over the last few decades. Economic liberalization—especially the privatization of major public companies and the virtual closure of the state mining corporation—meant that the size and responsibilities of the state diminished. No longer was the state the sole arena—or at least the principal one—in which struggles took place for the allocation of resources in society. It also brought about the effective demise of the mineworkers' federation as the "prime" social movement, reducing thereby the political importance of the once-powerful Central Obrera Boliviana (COB). The 1980s also brought important changes in society. Other sectors moved into the space left by the mineworkers, notably the peasants and *cocaleros*. Urbanization and the expansion of education had important affects in changing traditional forms of status. New spaces for participation emerged, not least following the Law of Popular Participation in the 1990s. The increased salience of indigenous politics brought important changes to the discourse of popular politics. The expansion in the number and activities of nongovernmental organizations (NGOs) brought new intermediaries into play in state-society relations.

Such changes also affected the political sphere, particularly in the intermediation between state and society through political parties. The system of pacts and coalitions that underpinned political stabilization from 1982 onward did so at the expense of parties' representative function. Alternating in power and pursuing similar policies, traditional parties came to be seen more as clientelist machines distributing state patronage than as vehicles by which society might influence state policy. But whereas in some other countries in Latin America this led to the virtual collapse of party systems, in Bolivia the genesis of the MAS provided a new mechanism for articulating social discontent. Although the MAS is in many ways still an umbrella organization for a variety of social movements, its experience of electoral involvement and then victory has lent it certain attributes of an organized political party.

In chapter 6, George Gray Molina, from the United Nations Development Program (UNDP), seeks to rethink some conventional notions about state-society relations. His chapter considers some of the more fundamental conclusions of an ambitious and far-reaching study carried out by the UNDP office in Bolivia on "the state of the state" (UNDP 2007). This invokes the need for a new compact or modus vivendi between a state that is not always as weak as is made out and a society that is not always so strong. He argues that the election of the MAS government, along with the convening of the Constituent Assembly, provided an arena for such a compact to emerge, one more in tune with the country's pressing needs over a wide spectrum of important policy areas. He therefore asserts that a new and lasting equilibrium is achievable.

In chapter 7, Franz Barrios takes a more pessimistic view of the chances of such a harmonious outcome emerging. He stresses the dangers of what he sees as the overpoliticization of the state as a consequence of the increased influence of social movements in spheres of decision making. He points to a number of areas where he feels that the Morales government has embarked on a dangerous path which threatens to undermine the rule of law in Bolivia. Barrios bases his argument on the need to "protect" certain areas of state activity from the intrusion of politics and to maintain what he calls (using the Greek sense of the term) an "apathetic" state which is isolated from the passions and feelings aroused by politics. Bolivia, he says, is at risk of becoming a "pathetic" state, a plebeian democracy in which all decision making becomes politicized.

State-Society Relations in Bolivia

The Strength of Weakness

GEORGE GRAY MOLINA

Although Bolivia is regularly included in lists of weak, unstable, and non-transparent states on the one hand (e.g., Foreign Policy Magazine 2007; Transparency International 2007; Kaufmann, Kraay, and Mastruzzi 2007, among others), and in lists of strong, mobilized and revolutionary social movements on the other (Hylton and Thomson 2007; Petras and Veltmeyer 2005; Kohl and Farthing 2006), seldom are the two linked explicitly, whether historically or normatively. In recent years, much attention has shifted to the relative strength of social movements and the weakening of traditional political parties, democratic institutions, and the rule of law, among other dimensions of the state-society balance. For some, this is proof of a new historical era; for others, the sign of a particularistic yet ephemeral form of populist politics.

Here I would like to take a step back from the current debates and center attention on the nature of state-society relations in Bolivia. The historical record suggests that in Bolivia a form of the "weak state/strong society" hypothesis holds, despite state-building efforts in the mid-1950s and in the mid-1990s.[1] The nature of this relationship, however, has not been sufficiently discussed in the mainstream political-science literature, which has tended to focus on what was missing from democratic state building rather than on what is driving the specificity of state and societal development in Bolivia.[2] The historical form taken by a "weak state/strong society" trajectory in Bolivia helps to explain a number of features that puzzle social and political analysts and policymakers—among them, the absence of widespread violence in a society marked by pronounced ethnic cleavages, social inequality, and regional imbalances. The modus vivendi adopted by the Bolivian state includes various forms of institutional pluralism that accommodate social pressures from above, and a society that takes on many features of de facto statehood from below in areas such as the administration of justice, natural resource management, and political self-rule (Gray Molina 2006a; UNDP 2007). The state is neither as weak as many political analyses would suggest, nor is society as strong as many would like; the Bolivian modus vivendi was based on shifting alliances of power between elites and social actors throughout the twentieth century.

And while the state-societal modus vivendi has kept the peace for over a century, recent events suggest that this form of governance is ill-equipped to manage the tasks of an increasingly urban, cosmopolitan, intercultural, and global society and economy (see Gray Molina 2006b). The challenge for Bolivia in the future is not as easy as simply strengthening the state, either in the progressive strong-state mold or in the liberal rule-of-law sense. The most difficult challenge, it would seem, is for Bolivian social and state actors to construct a renewed modus vivendi able to tackle a set of important and intractable problems: population pressure over natural resources, increased social services for a new urban populations, and intercultural politics in the public sphere, among others. Such a new modus vivendi, many hoped, would be crafted in the Bolivian Constituent Assembly. These are the challenges faced by this generation of Bolivian citizens, and make up many of the unresolved tensions discussed in this volume.

Three Paradoxes from State-Society

As suggested by the historical chapters by Rossana Barragán and José Luis Roca, Bolivian state formation can be described in terms of a long-term process of state bureaucratic, legal, and ideological development.[3] The institutions and practices of the Bolivian state developed in fragmentary form, from the remnants of colonial patterns of dominance in the eighteenth century, liberal institutions of the republican era in the nineteenth century, through the innovations of the national revolution in the 1950s and the most recent reforms of the 1990s. Each wave of state reform was accompanied by a new understanding of what the limits and scope of state action were, but also what actual institutional or legal state presence meant for rural or provincial society.

The Bolivian Human Development Report of 2007, *El estado del Estado* (UNDP 2007), posits the idea of a "state with holes" to describe this gradual process of state construction. Implicit in this description is the recognition that state-building in the nineteenth and twentieth centuries was not a linear process of territorial extension of the powers of a preexisting state. It was, rather, "a process of negotiation of the limits, the boundaries of state legitimacy and action" (Barragán and Péres 2006) that suggests that several of the dimensions of stateness were disjointed for any given population or aspect of state power.

The Bolivian state may have extended via military garrisons, schools, health posts, or judicial courts sometime in the nineteenth century, but it has also taken over a century for the legal dimensions of the rule of law and the ideological dimensions of a modern nation-state to exercise effective dominance over other forms of communal, patrimonial, or local rule. The disputed nature of legitimate state power continues to play a part in present-day Bolivian politics. The disjointed nature of the Bolivian state can be traced to important moments in state bureaucratic, legal, and ideological construction. Three of these linger in ongoing debates on whether there are historically unresolved tensions in state-society relations: the *república de indios y españoles* of the eighteenth century (see Thomson 2003), the land and taxation pacts between *ayllus* and the state in the nineteenth century (Platt 1982), and the experience of dual powers between miners and the MNR in mid-twentieth century (Zavaleta 1987).

The discontinuous nature of state-society relations suggests a number of puzzles and paradoxes for the present. Among these, perhaps the most important is how such a poor, unequal, and ethnically and regionally divided society could have kept the peace in the nineteenth and twentieth centuries. The absence of widespread violence, civil war, or ethnic strife in a society renowned for its history of revolution, rebellions, coups d'etat, and military rule can be addressed by more specific questions concerning state and society relations.

The first question is: If the Bolivian state is so weak, how did political elites govern in the twentieth century? Bautista Saavedra, president from 1921 to 1925, in 1917, said, "The most substantial mistake of democracy, as we have come to understand it, has been in having proclaimed equality as a defining principle. Nature is invoked in support of this principle, but nature, which exhibits a beautiful harmony of inequalities, does nothing but continually shatter this illusion, because a regime of freedom cannot be anything other than an environment of thriving inequalities" (cited in Irurozqui 1994). Bolivia's weak elites—silver magnates in the late 1800s, tin barons in the early 1900s, middle-class politicians of the Movimiento Nacionalista Revolucionario (MNR) in midcentury, agribusiness landowners in the 1980s and 1990s—all faced the common dilemma throughout the republic of how to govern.

Unlike other Latin American elites who built up their economic and political power through long-lasting alliances with the church or foreign powers, or imposed power almost exclusively by force, Bolivian elites fought their hegemonic power battles mostly alone, and for the most part, divided. Saavedra's "harmony of inequalities" invoked by historian Marta Irurozqui (1994)—a pattern of elite political accommodation that sustains social and economic inequality—is a common thread up until the Chaco War in the 1930s.

Afterwards, the harmony of political accommodation faced a foundational turning point. The national revolution in 1952 transformed the social and political scenario from the 1950s onward. A consequence of increasing pressures for popular participation and discontinuous state development has been the state's delegation of spheres of authority and dimensions of power to civil-society organizations by means of multiple institutional mechanisms. Institutional pluralism in the rule of law—dual power, worker comanagement (*cogestión obrera*), oversight committees, delegated taxation, communitarian justice—have resulted not of state failure but from the state's engagement with civil society in its ethnic and regional diversity.

In this view, the proliferation of parallel institutions is not a short-run dysfunction of state building but rather a structural feature of political accommodation under weak elites. The Bolivian state's institutional pluralism does not mean the state abdicates from exercising authority altogether; it instead engages in an indirect form of rule that involves multiple local agents or partners. This is, without a doubt, one of the most long-standing legacies from Spanish colonial rule in present-day politics.

Another effect of institutional pluralism is that the Bolivian state allows a considerable amount of de facto autonomy at the local and regional levels of government. Many regions and indigenous communities already exercise a considerable degree of self-government and autonomy from the central government in what might be described as a de facto weak-state devolution scheme. The Popular Participation reform of the 1990s provided a flexible—yet restricted—framework for regional and indigenous self-government practice (see Gray Molina 2004). Future moves toward decentralized self-government will have to account for this long-term historical process. Regional and indigenous autonomies, in particular, have much to build upon from past practice.

Institutional pluralism is not exempt from problems. One is that the proliferation of autonomous institutional rules tends to fragment the national public sphere, including areas where the joint construction of legitimacy, authority, and sovereignty are required to deal with national questions. There have been many cases of judicial or natural resource disputes between communities, peoples, or groups that could not be addressed because each challenged the legitimacy of the rule of law as applied to their specific circumstance. For many problems internal to a group or community, customary law has sufficed; for disputes between groups and communities, however, the cost of institutional pluralism can be high. Factional disputes over the nature and scope of the rule of law are often the rule, rather than the exception, at the national level.

A related question on institutional pluralism is whether it is withering or whether it is a structural feature of the state. The historical view is that the continuous process of negotiation over the legal and bureaucratic extension of the Bolivian state has resulted in an ongoing process of accommodation, both for political institutions and for political practice. The state should not, in this view, be seen as unfinished or uninstitutionalized, but rather as institutionalized along different lines. Rather than conforming to a pure type of political regime—liberal, socialist, or communitarian—the Bolivian state is a hybrid that has become a national-popular ideological umbrella. Hence, monolithic descriptions of the Bolivian state—as a neoliberal, populist, or colonial state—tend to misrepresent the nature of state-society relations as they exist in fact.

While institutional pluralism is the predominant feature of political accommodation in the twentieth century, a feature less commented upon is the way in which civil-society organizations such as NGOs, churches, neighborhood councils, international donors, unions, and indigenous *ayllus,* among others, have taken on statelike authority with respect to matters such as the self-regulation of land and natural resources, self-legislation concerning civil disputes, keeping the peace, and enforcing customary law. Such "state holes," places where bureaucratic or legal state presence is tenuous, are places where authority, legitimacy, and sovereignty are continuously contested. For some, this is evidence of a failed or weakened state that should be filled with liberal democratic institutions. For others, it is evidence of indigenous and popular self-rule, self-government, and self-legislation. I would like to argue that such state holes are evidence neither of the weakness of the state or the strength of society, but rather evidence of a peculiar balance of power between state and society that emerges from the discontinuous construction of state authority.

A more important question to ask is whether state holes are ruled by particularism or by some sense of public rule. Particularism is a form of poli-

tics that privatizes or hoards power in the hands of the few and includes a
number of forms of patrimonial politics, clientelism, and *caudillismo*. Public
rule can be defined as a form of politics that is open, public, and binding,
even among adversaries or rivals. It includes the rule of law as traditionally
discussed in the political-science literature, but it may also include forms of
customary or local law that do not inhibit open and public deliberations over
political power. The public or private nature of state holes is something that
is open to empirical verification. It is observable in the way local leaders are
appointed and how they exercise local, regional, and national power.

   *The second question is this: if society is so strong, why did ethnic politics
not prevail in the twentieth century?* "To speak of campesino struggles in
Bolivia requires a clarification. The term campesino, officially adopted in
this country after the 1952 revolution, usually masks the contents that developed in the struggles of rural populations that were predominantly indigenous," points out Silvia Rivera Cusicanqui. "One of the fundamental contradictions generated by the 1952 revolution was the failure of its project to
achieve cultural homogeneity" (1984, 1, 4). From the flip side of the state-
society equation, the important question must be how social, indigenous,
and popular mass movements contest power, rebel, and operate within the
framework of a national-popular order, and not vice versa. In particular, a
question that has regained relevance in recent years is why ethnic politicization happens in certain periods of time, rather than continuously throughout
the twentieth century. A starting point for this discussion is a review of the
invisibility of ethnic politics in the 1950s, its revival in the 1970s, and the
construction of a new form of multicultural politics in the 1990s.

   The national revolution framed popular struggles within a national-popular, rather than an ethnic or regional, political project. Silvia Rivera encapsu-
lates this problem in a single proposition: "the disappearance of the indigenous" in the context of a mestizo hegemonic political project (Rivera 1984, 1).
The revolution constructed a new vocabulary that emancipated indigenous
citizens from colonial forms of labor exploitation, but pointed to a new cohesive identity that was linked to the working classes, peasantry, and a national
bourgeoisie. The campesino played a key role in defining the identity of the
protagonists of the revolution's most important action: the agrarian reform
of 1953. A significant feature of this was the dissolution of all forms of agrarian labor exploitation, coupled by the massive redistribution of land over a
period of thirty years. However, the agrarian reform decree also erased all of-

ficial mention of Indian peoples and the Indian race, or Aymara or Quechua identity.

As Xavier Albó suggests in chapter 1, the campesino syndicates, created to redistribute land, were to provide a long-lasting link between the MNR and the rural society and economy for nearly half a century. The disappearance of the indigenous as a discourse largely follows from a very concrete practice of land redistribution, union co-optation, and MNR political hegemony in the mid-1950s. The 1964 coup that ended MNR rule strengthened the agrarian union leadership through a national-level military-campesino pact.

The breakdown of this pact, illustrated by the bloody confrontation between the military and campesinos in Epizana, Cochabamba, in 1974, was itself the cause of a new cycle of ethnic politicization in Bolivia, led by the Aymara Kataristas in the mid-1970s onward. An ascendant indigenous movement, loosely held together by Aymara intellectual Fausto Reinaga in La Paz, proclaimed a new political manifesto, the Tiwanaku Manifesto of 1974, which cut ties with the campesino syndicates and left-wing Marxist and socialist parties. The manifesto contains a stringent critique of the national revolution, its homogenizing effect over indigenous peoples, its Spanish-dominant education, and its co-opted agrarian reform.

Reinaga's legacy, however, crystallized more effectively within the agrarian union system, via young Aymara migrants and agrarian leaders who formed a cultural center-turned-indigenous-movement in the mid-1970s. The Kataristas revived the political and historical significance of the 1781 siege of La Paz by Julián Apaza (alias Tupac Katari) with a critical reading of more recent history—particularly the legacy of MNR and left-wing clientelism and paternalism in Bolivian politics. In April of 1978, the Katarista movement—then vying for control over the Confederación Nacional de Trabajadores Campesinos de Bolivia (CNTCB)—split into two rival factions: an indigenous faction led by Genaro Flores and Víctor Hugo Cárdenas, who founded the Movimiento Revolucionario Tupac Katari (MRTK), and an Indianist faction, led by Constantino Lima and Luciano Tapia, who founded the Tupac Katari Indian Movement (Movimiento Indio Tupac Katari, MITKA).

This split reflected more than personal or internecine disputes, as each faction conceived of ethnicity, indigenous, and *indio* in different terms. The MRTK was to become loosely associated with left-wing parties in the Central Obrera Boliviana (COB) and, eventually, with national parties such as the MNR (see Albó 1993). MITKA, on the other hand, rejected *q'ara* (Western, white) left-wing parties and promoted an autonomous political agenda from within the union system but not through alliances with traditional political parties. The indigenous faction, under Victor Hugo Cárdenas in the early 1990s, synthesized a pluri-multi agenda of unity in diversity, while the Indianist faction, though fragmented, was resuscitated by Felipe Quispe in the late 1990s, proclaiming the end of pluri-multi and the beginning of the reign of "two Bolivias."

An important question for the period from the late 1970s to the mid 1990s is why episodes of ethnic politicization did not lead to the establishment of ethnic-based political parties that could institutionalize ethnic differences within the formal system of democratic governance. The poor performance of indigenous parties such as MRTK and MITKA, in light of the strength of indigenous social movements, is perplexing. Although Katarista movement exercised prominent influence within the campesino syndicates, it never surpassed a 3 percent of the vote between 1979 and 1989. Bolivia's demographics would seem to favor ethnic representation, as nearly two-thirds of uninominal circumscriptions (constituencies) are predominantly Quechua, Aymara, or lowland indigenous districts. It is possible that indigenous political participation was hindered by institutional design, by way of electoral engineering. However, the scant appeal of ethnic political parties might be explained, rather, by a system of clientelist and corporatist inclusion inherited from the early 1900s and developed by the near-hegemonic MNR in the mid-1950s.

While ethnic political parties never caught on in the Bolivian highlands or lowlands, ethnic representation has increased steadily, first in municipal politics, and since 2002, in national politics. As of 2005, nearly one-third of congressional districts were represented by indigenous deputies or senators, another third by urban-based popular worker or informal sectors, and most of the remainder by middle-class mestizo representatives of the traditional political class. As pointed out by Ricardo Calla (2003), however, the mainstreaming of indigenous political demands—constitutional reform, land tenure reform, bilingual education, and formation of a constituent assembly— was achieved mostly by indigenous social movements on the streets, rather than in Congress. Since the early 1990s, indigenous movements have successfully introduced a multiethnic political agenda in Bolivia. The slow pace of reform and progress in this direction lies behind the backlash against conciliatory and reformist proposals.

The social mobilization and unrest of September of 2000 marked a turning point for state-society relations in general, but more specifically for the pluri-multi conception of politics promoted by the political and institutional reforms of the 1990s. Felipe Quispe, Aymara leader and secretary general of the Confederación Sindical Única de Trabajadores Campesinos de Bolivia (CSUTCB), amplified campesino perceptions that the political reforms of the 1990s were not procampesino or pro–indigenous reform. Rather, they "introduced the political system into the *ayllu*" (Quispe 2000). Although the social movements behind the mobilizations of September/October 2003 harked back to a long tradition of social contestation, many of those on the barricades were people shaped by the legacy of these reforms.

Decentralization, in particular, exacerbated problems of state control over political and economic development in the northern Altiplano, and helped revive mestizo and community political power across the whole Altiplano. The shift of power toward local councils weakened the earlier system of corporate campesino negotiation and provided a reminder to community organizations that the new sources of power lay in the hands of local politicians, NGOs, and development agencies. The September 2003 road blockades tipped the scale back to older-style corporatist negotiations between the CSTUCB and the central government. Between 2000 and 2002, the list of agrarian demands grew from a short petition to a ninety-point manifesto. An immediate effect of the September protests was a significant change in the discourse concerning national politics and nationality. In Quispe's words, heatedly debated in the Bolivian media, "two Bolivias: one Indian, one *k'ara*" had been pitted against each other since colonial times.

The two Bolivias conception broke with the more consensual pluri-multi ideas of previous years. It also triggered a backlash against multicultural politics from public-opinion leaders in the urban media. The notions of easy co-existence and unity in diversity were perceived as naïve and distorting of the true shape of power relations which favored definite moves toward a modern and liberal, or at least formally liberal, state. The two Bolivias discourse revealed an additional faultline in the Bolivian political debate, between those who value the idea of nation as a normative political goal and those who perceive talk of nationhood or nationality as archaic. In a sense, the idea of a nation as a shared set of secular or nonethnic doctrines (as suggested by the pluri-multi conception) never did exist.

As we saw in part 1 of this volume, the 1952 national revolution set forth a relatively clear vision of a national bourgeois, committed to mestizo cultural ideals and middle-class political values. The class alliance promoted by the MNR in the wake of the nationalization of the mines and the agrarian reform was highly effective at defining the nation in contrast to a paradigmatic "antination"—the tin barons, foreign oil companies, and bourgeois politics. Pluri-multi discourse on nationality struck a chord with opinion leaders and intellectuals who advocated the predominant language of liberal and democratic politics, while it alienated traditionally nationalist advocates, who understood nationalism, ethnicity, and class relations in urban, mestizo terms (see García Linera et al. 2000).

Disillusion with democratic politics (expressed through the public opinion polls) led to the election of President Evo Morales and subsequently to that of a constituent assembly, in what might be regarded as a highly legalistic form of popular protest. A significant feature of the recurring demand for state-led social and political inclusion is that practices or conditions that seem antithetical to social integration in the short run—weak and uneven state reach, weak political authority—are often conducive to longer-run processes of resilient political change. In this view, the continuous process of state reform and social protest that characterizes Bolivian lawmaking and policymaking is an integral part of a longer-lasting equilibrium.

Popular mobilization, contestation, and rebellion thus often drive social change, while constitutionalism and reformism internalize changes and prepare the ground for further distributional struggles that play out over long periods of time. The withering of a system of corporate inclusion is one such struggle, supplanted by a more fragmented and open-ended system of territorial representation. The move from functional to territorial representation has involved the exclusion of many time-honored forms of social mobility and political inclusion, including the transformation of the military, political parties, and popular organizations.

The third question is this: if the legitimacy of law is so weak, why is constitutionalism in such high demand? Article 1 of the regulations governing debate in the Constituent Assembly defined that body as *"originaria* because it springs from the will to change of the people, as the holders of the Sovereignty of the Nation. The Constituent Assembly is an extraordinary political occurrence that emerges from the crisis of the state, caused by social struggle, and it is installed by popular mandate. The Assembly has . . . as a mandate the transformation and construction of a New Bolivian state."

After eighteen constituent congresses or assemblies in a little over 180 years of republican existence—about one per decade—an important question arises as to how legal reform, laws, and constitutionalism acquire legitimacy in public opinion and in political culture. Recurrent cross-country indices on transparency, public sector corruption, and low-intensity conflict might suggest that Bolivians are lawless. However, we might view instead Bolivia as possessing a culture of legality that requires further explanation. The implications of this paradoxical relationship between the idea and practice of law—in particular the rule of law—in a democratic state merit exploration.

While many of these questions are considered in the chapters by Eduardo Rodríguez Veltzé and Luis Tapia, I highlight here some empirical findings from a recent study by UNDP-IDEA (2007) about the nature of discontinuous state-society relations in Bolivia. These touch upon three interrelated themes of legality: how Bolivians relate to the concept of law as an imaginary or social representation, what accounts for the simultaneous observance of law as an instrument of societywide legitimation and its transgression in everyday practice, and how we are to understand the resurfacing of the legitimacy of legality in times of profound political crisis.

The UNDP-IDEA study deconstructs social representations of legality, including the discursive associations that Bolivian adults make with the idea of law. The phrases most associated with legality in Bolivia are not, as one might suspect, based on rights and obligations of free citizens, but rather on the idea that the law is "a means to enforce order" on the one hand, but that "laws are not enforced" on the other (64). The first idea squares well

Table 6.1. Who enforces the rule of law most regularly?

	Always	Most of the Time	Regularly	Sometimes	Never
Politicians	2%	9%	23%	38%	27%
Judges	3%	16%	24%	35%	18%
Lawyers	3%	15%	23%	37%	20%
Civil servants	2%	13%	23%	39%	34%
Police	3%	14%	20%	34%	29%

Source: UNDP/IDEA (2007).

with the larger social representations of the state and the constitution, which tend to privilege the exercise of power over previously existing communities and peoples. The discontinuous reach of the legal dimension of the state is seen as a way of enforcing order over citizens and groups, rather than on behalf of them. The second idea is common sense in Bolivia and most of Latin America (see Méndez, O'Donnell and Pinheiro 1999). That laws are not enforced seems to link back to the historical fact of dual legal orders, first- and second-class citizens, and privileges with respect to the rule of law. As Getúlio Vargas put it, "for my friends, everything; for my enemies, the law."

In part, Bolivians feel that laws are not enforced, because most feel that "laws are unjust" and that "unjust laws may be broken" (UNDP 2007, 78). Bolivian public opinion has identified the worst transgressors as "the rich" and "politicians" (79). If a majority of public opinion believes unjust laws can be broken and feel that the rich are the worst transgressors, the binding legitimacy of the law is weakened for every sector of the population. These findings are no doubt useful, but studies of social representation point only to the discursive aspects of the legitimacy of law. Beneath imaginaries, discourses, and common wisdom are practices that perpetuate the delegitimization of the law in Bolivia. This is perhaps, the most difficult issue to confront.

When we turn to the issue of practices of legitimacy and transgression, we see that most Bolivians continue to advocate "universal" enforcement of laws (72) while at the same time reserving the right to transgress, protest, or overturn law through customary or particularistic political practice. To understand this paradox, we must look not at the legal system itself but the way that law gains legitimacy in a weak state/strong society setting. As discussed above, this is more about state building as a legitimate relationship than it is about state building as an extension of the bureaucratic or meritocratic reach of the state. The rule of law is not weak in Bolivia because of a failure to reach the population but because of a failure to assert binding legitimacy when it does so.

The very process of drafting the Bolivian constitution in the 2007 Constituent Assembly provides an example of this. The approval process tackled not just the requirements of internal legitimization (two-thirds majority rule and referendum), but also those of popular legitimization (popular mobilizations, strikes, conflict). Approval of the most important pieces of legislation moved, in pendulum fashion, from assembly agreement among moderates, to street mobilizations led by radicals, and back to final agreements among moderates. On many occasions—including the approval of autonomies, the issue of which city should be capital (*capitalidad*), and the question of re-election, the key legitimizing factor was the reaching of internal agreement after external shows of popular and regional political power had played out. In a sense, the popular-legal pendulum is the institutionalized way of advancing reform legislation in Bolivia.

The consequences of the legitimacy of legality debate for Bolivian democracy are far from inconsequential. It would seem that the Bolivian modus vivendi of political accommodation is based both on a culture of popular mobilization and a culture of constitutionalism that forges a flexible practice of legality. The thin line dividing legal from illegal practice is ever important, as witnessed by the legalistic tiptoeing of every Bolivian president since 1982. However, the political modus vivendi is clearly based on an instrumental use of balance-of-power politics, not on the universal or liberal recognition of the rule of law. Invariably, minority politics challenge not only laws but the rule of law in general, making it difficult to "agree to disagree" in accordance with what we might describe as liberal or deliberative democratic politics. How, then, should we characterize Bolivian democracy in terms of the weak state/strong society paradigm?

Perhaps the key issue distinguishing Bolivian democratic politics in Latin America is the system that grants legitimacy to a tenuous legality. The system might be described as an institutionalized form of popular politics-cum-constitutionalism. The drawbacks of such a system are many: the lack of binding rules of the game for democratic contestation mean that every legal statute is suspect. The discontinuous territorial reach of legal rule means that in many places particularism, communitarianism, or the rule of the strongest applies. In other instances, it is hard to make the case for depoliticized spheres of government or civil service. The benefits, however, are also conspicuous: the Bolivian modus vivendi avoids political violence by means of pluralistic accommodation, the regional and ethnic tensions that threaten democratic politics from time to time are usually subsumed into a larger national-popular umbrella of political legitimacy, and cross-cutting cleavages stabilize what might otherwise evolve into highly conflicting and polity-threatening political divisions. The construction of binding legal rules of the game continues to pose a significant challenge for Bolivian democracy. Some steps have been taken to accommodate pluralism, but more is needed to ratify the common core of constitutionalism that keeps the system together.

New Challenges for State-Society Relations

The discontinuous extension of bureaucratic, legal, and ideological state power in the nineteenth and twentieth centuries has important implications not only for the way Bolivian society processes social and economic conflict but also for how it meets new challenges. At least two consequences of the "state with holes" hypothesis are considered here. The first is that the institutional pluralism that promotes power sharing and political accommodation among highly diverse and heterogeneous ethnic and regional actors is a structural feature of the Bolivian state, and not an anomaly. Such pluralism is neither the result of poor institutional design nor of faulty implementation, but of a particular modus vivendi—weak elites accommodating to strong regional and ethnic societies. The second consequence is that in places and dimensions where state reach is weakest, grassroots and local organizations have taken on statelike qualities and exercise statelike authority. Neighborhood associations, campesino unions, and Aymara *ayllus* each take over functions—symbolic and institutional—of natural-resource management, the administration of justice, and peacekeeping that are traditionally reserved for the national state.

These features summarize what we might call the "strength of weakness" of the state and society in Bolivia—a political modus vivendi that avoids violence but fails to resolve so many of the social and economic distributional issues that are pending. The question that motivates these concluding remarks, however, is whether this modus vivendi can successfully address the new challenges that emerge from domestic and global change. While highly localized bilateral negotiations of authority between state and society have accommodated differences and provided a flexible framework for democratic politics in the postnational revolutionary era, many of the most pressing questions today are neither localized nor are they bilateral. There are several examples of such issues to be considered.

For example, natural-resource management under conditions of population growth, requires a national consensus on conservation, biodiversity, and land management that surpasses local interests or the particular interests of *colonizadores* (migrant peasants to the jungle lowlands), cattle ranchers, or lowland indigenous communities. Conflicts in 2007 between *colonizadores* and indigenous communities over the Madidi National Park in La Paz department are a case in point, as are the confrontations between landowners and campesinos in San Julián in Santa Cruz to secure land rights (see UNDP, in press). Neither of these tensions can be tackled by localized or short-term interventions, and neither is likely to be solved by the use of superior force. A new environmental policy, based on a shared notion of a common or public good, will push the limits of the current modus vivendi in ways not witnessed since the March to the East (*marcha al oriente*) of the 1950s.

In addition, the extension of social services under a universal health package, in a country were one-third of all citizens are temporary or permanent migrants, cannot rely on fixed territorial transfers of the sort used heretofore to temper rent-seeking redistribution (see UNDP 2006). To the extent that population growth and movement become more dynamic, the move from territorial to individual or group-based entitlements will pose new challenges to the existing modus vivendi. Rather than negotiate fixed intergovernmental transfers from national to local levels of government (which tend to reinforce the strength of elite political accommodation with local leaders), future social policymaking will increasingly deal with individuals or families—including female-headed households, migrant extended families, and proxy communities. The political economy of negotiation will veer from territorial to functional forms of politics.

Reconciling multicultural differences into sets of mutually recognized—intercultural—procedures for resolving disputes over property, civil, and even penal issues is a further challenge to the existing modus vivendi (see Gray Molina 2006d). Recent discussions of a fourth power of social control that would provide popular checks and balances over the executive, legislative, and judicial powers would seem to test the limits of multicultural institutional design. Closer to local and regional interests are the debates over the structure of overlapping regional and indigenous autonomies (see Albo and Barrios 2007). Whether an asymmetric form of decentralization can actually deliver the flexibility required for such contested issues such as natural resource administration, land taxation, migrant community benefits, and political representation is at stake under the new constitution.

Each of these issues will test the existing "state with holes" in theory and in practice. As noted with other such state-building reforms, such as Popular Participation or the education reform in the 1990s, the new challenges raised by an increasingly mobile, intercultural, and global population are sure to realign the balance of powers between old and new political elites, and between old and new social actors. This might be the very feature that explains why popular mobilization, rebellion, and organized contestation are structural characteristics of state and institutional development in Bolivian society. They describe not the exception, but the rule with respect to how a heterogeneous society exercises self-government in the midst of social conflict. Not all of the features of the ongoing modus vivendi are democratic, virtuous, or even fair. They do, however, suggest a resilient form of politics for a society with a penchant for continuous social and economic change.

7

The Weakness of Excess

The Bolivian State in an Unbounded Democracy

FRANZ XAVIER BARRIOS SUVELZA

> I believe that we cannot wait for the laws to be implemented; we must continue to make political decisions. Our supreme decrees are said to be unconstitutional, it will be the people that judge, and in this way we will continue identifying the enemies that do not want change.
>
> EVO MORALES, during the visit by Hugo Chávez on August 10, 2007, Entre Rios, Bolivia

The process of social and state reform that Bolivia is currently undergoing has finally exposed a structural tension within the state, one long ignored by the Bolivian intelligentsia. This structural tension, revealed by the current process of upheaval, can be reduced to a fundamental dilemma concerning the *style* of the state, a style characterized by refusal to insulate certain areas within the state from the influences of democratic opinion and the political process.

According to classical post-Aristotelian Hellenic philosophy, it is possible to shelter what I will call *a-democratic* and *apolitical realms* within the state. By this I mean public institutions, such as an electoral commission, which have authority and a designated role but which are supposed to be insulated from routine democratic politics. The Stoic school advocated distancing oneself from one's impulses, pleasures, and inclinations, from one's passions be they good or bad, converting what it called *apathy*—defined as freedom from feeling, or passionless existence—into an ethical principle to govern human conduct (Hegel 1986, 283; Russell 2004, 255; Kranz 1986).[1] As will be developed further, the a-democratic and apolitical spheres within the state reproduce this principle, encompassing areas within the state removed from the influence of impulsiveness and emotionalism. By contrast, I use the word *pathetic* in the Stoic sense (of a condition arousing strong emotions) to refer to a style of state where democratic and politicized forces have come to permeate the state: the very opposite of the apathetic style.

In the apathetic style of state, it is possible to find certain spheres related to state decision making that are protected from the democratic and political process, even though the state, taken in its entirety, can still be characterized as democratic. This form of power limitation differs from the classical horizontal type of checks and balances between executive and legislature, in which the judicial power is a final, insulated, and unique stronghold binding and dividing them in a particular manner. From a new perspective—which I call the "oblique" division of state power—the judiciary is the key to discovering a new dimension of division of powers that is as significant as the horizontal.[2] The contention here is that the current process of change in Bolivia involves a tendency, concerning this oblique division of power, to reshape the style of state in the direction of an unbounded and unconstrained democracy, one lacking restraint on the passions—what we might call in Stoic terms a pathetic state. It is necessary to first understand the relationship between democracy and the rule of law and then apply these theoretical considerations to the Bolivian case.

What Democracy Is and Is Not

The hypothesis that democracy is largely synonymous with the rule of law, or that the latter is simply one more feature of a democratic system, is a key impediment to understanding the role of a-democratic and apolitical realms within a democratic state. This confusion between democracy and the rule of law has been encouraged by a number of well-known authors. For example, although some of Norberto Bobbio's work recognizes that the decisive element of democracy is the involvement of very large numbers in decision making, he nevertheless inclines toward viewing democracy as the rules that define who is authorized to make collective decisions and the procedures which they adopt.[3] This emphasis on rules and procedures leads Bobbio to assert that democracy is a confluence of rules intended to solve conflict without violence. He goes on to write that "democracy is the government of laws *par excellence.*" But as we see below, the simple fact of the existence of rules tells us precious little about the application of the rule of law, even where these are respected.

Following this erroneous equation of democracy with a rule of law, we find democracy considered as a form of limited government, as if notions of self-restraint or moderation were inherent in the concept (Weingast 2005, 245). Karl Popper contributes to the blending of these concepts, asserting democracy to be a type of government defined by an institutional frame-work that permits reform and alternation of those who govern without the need for bloodshed (Popper 1971, 124–26). But if a constitution were clearly to establish the right of an aristocracy to govern, and if the weight of tradi-tion ensured such a rule or convention were applied, respected, and even defended by the society without violence, we would not consider this to be a democracy simply because of the existence of a framework of rules peace-fully abided by. This would be so even if it were clear that these same rules impede the people—for better or worse—from having any influence over matters of state. In such a case, we would have a state of law, but it would not be considered democratic.

Ralf Dahrendorf reveals the first fissures (though not very explicitly) in this identification of democracy with the rule of law. He still advocates a definition of democracy in line with Popper's (transition without violence) and adheres to the idea that it is the moderation of power that lies at the heart of democracy. But he then asks—how can the people have a voice in this process?—introducing thereby an analytical approach that distinguishes de-mocracy from other concepts such as the rule of law. He recognizes that the rule of law is as much part of the liberal tradition as the democratic; *inside* of what he terms a "liberal tradition," democracy and the rule of law are not simply one and the same, and "the rule of law tells us little about how to guar-antee the participation of the *demos* in the democratic process" (Dahrendorf 2003, 12, 13).

Other authors (e.g., Löwenstein 1994, 12–67) push this distinction further, reinforcing the point that a state governed by law does not inevitably involve the attributes of a democracy. Carl Schmitt, for example, rescues democ-racy from the idea that it contains all that might be considered the best of all worlds, opposing those who would identify it with "liberalism, socialism, justice, humanism, peace or international fraternity" (Schmitt 2003, 225). He argues that democracy is only a political principle, and only when linked to the implantation of a liberal component will it generate a tendency toward moderation. Underlying the political principle of democracy is a tension over the composition and identity of "the people" that can give rise to conflictive relations between actors. Schmitt seeks to distinguish between the political dimension, on the one hand, and the liberal, rule-of-law state, on the other. He sees the latter as encapsulating the principle of the division of powers (the classical horizontal triad) and the primacy of individual liberty (Schmitt 2003, 126). This reasoning allows for a clear separation between the checks and balances aspect of the liberal state and the democratic component. However, it involves new problems when it comes to making the separation of powers and the perfection of individual freedom operational by presupposing that liberalism is apolitical and that the horizontal division can be equated to a state of law.

This theoretical differentiation of the democratic from the rule of law is crucial in analyzing state reform in Bolivia after 2006. My contention here is that in contemporary Bolivia the democratic impulse is tending to engulf the rule of law; only by distinguishing them conceptually can we understand that it is possible to have a flourishing democracy and at the same time an erosion in the rule of law, just as it is possible for the rule of law to trump democracy. This conceptual disassociation makes clear how it is possible that the rule of law is being subverted (and even more so political liberalism) at a time when Bolivian society is becoming more democratic. The distinction also enables us to guard against an alternative theoretical error now in vogue: namely, the denial of the democratic character of Bolivia's current political innovations. To borrow Giovanni Sartori's phrase, "The maximization of democracy seeks to . . . limit the guarantees embodied in liberal constitutionalism" (Sartori 1995, 239).

In order to grasp the democratic principle, we must give detailed consideration to the identity of its subject, the issue of estrangement and alienation, and finally to questions of procedures. The category of "the people" as the democratic subject poses a theoretical problem. Certain definitions of the democratic principle, such as Aristotle's, broadly identify "the community" as the oppressed or marginalized classes (Strauss 1978, 6). This could be a large group of excluded people who conclude that the only way to improve their situation is by leveling downward; for them, democracy means that the moment has arrived for the oppressed to defend their self-interest. This is what Aristotle meant when he referred to democracy as a defective version of a polity; government of the many may not be the same as pursuing the common interest of all (Kranz 1986, 253ff). This variation can be termed a *plebeian democracy*, and it captures the particular democratic outlook that inspires the MAS (Movimiento al Socialismo) in Bolivia.

Not even a plebeian democracy can avoid the need for the leadership of an elite that speaks and acts in the name of the oppressed. As such, the problem of estrangement and alienation is integral to any discussion of democracy, and even more so when the plebeian element is so closely associated with the idea of direct government. By estrangement and alienation, I mean the process by which real power is assumed by a small clique, which otherwise talks in the name of the poor. This involves an abrogation of power rather than representation as such. Procedurally, plebeian democracy must also resolve problems that arise from practices of direct democracy. The defining feature of democracy in ancient Greece lay in its direct government.[4] Its modern Bolivian equivalent, perhaps, is that "social actors will evaluate the ministers" (a dictum rarely realized in practice). The obstacles that confront direct government not only arise from considerations of scale but also from the consequences of political estrangement and alienation that inevitably lead to the creation of inner circles of power within a worker-peasant state. The direct unity of the people and government may be affirmed symbolically, but in practice, this relationship is rarely genuine.

In contrast to plebeian democracy stands what might be termed "citizen democracy." Here the democratic subject is not the poor, but rather a mass group of citizens who exert influence through legitimate channels of universal suffrage. To use the adjective *citizen* does not preclude the possibility that such a democratic modality may reinforce the privileged position of certain groups in society—a possibility that neoliberal ideology and its conservative adherents prefer to obscure. When a citizen democracy adopts policies in favor of the poor, it does not imply it has become a plebeian democracy, because the poor are not *the* preferential subjects of the citizen-democratic state. They are merely, in some cases, the beneficiaries of public policy. Procedurally, in contrast to plebeian democracy and direct government, citizen democracy encourages representative channels. Although it does not entirely discard direct popular rule as a channel of participation in state decision making, citizen democracy seeks to overcome the limitations of this form of influence.

Whether government is plebeian or citizen oriented, when the democratic and political spheres exceed their domain the style of state becomes pathetic rather than apathetic, such a situation leads political and democratic actors to penetrate and seek to capture the state whenever possible. The alternative style of state attempts to insulate those spheres that *can be considered to protect the democratic principle* from being directly overwhelmed by democratic and political forces.

In a democratic state, there will inevitably be decisions that are made with some degree of linkage to the popular will. But the state also needs to make certain decisions in a premeditated manner, removed from the people, in ways that do not call into question its adherence to democracy as such. It is therefore no failing of the system if certain types of state decisions are taken with only minimal consideration as to the electorate or the people. Indeed, there are many routine instances of this happening in public policy. It is also conceivable that technical decisions can be political decisions, even though they are made in an apolitical manner. For example, central banks and constitutional courts tackle conflictive subjects that stand to benefit the interests of particular groups, yet in ways that are carried out in a technical and independent manner. Other decisions, such as public auditing, involve independent control mechanisms that are explicitly nonpolitical.

Given the complex pattern of diverse policy spheres, we need to be able to refine our understanding of systems of control within the state. That those a-democratic and apolitical systems must be appointed by and accountable to a sovereign authority is beyond dispute. But there are numerous spheres of decision making that need to be kept a-democratic and apolitical in order to carry out certain types of essential state functions. While it would be a mistake to separate out both these components to an absurd degree, they need to be kept distinct, despite their inevitably related practical and philosophical interconnections.

Bolivia's New Pathetic Democracy

The Government of the Social Movements

The doctrinaires of the regime in power in Bolivia since 2006 have devoted a great deal of attention to social movements. These take various forms but include indigenous movements, union organizations, and ad hoc groupings that have emerged in defense of natural resources. This exalting of social movements, both in theoretical as well as practical terms, has led to an attack on the meritocratic appointment of state officials. The Constituent Assembly is a second important element in Bolivia's shift toward a pathetic style of state. Elected in 2006, this body has acquired metaphysical dimensions as against the "constituted power," leading even to conflicts with Congress. However, we will focus here on the war of nerves between the assembly—the "constituent power"—and the judicial branch, which, while part of the constituted power, is also a significant element of the a-democratic and apolitical functions of the state (see chapter 8 for an alternative discussion of the concepts of constituent and constituted power as they relate to the Bolivian case). The tussle arose when the Bolivian courts pronounced judgment on the procedural failings of the assembly with respect to its own regulations.

The third variable is the so-called fourth power of society, whose remit would be superior to the other, more classical powers of the state. According to one scheme, put forward within the Constituent Assembly, this would be composed of representatives of Bolivia's social movements, giving them supreme authority over the rest of the state. In practice, this proposal was not included as such in the final constitutional draft. As we see more fully below, the concept of a fourth power—superior to the other three—would clash with the jurisdiction of the Constitutional Tribunal, a body created as a result of the constitutional changes in the 1990s, to resolve disputes over constitutional interpretation. From the standpoint of the apathetic state, the tribunal seems to be the closest we get to a power that is superior to the other three powers of the state.

In each case, we observe a diminution of the a-democratic and apolitical functions of the state.

The doctrine of the Morales government asserts that what emerges from the historical changes taking place is a state *of* the social movements (García Linera 2007, 164, emphasis added). The supposition here is that the state is, in essence, antidemocratic, and that the imprint of the social movements is such as to give them the last word in decision making (García Linera 2007, 165). This is because when in opposition to the state prior to 2005, these movements were synonymous with democratization and socialization. The regime provides unmistakable evidence of trying to involve its social base in the administration of the state. The appointment of ministers of genuinely plebeian origins, at least in Morales's first cabinet, is evidence of this. "*Evismo*" would stand out from earlier left-wing experiences precisely because it endows those social movements with "access to levels of state decision making"—a process of change that vice president Álvaro García Linera sees as being of global resonance (García Linera et al. 2004, 18).[5]

The aim here is to achieve "the wholehearted self-representation of those social movements." In this way, Bolivia will become "a unique example worldwide of social movements managing to take control of the state" (García Linera 2006). The regime wants its project to be understood as being a consequence of the earlier broadening of popular decision making in the affairs of state that reinforced democracy and that resulted from the multiplicity of social movements that emerged after 2001. This is premised on the view that the organization of such movements and the way they conducted themselves could—under specific conditions—lead to a "re-design of the state . . . in ways that differ from all the other sorts of republican state we have known hitherto" (García Linera et al. 2004, 20). The doctrinaires of the regime hold that it is the social movements which should guide the process, not the state. But because the state is indispensable, or at least a necessary evil, they therefore uphold the idea of "the state *of* the social movements."

This sort of vision brings into focus some of the points made above in our discussion on democracy. The appeal to direct democracy reverberates here, irrespective of whether this is more declaratory than real. Furthermore, the term *social movements* clearly invokes a plebeian type of democracy. Even the fact that this particular democracy comes about by virtue of a government led by an elite of trade unionists and left-wing intellectuals (who actually run the bureaucratic structure to the benefit of the excluded) does not impair the nature of this democracy, even though it is clear that it is not the excluded who actually govern. This is because the massive electoral legitimacy, the penetration by organizations that represent the social movements, and the enunciation of pro-plebeian policies together confirm the plebeian-democratic nature (not necessarily liberal and still less constrained by the rule of law) of the regime taking root in Bolivia.

To some extent, the social movements take on the characteristics of a classic revolutionary proletariat; it is thus not surprising that they are described as being "the nucleus of leadership, both political and moral, for the rest of the country" (García Linera et al. 2004). Thus it is that the common people, the plebe, penetrate areas of state decision making, not only in a formal, doctrinal, or rhetorical sense but also in ways that have real effects on the way the state is managed. Such ideas support the view that since the state is by definition a monopoly, it is seen as something homogenously corrupt (García Linera 2006), a space that can be evenly taken over, without proper consideration of how this might affect its specialized functions and dynamics. Such ideas differ radically from those theories of decision making that see the state as a complex piece of machinery that brings together different domains of decision making in ways that break down subjects and agents in line with state policies. What we have here is a political philosophy that stems from the overly simplistic premise that, since the state is ailing from top to bottom, it is therefore in need of drastic overhaul.

Bolivia's official doctrine posits that tension will persist between the vice-ridden state and the virtuous agent known as the social movements (García Linera 2006, 165). In fact, this is a sophism to conceal the fact that the "state of the social movements" is something unobtainable, possible only in the bolder imaginings of a certain type of intellectual. Still, it is sufficient to justify, promote, and carry out the progressive dismantling of those parts of the state that we have called a-democratic and apolitical. That the measures undertaken by the regime are responses to pent-up social pressures is no proof that it is the social movements that govern directly, as the official line would have us believe (García Linera 2006, 165–66). The conciliatory measures taken are perfectly compatible with the idea of a governing elite that heeds such demands. Nor should it come as any surprise that many social movements, often indistinguishable from leadership elites, should make extreme demands that the government has ended up rejecting. Again, from the opposite direction, in depicting the process in Bolivia, it is equally relevant that the measures taken hitherto express a plebeian notion of social change. Indeed, it would be unfair not to recognize the fact that the regime has taken concrete steps to promote the penetration of social movements into the decision-making system.

Summing up, the theorization of social movements is closely tied to their presence within the state (García Linera 2006), hence the argument by those in power that the institutions of the state should be transformed in ways that "favor the social movements and civil society." The way in which democracy has overflowed into the decision-making sphere, to the detriment of a-democratic and apolitical state functions (and a consequent change in the separation of powers) is also exemplified by the notion in official discourse that the nationalization of hydrocarbons came about after deliberation and consultation with social movements.

This sort of simplistic analysis, coupled with the notion of the state as an instrument or necessary evil in order to "live well" (*vivir bien*), helps explain why the official doctrine perpetuates a long-established contempt for a meritocratic state machine. One of the most evident signs of the dismantling of the a-democratic and apolitical spheres of the state is to be found in an answer proffered by the regime's main doctrinaire to the question of whether it is true that the political process is guided by the social movements. He argues that the proof of this is the fact that "the mechanism used to appoint officials to the public administration involves the social movements" (García Linera 2006, 166). This, he proudly asserts, contrasts with the previous model in which relatives or friends of the traditional ruling-party cliques rose to powerful positions. Now, by contrast, "to reach the public administration it is necessary to have the support . . . of the peasant confederation." This answer indicates no awareness, however, that the problem of having a professional state apparatus has not been resolved: all that has changed is the agency through which the dismantling of the a-democratic and apolitical sphere of the state takes place. The problem, indeed, has been made worse by the application of a highly popular notion of government austerity involving salaries in the public sector being reduced.

A Constituent Assembly with Metaphysical Powers

The drive toward a thoroughgoing overhaul of the constitution through a constituent assembly emerged from the social mobilizations that took place from the late 1990s onward. Bringing with it the demand for greater democracy, from the outset the assembly gave rise to a doctrinal affray with radical and left-wing intellectuals seeking to give it such powers as would threaten the principle of power limitation in general and apolitical decision making in particular. Indicative of this ideological struggle was the declaration that the assembly was *the* constituent power. Such metaphysical attributes were made explicit in the regulations for the assembly, which state, "It is legitimately superior to any constituted power" (Article 1 of the General Regulations for the Constituent Assembly). Previously, Law 3364 convening the Constituent Assembly had stated that it was "independent . . . , neither does it depend nor is it subject to the constituted powers" (Article 3 of Law 3364).

The way the assembly has evolved has been somewhat different. To start with, there are few in Bolivia who would now dissent from the view that the assembly was subjected to instructions from those in government and from opposition parties. When the original deadline passed, after a year of meager results, the ruling party negotiated a law with the main opposition party in Congress extending the assembly's life. This hints at its derivative nature. Our main concern, though, is the tension between an assembly with such metaphysical attributes and the judiciary. By way of example, the executive power encouraged the assembly not to heed the judgment of a tribunal that had pronounced on a complaint that the ruling party majority had violated the regulations which the assembly itself had approved by refusing to debate a particular polemical issue.[6] This was not the first time that the Bolivian judiciary had sought to control the assembly's actions when it believed these had overstepped the legal bounds of its mandate. It upheld a previous complaint when, in one of the special commissions, the official majority used its voting strength to avoid a dissenting minority report reaching the plenary session.[7] Here we have a further instance of the retraction of judicial orders, orders that are essentially a-democratic and apolitical. The logic of the pathetic type of state is that the law should be heeded because it is an expression of the popular will. This is quite different from the concept of law mentioned above, in which it is the expression of the rule of law.

The words of the vice president are suggestive here. During this particular judicial polemic, having proclaimed that "institutions should respect the law," García Linera was asked if this meant adhering to the rulings of the Constitutional Tribunal. He answered the journalist with the following question: "Was the ruling of the court a law?"[8] This suggests that the laws need to be respected when they form part of a program of revolutionary change, but not when they are the decisions of jurisdictions which, according to the vice president, are mere moral appeals without binding force. The official explanation for this indifference toward judicial decisions concerning the Constituent Assembly is that the latter is the expression of the "supreme sovereign power," and because it is "plenipotentiary" it cannot accept "the interference by another power of the state."[9]

The Fourth Power: Social Control

The coming to power of the MAS gave an impulse to what may be termed as the Jacobin rhetoric of the vice president, who, two years earlier, proposed the formation of a "directorate" of social leaders in order to program action toward the Constitutional Assembly (García Linera et al. 2004).[10] At the beginning of 2007, this took the form of establishing the National Coordinator for Change (Coordinadora Nacional para el Cambio, CNC) to be organized on a territorial basis. According to the president, the CNC would defend the reforms of his government.[11] But, as is often the case with pathetic styles of government, there was no announcement as to how this would work in practice.

It is worth recalling that the introduction of the CNC took place at the time of the killings at the Huanuni mine, a serious reverse for the Morales administration.[12] Paradoxically, this involved one social movement—the *cooperativista* mineworkers—who lost their influence in the cabinet when the minister of mines (one of their numbers) was subsequently dismissed. Since then, it has become clear that (for official doctrine at least), the *cooperativistas* no longer constitute a social movement. We can therefore see how they remain so if they fulfill particular social requirements, in this case by not going against the government and by aligning themselves with the unionized labor elites that back the executive. It should come as no surprise, then, when a top executive official (in declarations on the event of launching the CNC) said that "we aim to improve [the workings of] democracy with the involvement of *healthy* elements" (Garcia Linera et al. 2004, emphasis added).

Thus, an idea that first emerged as the "directorate," and then as the CNC, paved the way toward the Constituent Assembly espousing (over months of internal discussion) the notion of "the fourth *social* power of the state."[13] This power, evidently composed of social movements, "would control the powers of the state."[14] At times it appears as the "fourth power of the citizenry," and it is probable that other nonplebeian social collectivities would also participate in it.[15] For its part, the indigenous leadership of the western part of Bolivia went so far as to announce that this fourth power would be made up of "elders" (*sabios*) in a council of *amautas* (*consejo amáutico,* council of elders) whose jurisdiction would override that of other powers of the state.[16] At another moment, the fourth power was envisaged as taking an active role in political management as a sort of filter for the approval by the grassroots of proposed government legislation.[17] Referring to this fourth horizontal division of power, a MAS senator announced in mid-August 2006 that "its power is not and cannot be delegated . . . , and so the three existing powers have to recognize a fourth, primary power, which is the people."[18]

In the constitutional debates of September 2007 (when the full sessions of the assembly were suspended), the MAS delegates debated the "restatement" (*reposición*) of the idea of the fourth power, since it had lost some of its initial momentum during the preceding few months.[19] In the discussion over *reposición,* the idea was confirmed that the fourth power would exercise "political and administrative control over the executive, legislative and judicial powers" and that it would stand above the classic powers since it was "conceived as a power of the people."[20] However, when the ruling party delegates put the finishing touches on their amended version of the complete text of their draft constitution, the initial intention to reinstate the issue of the fourth power was watered down. It is fair to point out that on a number of matters such as this, the ruling party has shown a notable degree of rationality and realism, to the point that some social movements consider the MAS guilty of "betrayal."[21]

Judging by the press statements issued in September 2007, the MAS's draft constitution had stepped back from the "fourth social power of the state," turning it instead into a "transversal mechanism of social control over all public office."[22] This would mean "comprehensive transversal social control by the natural organizations of the social movements." One of the reasons mentioned for this downgrading was the fear that institutionalization or integration into the structure of the state would have led to "bureaucratization and political dependence." From an operational standpoint, it would have worked through assemblies at different levels of government receiving reports from the public authorities.

This evolution in the official discourse about the fourth power of social control can be looked at in two ways: first, it entailed a distancing from more extreme imaginings whose implementation looked to be unviable; second, it represented a return to a scheme not new in Bolivia and whose effects had previously proved to be negative. So far as the latter is concerned, I refer here to the attempt to extend the idea of the "oversight committee" (*comité de vigilancia*), introduced under the 1994 Law of Popular Participation. This was a form of civil social control over municipal administration. Attention has frequently been drawn to the ineffectiveness, the duplication, and the partisan nature of this program. Furthermore, under the so-called National Dialogue Law of 2000, a dense network of legal norms was introduced at the territorial level for "organizations and institutions in civil society." These were to exercise the right "to recognize, supervise, and evaluate the results and impacts of public policy and of participatory processes in decision making" (Article 25 of Law 2235 of 2001).

Once again, as with the CNC, we see that all this sort of apparatus has had very little effect. Moreover, it is suggestive of the permanent tendency for Bolivian politicians, at any period, to seek to institutionalize complex and exaggerated mechanisms of social participation. In this regard, the MAS is simply sowing similar ideas on the soil of democratizing social imaginaries, fertilized by the country's social experience.

This brief summary of the supreme power of social control enables us now to look at one aspect of the idea of a social "super power" with jurisdiction over and above the conventional powers. This picks up on the endemic friction between the Morales administration and the Constitutional Tribunal. From the point of view of the a-democratic and apolitical spheres of the state, the tribunal comes closest to the notion of a supreme protector, or a "power over the powers." It is clearly autonomous of the people and social movements.

Drafts of proposals for constitutional reform, leaked to the press at the beginning of 2007, suggested that the Morales government proposed to get rid of the Constitutional Tribunal. These documents stated that the government would opt for the "the exercise of jurisdiction by means of social organizations."[23] They concluded that "the plurinational CPE [constitution] is the supreme law. No other law will be able to interpret it, regulate it, contradict it, or establish or say any anything contrary to it. Disputes with respect to its precepts, principles, mandates, and articles will be resolved by the sovereign people by means of referendum and/or the convening of a Constituent Assembly."

A climax in the confrontation between the regime and the Constitutional Tribunal came about with a case initiated in 2007 by Evo Morales against four tribunal magistrates who had taken office during the previous regime, at a time when such posts formed part of the partisan distribution of positions. On May 9, 2007, the tribunal upheld the constitutionality of Supreme Decree 28993 that enabled Morales to appoint four magistrates to the Supreme Court on an interim basis, but the court's decision then proceeded to make them retire on the grounds that they had exceeded their time limit.[24] Although in an agreement with the opposition, Morales finally ended up nominating new magistrates, abiding thereby with the ruling of the tribunal. He then decided to launch a trial of responsibilities (*juicio de responsibilidades*) against the four tribunal magistrates. In September 2007, the Senate, with an opposition majority, replaced the four magistrates that the president sought to put on trial.

The theory of spheres of decision making, presented as one of the underlying features of the oblique division of power in any state, has a particular value for understanding recent developments in Bolivia. Alongside the debate about separating democracy and the rule of law, we can see that the process under way in Bolivia is democratic, but in a very special way. Democracy here is taken to mean the unprecedented way in which the excluded and disadvantaged of society, and especially its indigenous peoples, come to assume a role that goes beyond mere symbolism; it is real and evident at key points of decision making within the state.

Accordingly, the process of transformation under way in the country involves elements of inclusion in a society with many social barriers. This does not mean that within this democratic metabolism there are not elements of estrangement and alienation. So, when the critique of the Bolivian Right accuses the process under way of being undemocratic, this is not simply the result of the conflating of the concepts we have debated above. The Right, it would seem, is intent on negating any form of democracy of plebeian origin.

However, we have seen at the same time that whatever the peculiarities of this democratic process, it has not been able to provide, nor has it wanted to reconcile itself with, a reasonable level of protection of the a-democratic and apolitical spheres of the state. We have seen this in theory and in practice with respect to examples of the social movements dismantling a regime of state officeholding. We have observed the same thing with respect to the metaphysical status attributed to the Constituent Assembly and how this led to challenges to the rulings of the courts. Finally, we have seen it in relation to the fourth power of social control, a source of tension with the existing Constitutional Tribunal.

This clear retraction of the a-democratic and apolitical spheres of the state helps produce what we have called a pathetic style of state. This is simply an observation that does not necessarily seek to imply that it is an undesirable situation per se. It remains to be seen the extent to which this style of state may have a deep social justification. Bolivia's own experiences and its idiosyncrasies as a nation may mean that it has no reason to assume that the experience of other countries in combining democratic rule with the rule of law and a liberal system is the best course to adopt.

PART IV

The inauguration of a Constituent Assembly in the city of Sucre on August 6, 2006, raised hopes that the newly elected Morales government would deliver in the rewriting of Bolivia's constitution in such a way as to increase levels of participation in the politics of the country, especially among the urban poor and the indigenous population which had felt excluded from processes of deliberation and decision making. The Assembly would—within the allotted space of a year—accomplish the ambitious task of "refounding" the Republic. The law that paved the way to the holding of the assembly talked about its being *originaria*, meaning that it would embody the sovereign will of the people and therefore be juridically superior to the others powers of the state: the executive, the Congress, and the judiciary. In terms of its composition, the majority of seats in the assembly were occupied by the ruling MAS (Movimiento al Socialismo), and a goodly number of MAS *constituyentes* were of indigenous origin or from the social movements that provided the party with its popular base.

This is not the place for a detailed account of the proceedings in Sucre, save to say that the process of redrafting the constitution proved acrimonious and polarizing, with the MAS failing to deploy its majority in a skillful and persuasive manner and instead prompting an initially fragmented opposition to find common ground. Failure even to agree on basic ground rules eventually led to the postponement of the deadline for drafting the new constitution. At the time of writing, it was even unclear whether the assembly, as formally constituted, would achieve its mandated objective. The divergences exposed in the assembly reflected many of the cleavages described in this volume— differences of opinion that reflect radically different positions between members of the assembly and the parties to which they adhered. These differences were made more difficult to bridge because of the lack of trust on all sides, a mistrust that seemed to grow as time went by. Assuming that a successful constitution must enjoy the support of a broad selection of the political forces within a country, the experience in Sucre did not appear to involve a consensual meeting of minds.

The chapters that follow in this section of the book underline the importance of a constitutional tradition in Bolivia, notwithstanding the turbulence of its politics since independence and the frequent interruption of constitutional rule by military regimes of one sort or another. The constitution, too, has undergone repeated processes of alteration and reform, reflecting in part the emergence of new political actors and the changing priorities of society. Demands for the latest exercise in constitutional reformulation date from the 1990s, when the workings of Bolivian democracy came under mounting criticism from emergent social movements. These claimed that the existing system represented more the interests of a small elite than those of the majority of voters who are indigenous and poor. These complaints underscored the growing unpopularity of traditional political parties, whose links to society had atrophied, notwithstanding regular electoral competition. Ignored to start with, demands for a constituent assembly had become strident by the time Goni was forced to resign in October 2003. Indeed, the election of a constituent assembly was a key point on the so-called October Agenda, such that those in power could no longer ignore the appeal. One of Evo Morales's first actions in government was to announce the holding of elections to such an assembly.

Just as Bolivia has a long constitutional tradition, it also has a strong tradition of extra-parliamentary mobilization. This too goes back to the foundation of the republic—if not well before— and has emerged at various points, challenging the status quo in sometimes violent ways. Perhaps the most important eruption of this sort was the national revolution of 1952, in which the previous regime was swept away in an upsurge from below. The success of the 1952 revolution, and its significance in Bolivian politics since, had the effect of legitimizing the use of popular mobilization as a method to win social goals. It also enhanced the tradition of syndicalism in Bolivia with the establishment of the COB (Central Obrera Boliviana), which embodied a clearly revolutionary discourse. Until the demise of the mineworkers' union in the 1980s, unions generally were a key factor of power which no government could ignore. The weakening of union power (as well as that of the military) was a factor which helped underpin the restoration of constitutional power in the 1980s and 1990s. The renewed rise of social movements as of the late 1990s brought with it the revival of the politics of mobilization, not least among the *cocaleros* of the Chapare, Morales's power base that presented the old tradition of syndicalism in a new guise. Within the MAS, there is a strong current which believes that its political agenda will ultimately only be achieved through direct action, and not through constitutional bargaining and compromise.

Given the shortcomings of representational politics and this tradition of direct action, it is not surprising that there has been a shift toward instituting mechanisms of "direct democracy" in ways designed to increase political participation by ordinary voters. As the ex-president of the republic and former head of the Supreme Court Eduardo Rodríguez Veltzé shows in chapter 8, the use of referendums is not new, and the constitution has been amended in such ways to incorporate new forms of political participation. However, as is clear from other countries in Latin America, methods of direct democracy—particularly at the behest of incumbent presidents—can be used to enhance presidential control and weaken legislative and judicial counterbalances to executive power. There are indications that this may also be the case in Bolivia, where the legitimacy of the political class is often frequently questioned by those who do not belong to it.

The following chapters provide contrasting visions of constitutionalism and constituent power in Bolivia. Rodríguez Veltzé, a lawyer by training, held the post of president of the Supreme Court until 2005, when he became interim president following the resignation of Carlos Mesa (2003–2005). He emphasizes the need to preserve the rule of law in such a way that constitutional arrangements reflect the interests of society as a whole, and not just parts of it. The constitution, he argues, has to preserve democratic freedoms and individual rights, with the separation of powers and an independent judiciary as key elements in this institutional design. For his part, Luis Tapia, a sociologist from the Universidad Mayor de San Andrés with close links to the MAS, interprets the notion of "constituent power" in a somewhat different way from Rodríguez Veltzé, seeing it as the social force that led to the eventual convening of the Constituent Assembly. He locates it in the social movements that undermined the old order, raising the question as to whether the MAS—now in government (or the constituted power, as he puts it) will be able to maintain that dynamic of change unleashed by the ouster of Sánchez de Lozada.

The Development of Constituent Power in Bolivia

EDUARDO RODRÍGUEZ VELTZÉ

The viability of democracy in Bolivia has been undergoing testing ever since 1982. This has been the longest period of uninterrupted democratic constitutional government since the foundation of the republic in 1825. It has been during this period, much more than at the time of independence or during the unstable political history that followed, that the notion of constituent power—as used by Antonio Negri (1993)—assumes greater relevance. Negri defines this as "not only as the omnipotent and expansive source of the constitutional norms that permeate the juridical framework, but also the subject of what they produce." In other words, not only is constituent power the instrument that produces those norms; it is also the concept that orders and regulates political life in a democratic society. The concept of constituent power involves a paradox: on the one hand, it embodies the idea of absolute democracy, while on the other it presupposes the creation of limits and order over the exercise of power.

In practical terms, it is the processes or results of such constituent power in Bolivia's flourishing democracy that not only raise tensions and create crises of different types, but also reflect a maturing of that power. This is a complex democratic phenomenon, but one as important as the preservation of the system itself.

The theoretical approaches to the idea of constituent power are numerous. However, the contrast between its judicial and political components through time and space contribute to the analysis. In analyzing the origins of the republic, we notice, for example, how conceptual and theoretical models were initially transplanted in the way the republican constitution was devised. The European constituent power that inspired the architects of the Spanish American constitutions was not a product of the sort of conditions that prevailed in the new republics of the nineteenth century. The republics of Europe had experienced bourgeois revolutions, the state and many of its institutions were already in existence, and its societies were relatively homogenous in their culture and ethnic make-up. In Spanish America, by contrast, the communities of its multicultural and multilingual republics were dispersed over a much wider terrain and subject to the power of landowners, clergy, and the other facets of imperial power. Although it was a bourgeoisie, freed from monarchical control, that was the mainspring of constitutionalism, they did not act within societies that were in any way homogenous or where institutions were well established (Sachica 1985).

In no sense was the triumph of independence in Bolivia the result of a mature constituent power. Although military and political events led to the convening of a General Assembly in 1825 in which the independence of the "Bolívar Republic" was declared, it was a year later, in November 1826, that a General Constitutional Assembly approved the first constitution, devised in Lima with some modifications by Simón Bolívar.[1] This document lasted five years and since 1831 has been amended and reformulated through of a succession of assemblies, conventions, or legislative congresses: in 1834, 1839, 1843, 1851, 1861, 1868, 1871, 1878, 1880, 1938, 1945, 1947, 1961, 1967, and finally by the Constituent Assembly that began its labors in August 2006.

Generally speaking, these constituent conventions were summoned by a succession of regimes in order to justify, consolidate, or prolong themselves in power. According to Jorge Lazarte (2006), such assemblies were, in their various guises, "processes imposed from above, backed by ruling political elites, and, if we look at the dividing line between right and left, they were more a political monopoly of the right." The most significant of these was the so-called National Convention of 1938. Among other things, this reform introduced the principles of modern constitutional law, regulated the social function of property, established state ownership over natural resources, and incorporated the principles of labor law. Equally important was the Constituent Assembly of 1967, which systematized the political and social changes brought about by the 1952 revolution and which has endured up until now.

In promoting constitutional order, the constituent power used these successive assemblies to establish a democratic order that did not necessarily correspond to the complex diversity of the state and the actors within it. The other aspect of this power, the subject for whom the constitution was intended, continually demanded (with differing degrees of intensity depending on the correlation of power at any one point) a greater sense of empowerment or belonging within the prevailing constitutional order. The fragility of constitutional democracy, highlighted by the large number of de facto regimes, did little to help resolve such problems in the democratic order. For this reason, the last two decades take on particular significance, since the constituent power and the process of constitutional reform in different ways became the key to the future viability of democracy in Bolivia.

Emergent Democracy

Since the beginning of the 1980s, when Bolivia established a democratic constitutional order, there have been important structural and institutional changes in a number of different spheres. Many have worked well; others less so. If anything characterizes this period, it is the gradual consolidation (notwithstanding its incipience) of a democratic order, both in the access to political power and in how this power is exercised. We have seen the development of constitutionalism, which has both promoted change and been subject to the changes taking place. Democratization is revealed by the sequence of electoral contests, the plural and free way these have been conducted, the fairness of the results, the alternation in office, the social and political crises that have erupted, and, above all, the way in which these were resolved within a democratic framework. Specific mention should be made here of the most recent elections, those of December 2005, when the Movimiento al Socialismo (MAS) won 53 percent of the vote for the presidential and vice presidential slate of Evo Morales and Álvaro García Linera.

According to Carlos Toranzo (2005), the victory of Evo Morales can only be explained by reference to the state reforms of recent times, the spaces these opened up, and the political inclusion that resulted. "The historic election of December 2005 was nothing other than a democratic revolution, brought about through the ballot box, using the tools of representative democracy and not street violence." His emphasis here is appropriate. One of the features of Bolivian history has been the lack of any genuine attempt to overcome *anti-indígena* sentiment and the marginalization of the campesino. From the very origins of the republic, indigenous peasants made their participation felt, through uprisings, during the Chaco War, under the liberal state, during the national revolution, and in various other struggles. In alliance with mestizos, Bolivia's indigenous campesinos set in motion an unstoppable force toward greater political participation with the real option of winning power. According to Toranzo, this *mestizaje* is what defines or characterizes Bolivian society as "a nation of mestizos, of cultural intermixing, of ethnic, economic, political and social diversity, where what is most striking to the observer is precisely that *mestizaje*, that mixture and combination between Bolivians."

However, at the same time, Toranzo also notes that high indices of poverty persist, alongside feudal *anti-indigenista* attitudes. He describes how today the peasants and *indígenas* not only demand rights, land, territory, and respect for pluriculturalism and multiethnicity, but also the construction of a new and more inclusive state. Such demands, he argues, arise in a context where the majority of the population is mestizo, living in conditions of extreme poverty, and open to mobilization by a state that is now more democratic.

Barriers in Bolivia to the full exercise of the rights and obligations inherent in democracy were, and continue to include, exclusion; a limited commitment to democracy or to democratic values on the part of a large sector of the population frustrated by ever-growing poverty; the weakness of democratic culture and institutions, still tinged by authoritarian attitudes and *caudillista* patrimonialism; the development of a rentier (rentista) culture; and the concentration of power and privilege (as well as their abuse). In addition, Bolivia suffers the absence of transparency and accountability and the lack of timely and credible information on the part of the majority of voters that would enable them to evaluate the performance of those in power, not to mention to judge the appropriateness of specific policies and laws.

The situation is complex, but it demonstrates quite graphically the paradox of constituent power over time, based as it is upon the meeting of civilizations more than four hundred years ago. It began with the conquest and lasted throughout the republican era, and from the outset little was done to encourage a modus vivendi between pre-Columbian ethnic groups and those who had come to conquer. The length of time since the foundation of the republic invites profound reflection on attitudes of one toward the other. Today we appreciate better than ever the damage inflicted on those who were systematically kept excluded at the margins of national development. We can appreciate the moral blindness of those who, directly or indirectly, took advantage of this situation. And, on the basis of what has been achieved so far, we can see the importance of conciliation, in the hope of peaceful coexistence in ways that avoid expressions of blind hatred and sterile vengeance.

The Constituent Assembly and the Binding Referendum

The reestablishment of democracy in 1982 was grounded on full observance of the constitution, but the text of the constitution contemplated neither the notion of a constituent assembly nor a referendum as a means to amend or modify it. It laid down procedures for amendments that were regulated in the legislature, with the majority party or alliance ultimately deciding what could be done by way of constitutional reform.[2] Political events in the early 1990s—primarily demands for improvements to the electoral system and a more independent judicial system—led to the so-called Agreement for the Modernization of the State and the Strengthening of Democracy, to which the main political actors gave their consent in 1992. This established that the procedures used for constitutional reforms should be those laid down in the constitution.

The first change to the constitution began in April 1993, with the Law of Necessity for Reform (Ley de Necesidad de Reforma). It was finally approved by Congress in 1995, and then promulgated by President Gonzalo Sánchez de Lozada.[3] It introduced substantial reforms, including the recognition of the pluricultural and multiethnic nature of the country, a provision for the election of a proportion of deputies on the basis of one-person constituencies (*circunscripciones uninominales*), the creation of a Constitutional Tribunal, the introduction of a Council of the Judiciary (Consejo de la Judicatura), and the creation of the post of ombudsman (Defensoría del Pueblo). At the same time, the government enacted a series of economic reforms, characterized by the partial transfer of ownership of public companies and services to the private sector through the device known as "capitalization."

The effects of the so-called water war and other public protests in 2000 brought with them the first murmurings of the need for a constituent assembly. Initially, at least, there was little prospect of this happening, since, in February 2001, President Hugo Banzer proposed a text for constitutional reform that made no reference to the idea of an assembly, although it did include the introduction of referendums. In the wake of this initiative, the Citizens' Council for Constitutional Reform (Consejo Ciudadano para la Reforma Constitucional) was set up, which worked on a separate proposal incorporating a number of initiatives emanating from civil society.

A second reform thus took shape. However, this was a period of growing social agitation in which, because of the upcoming presidential campaign of

2002 and peasant mobilizations, the demand for a constituent assembly to overhaul the entire existing constitution became increasingly pressing. In August of that year, the second Law of Necessity for Constitutional Reform was passed, with some fifty suggested amendments.[4] Still, no mention was made of an assembly. Indeed, the legality of an assembly had been questioned by a number of the traditional political parties, and a year earlier the Constitutional Tribunal had turned down its immediate introduction in preference to using the derived constitutive power vested in the Congress as established by the legal order then in force.

The political and social movements that brought about the ouster and resignation of Sánchez de Lozada in October 2003 made a constituent assembly a cornerstone of the so-called October Agenda. President Carlos Mesa and the Congress responded to this political challenge by widening the terms of reference of the Law of Necessity and including within its text a reference to a constituent assembly.[5] This incision merits criticism, since it did not exactly follow the sequence set out under Article 230 of the Constitution, and the assembly was included as an organ of direct citizen government. In any event, the political climate at the time was such that its inclusion helped avert further confrontation on this issue. The second reform was approved in February 2004, and the revised text was then promulgated by Mesa.

The third and final reform of the constitution carried out under the derived constitutive power of the Congress during this interlude came about as a result of the political crisis of June 2005. Social protests and the crisis in relations between the executive and Congress led to Mesa's resignation as president, as well as that of Senate President Hormando Vaca Diez and Chamber of Deputies President Mario Cossio.[6] It was following this turn of events that I, then president of the Supreme Court, thus became president of the republic, and a new agenda—one of extreme urgency to find a democratic solution to the political crisis and to preserve democratic institutionality—emerged. This demanded the holding of fresh elections, not just for the presidency and vice presidency of the republic, but for the whole Congress, as well as departmental prefectures, the holding of a referendum on autonomies, and the convening of a constituent assembly. After laborious negotiations, this plan of action was finally approved. This meant that, at the same time, the legal constitutional procedures had to be set in motion for it to happen.

The first issue, the general election for members of Congress, president, and vice president, was resolved through an amendment to Article 93 of the constitution, which sets out the rules on bringing forward the presidential succession in case of absence or impediment of the vice president, and then—successively—of the presidents of the Senate and Chamber of Deputies, and finally the president of the Supreme Court of Justice.[7] Paragraph 3 previously stated that, in case of the succession of the president of the Supreme Court, "if less than three years of the presidential term has elapsed, there will be fresh elections for president and vice president only to complete that period." This particular stipulation raised two critical difficulties: one which restricted election to the posts of president and vice president, and the other which restricted the period over which they would exercise their functions (once elected) to a period of less than three years. This was a combination which did nothing to resolve the problem of representation in Congress, and nor did it provide a solution to the crisis of governability. The amendment resolved this difficulty by introducing a more practical wording: "In the latter case [the succession of the president of the Supreme Court], new general elections will be called immediately, and these will be conducted within 180 days of the elections being called."

The second issue related to the election of departmental prefects. This had been demanded by the regions as part of a shift toward greater decentralization and regional autonomy. It was resolved by the Congress by passing a law of constitutional interpretation (*ley interpretativa*) that stated that the presidential appointment of departmental prefects would take place after their direct election under universal suffrage by a simple majority, and their term of office would be for five years and their election would take place at the same time as those for municipalities.[8]

The use of derived constituent powers by the legislature underwent an interesting process of evolution over this period. It began with these being exercised through two rounds of constitutional reform, whose orientation would clearly reflect the concerns of the government of the time. The way in which the Law of Necessity was formulated and subsequently dealt with in Congress responded to the political demands of the time, in as much as the constituent power was exercised by consensus emerging from and seeking to resolve bouts of intense political crisis. So it was that the idea of the Constituent Assembly, the election of prefects, and the calling of general elections in cases of succession were incorporated. Equally significant was the power of the Congress to interpret the text of the constitution, facilitating political solutions within a framework of constitutionality in such a way as to guarantee legitimacy. This practice effectively overruled the idea of the Constitutional Tribunal as the sole and supreme interpreter of the constitution.

The crisis of representation in the political system and the collapse of the system of pacts orchestrated by the traditional parties gave rise to demands for greater citizen participation.[9] The growth of the mass media, the spread of democratic values in recent years (especially unrestricted freedom of expression), and the increase in citizen demands across a range of issues all encouraged the development of public participation. These involved public rallies (*cabildos*), plebiscites, referendums, and the right of citizens to launch legislative initiatives. Indeed, the constitutional changes brought about in 2004 introduced the idea of the citizens' initiative and referendums as forms of deliberation and government by the people, in line with Article 4 of the constitution.[10] Bolivia held an important referendum in 2004, in which the majority upheld a number of key constitutional changes that helped strengthen the democratic state. These included the establishment of a system of constitutional guarantees, greater powers for Congress, administrative decentralization, limitations on presidential reelection, the establishment of the office of comptroller-general of the republic (Contraloría General) and university autonomy.

In May 2004, to comply with the October Agenda that emerged after the fall of Sánchez de Lozada, the government called for a binding referendum on five questions relating to hydrocarbons policy: changes to the existing law, the recovery of national ownership of hydrocarbon resources, the refounding of Yacimientos Petrolíferos Fiscales Bolivianos (YPFB), the use of gas as a negotiating tool to regain access to the Pacific Ocean, and four issues about the consumption and the industrialization of gas, its taxation and the use of the benefits derived.[11] The referendum elicited a "yes" vote to all the questions posed, with majorities in favor ranging from 58 to 92 percent. It paved the way for the reform of the Hydrocarbons Law, promulgated by Congress in 2005.[12]

In response to political agreements arising from the crisis of 2005 and the long-standing desires of Bolivia's eastern departments, a law was passed on March 6, 2006, that called for an additional national referendum on departmental autonomies. This stated that the result would be binding on the Constitutional Assembly and in those departments where a "yes" vote prevailed. It also prescribed the wording of the referendum and set July 2, 2006, as its date.[13] The departments of Santa Cruz, Beni, Pando, and Tarija voted in favor of autonomy, while La Paz, Cochabamba, Oruro, Potosí, and Chuquisaca voted for the "no" option. The tensions to which this gave rise soon became evident. The government took an antiautonomy line, causing an unnecessary political and regional breach with the departments of the eastern part of the country. The assembly was finally unable to provide a solution mutually acceptable to both positions, a divergence with unpredictable consequences for the unity of Bolivia.

The notion of citizen participation in political decision making has therefore become established. Indeed, the text approved by the Constituent Assembly would need to be submitted to a constitutional referendum. The executive has also taken the initiative to incorporate a recall referendum into the text of the constitution as a democratic means of resolving growing tensions between the government and elected departmental prefects, especially those not belonging to the ruling party.

The constituent power may find, in the referendum, an extraordinary source of the sovereign will; it contributes to the deliberative process, it is inclusive, and it encourages democratic participation. However, prudence needs to be exercised in how this form of democratic participation is put into action, especially with respect to the nature, scope, and outcomes of referendums. As John Morison points out (2004), it might be possible to design a complete system of citizen control in decision making, as was the case in ancient Athens, but it remains to be seen if such a highly developed form of democracy is either practical or acceptable.

Having negotiated an agreement with Congress, the transitional government thus established the bases for holding a referendum on autonomies and for convening a Constituent Assembly.[14] It initiated discussion about the practical norms to be adopted for both. The most controversial issue concerned the regulation of the Constituent Assembly. A preliminary proposal suggested adopting special constituencies of indigenous or *originario* peoples, but this was subsequently dropped. On March 6, 2006, the Congress—in an unusual gesture of consensus—approved the Special Law Convening the Constituent Assembly (Ley Especial de Convocatoría). Passed by a two-thirds majority, this defined the nature and number (255) of assembly members, the place where the assembly would sit, its independence of the other constituted powers of the state, and its sole aim of revising the constitution in its entirety. It also established rules regarding the election of members, as well as the organization and workings of the assembly. It specified that the text of the new constitution would be approved by a margin of two-thirds of those present' and that subsequently the executive would call a referendum on the constitution so that, in a period of no more than 120 days, the people—by an absolute majority—could endorse the text.[15] Should they fail to do so, the existing constitution would remain in force. Elections were then held for members of the assembly on the date set, as well as the referendum on autonomies. They were conducted in an orderly fashion, paving the way toward this new phase of change.[16]

Following an auspicious inauguration in Sucre on August 6, 2006, the assembly soon became bogged down in an interminable wrangle over the rules of procedure, particularly the method by which the text of the constitution would be approved. Finally, in December 2005, the majority ruling party approved the general set of rules governing debate in the assembly, giving rise to a huge polemic over two articles. One (Article 1) declared that the assembly was originaria.[17] The second (Article 70) ruled that the decisions of the assembly would be made, as a general rule, by an absolute majority of votes both in commissions and the plenary, restricting the two-thirds vote to the final text in a plenary session.[18]

In January 2007, the urban population of Cochabamba joined in with the tide of opinion, leading to violent clashes between urban residents and *cocalero* campesinos. Early in 2007, the civic and municipal organizations of the city of Sucre launched a campaign to recover its status as the "full" capital of Bolivia in the new constitution. This provoked a confrontation with La Paz. Unable to fulfill the deadline for completing the constitutional text, the time limit had to be extended from August 6 to December 14, 2007. Inasmuch as the conflict over the *capitalía* turned violent, the sessions of the assembly had to be suspended. With the new deadline looming, the assembly decided to resume sessions in the relative security of a military installation under the protection of the armed forces, but without the presence of the opposition. On November 24, 136 of the 235 assembly members approved (without debate) the reports of the twenty-one commissions. This aroused further protests from the opposition, with the declaration of regional strikes in support of the departmental autonomies. Thus it was that the assembly met once again on December 8 and 9, this time in Oruro, with the protection of progovernment forces. In a session lasting only a few hours and in the presence of only the MAS and its allies, detailed approval was given to the 411 articles of the draft constitution, which would then be submitted to a referendum. The opposition and the regions opposed to the government thereupon rejected the proceedings and approved the texts of their own statutes of autonomy.

In this context of ever-growing tension, neither side seemed willing to back down and compromise, but neither did they have the ability to impose their will without resort to violence. However, the situation gave rise to both domestic and external efforts to promote dialogue. A series of meetings got underway in January 2008 between Evo Morales and the prefects to explore political solutions to the crisis. However, these failed to resolve a growing stand-off between the government in La Paz and the opposition in Santa Cruz. The assembly had failed in its task of reaching a text based on consensus; the final draft was not based on agreements encompassing a vocation for peaceful, democratic, and equitable coexistence among all the actors, irrespective of their ideological positions.

It was therefore clear that there was a deviation from the constitutional will expressed at the time of the assembly's installation. The rules and regulations guiding its conduct were systematically breached so as to limit discussion and to end with the approval of a final text in the absence of judicial, legislative, or political mechanisms to restore it to its rightful course. This was made worse by the resignation of the magistrates of the Constitutional Tribunal, alleging political pressures brought against it by the government. The assembly thus proved unable to bring together and compatibilize divergent visions about the future of the country. Nor was it possible to resurrect the initial agreements reached in some of the commissions and in the attempts to reach supraparty agreements. Indeed, unexplained divergences appeared in the text, and the situation was not conducive to considering these observations.

Although there had been an agreement post-2003 to set up a "preconstituent" arena to prepare the rules of the game, this was not taken seriously, and when it was promulgated, the law convening the assembly was interpreted differently by the various parties, notwithstanding the intelligent way it was drafted. Irrespective of the polemic surrounding the wording of the regulations, the nature of the assembly and the methods employed for the approval of resolutions (including the final sessions whose legitimacy and legality was questioned by significant sectors of the population), it is clearly essential for all parties to restore the will to build a new constitutional order. Otherwise, formulae imposed without consensus, even on the basis of circumstantial majorities, will lack legitimacy. They will violate the fundamental essence of a constitution which—and it hardly needs restating here—provides the basis for peaceful and fraternal coexistence between all without exclusions and on the basis of clear rules for the rational exercise of public power. The president of the republic, the Congress, the assembly, political leaders, prefects, civic committees, and civil society all have a duty to demonstrate this vocation for reconciliation and fraternity. In practical terms, this means discussing the norms involved and reformulating them in a more intelligent way so that no one feels either victor or vanquished. Many people have lost their lives in recent times as a result of rancor and violence; we have to avoid further casualties, particularly any such rift that threatens to split the country asunder.

Jurisdictional Control and Constituent Power

An inseparable corollary of the theory of constituent power is judicial control over the normative will, both with respect to the procedures to be followed in producing it or changing it, and, eventually, over what it consists of and the effects it may have on those who are the subjects of the legal and constitutional order. The relation between the two depends on the extent of this control, or constitutional jurisdiction, and it has varied a great deal. The first Bolivian Constitution of 1826 included a three-chamber legislative power, with a chamber of censors whose duty was to watch over compliance with the constitution and the legal order, and to act as a prosecutor before the Senate in cases where the executive infringed these. Subsequent reforms, in 1851, granted the judiciary—through the Supreme Court—this role. The responsibility for exercising judicial control over constitutionality was then transferred to the Constitutional Tribunal in 1998. Its authority was based on the clause that upheld the supremacy of the constitution over aspects of the national juridical framework, and the duty of the courts, judges, and other authorities to uphold it over above all other laws or other types of resolution (Article 228).

Political control over constitutionality has also remained in force to date. From the reform of 1839 onward, the Congress has had the power to pass laws that interpret the constitution by means of special laws that require a two-thirds majority. These cannot be vetoed by the president of the republic. This scheme for the control of constitutionality—both judicial and political—was something of little importance, at least up until the creation of the Constitutional Tribunal. The return to democracy did much to establish a more solid and credible system for the protection of basic rights. It brought with it the restoration of full constitutional rights and guarantees. It also renewed guarantees of judicial autonomy, and it rendered the system of constitutional oversight through a specialized tribunal more sophisticated. It also brought (among other things) the constitutional independence of the public prosecutor's office (Ministerio Público), the establishment of an ombudsman (Defensoría del Pueblo), the modernization of the penal system, and improvements in the rules governing judicial appointments. Yet, it is undeniable that the Bolivian judicial system still faces enormous challenges in terms of accessibility, predictability, and efficiency in every sphere, from the preservation of constitutionality down to the level of communal justice. All play an essential role in maintaining the democratic essence of constituent power (Rodriguez Veltzé 2004).

As elsewhere in Latin America, Bolivia has made some useful contributions to constitutional justice. As Fernández Segado (2006) notes, Latin American countries constitute "a real constitutional laboratory as regards control over the constitutionality of the laws and of other acts of power." This valuable diversity, particularly given its evolution in recent times, is of great use in addressing the workings and the powers of the judiciary, and particularly its powers in exercising control over constitutionality. Also valuable will be the critical appraisal of constitutional jurisdiction in Bolivia. Among the issues to deal with here, one could mention that of conflict between the Constitutional Tribunal, the Supreme Court, and the ordinary courts over the extent of constitutional oversight, their rulings versus precedent (res judicata), and the very nature of that control. Should this function be concentrated in the Constitutional Tribunal as the sole and supreme interpreter of the constitution, whose rulings have binding force? Or should it be shared and diluted among all authorities and judges who have to apply the constitution over and above other rules, and with the legislature, given its role as derived constitutional power and its attributes in exercising political control over such scope through interpretative norms?

In any case, it is important to stress that the judicial system of constitutional control in Bolivia contributed decisively and positively to strengthening the rule of law and, specifically, during those crises of governability that put the survival of constituent power to the test. The Constitutional Tribunal contributed significantly to helping resolve the controversies that arose around the December 2005 general elections and the election of prefects which gave rise to legal challenges.

The tribunal embodies the notion

> of a rule of law characterized by the subjection of both public powers and citizens to the juridical order, to the maximum norm of this superior order which, from a moral and political standpoint, affirms and guarantees values considered essential for social coexistence and the recognition of the fundamental right of the citizen to participate in the conformation of public powers, both as elector

and as a person elected. This understanding is based on the principle of popular
sovereignty, a principle that cannot be delegated, and on the importance of the
suffrage, the cornerstone of the system of representative democracy, founded on
a vote that is universal, direct and equal, individual and secret, free and obliga-
tory. It is also based on public oversight and proportional representation. Consequently, in the Bolivian constitutional model, there can be no rule of law without
democracy, and no democracy without the rule of law (Durán Rivera 2005).

The tribunal dealt speedily and opportunely with four rulings concerned with
strengthening of the rule of law and democracy: (1) SC 0066/2005, on the issue of the proportional distribution of seats in Congress; (2) SC 0075/2005,
on the election of prefects; (3) SC 0076/2005, on the general elections; and (4)
SC 1392/2005-R, regarding voting by Bolivians living abroad. Together with
other rulings from previous years on the democratic system and presidential
succession, these constituted (in the view of the tribunal's magistrates) "the
most solid and faithful contribution that the Constitutional Tribunal has
made to the state of law and democracy in Bolivia" (Durán Rivera 2005).

The extent of constituent power at times when an assembly is producing a new constitution is extraordinary, since it is during such times that
this power finds its maximum normative expression. At the same time, it
is incumbent on the subjects to take part in and exercise this power; the
whole citizenry must express a democratic will for peaceful coexistence that
is not only written down, but also agreed upon and then complied with. As
Michel Foucault (1995) points out, we enter "the great game of history" in
which whoever is master of the rules, whoever takes the place of those that
use them, whoever disguises himself to pervert them, whoever uses them for
purposes for which they were not intended, or whoever uses them against
those who had constructed them "will make them work in such a way that
the dominant find themselves dominated by their own rules." In the exercise
of constituent power, it is necessary to assimilate the experiences, feelings,
and theorizations that are most constructive and conducive to building a
more just and democratic society; power is constructed and works through
a multitude of power relations, not just as a consequence of the individual or
collective will (Foucault 1995).

As Salvador Nava (2003, 13) puts it, the relationship between constitution and democracy is a marriage that "is not straightforward, since tensions
erupt when the expansion of the former undermines the latter, or . . . when
the strengthening of the constitutional ideal puts the brakes on democratization." It is the constituent power that helps to produce a synthesis of legal

security, often absent during periods of democratic development and major legal change. It is the result of the will to preserve the rule of law, mirrored in a constitution that vouchsafes guarantees of freedom and individual rights, including the separation of powers (with all its controls and counterbalances) and an independent judiciary that is both accessible and efficient in dispensing justice. Other equally important elements should also be borne in mind: submission to the principle of legality, to legitimate norms that are not just a product of the discretional will of those that govern; oversight and control of public and private power in pursuit of the collective interest and the defense of democracy; the ability to generate policies that engender human development; and the supremacy of fundamental rights.

In any event, the constitution is never a prisoner of its own text. Bolivian society will continue to define it, taking the past into consideration but above all looking to the future; its memories are no less illuminating than its gaze into the future.

9

Constitution and Constitutional Reform in Bolivia

LUIS TAPIA

In order to understand the current phase of political reform in Bolivia, we must first examine the relationship between the way in which Bolivia is constituted or constructed—its social and political composition—and the political constitutions that have defined government institutions and legality through different periods of its history. We must then draw a distinction between constituent power and constituted power, and the dynamic between these two as regards our first theme: that is, the way the country is constituted.[1]

The first constitution of the Republic of Bolivia took little or no notice of the degree of cultural diversity to be found in the country, almost entirely ignoring the majority of the population. The constitution defined a set of institutions in ways that were more-or-less modern and liberal—for instance, establishing the separation of powers—but made no reference whatsoever to the existence of other social and political structures that had persisted throughout the colonial period, except inasmuch as they were included in certain aspects of the juridical framework it established. These mostly had to do with establishing the tax status and obligations of indigenous peoples within the new state while simultaneously denying them political or citizenship rights.

The constitutions of the nineteenth century acknowledged a political change—the replacement of Spanish colonial power by a new state that responded to the dominant economic and social power groups within it—but brought no social change as such. That independence took place without changing the social structure is reflected in the constitutions of the time, conceived as these were more as a political transformation than a social one. This was certainly the case up until well into the twentieth century. The 1938 Constituent Assembly was the first instance of an element of social change being acknowledged. This involved the recognition of certain social rights, and it therefore widened the scope or competence of the state beyond that of its previous liberal role as overseer and legislator to that end. Even then, in the 1930s, it was more a question of widening the functions of the state rather than tackling the colonial heritage of the liberal state. We can now see how, at that time, the changes to the constitution mirrored some of the social changes under way in developing citizenship in Bolivia as elsewhere. This formed part of a much longer cycle of crisis in the structure of the state and the development of conditions that would lead to the 1952 revolution. It is perhaps symptomatic that the social changes brought about by 1952 were not accompanied by any changes to the constitution such as to reflect the new configuration; this only took place years later (1967) during the phase of counterrevolution. Generally speaking, and in contrast to these historical developments, the holding of a Constituent Assembly in 2006 and 2007 ran pari passu with processes of political and social change, but in ways that are extremely complex and involve changes and contradictions that this chapter seeks to analyze.

Constituent Power and Constituted Power

To analyze the relationship between the way a country is constituted or constructed and its political constitution, it is helpful to start by drawing the distinction between constituent power and constituted power. A constitution is the overall political form assumed by a constituted power. It outlines its jurisdiction and designs a system of structures that define the existing political order and the way it is governed. It also defines the way in which it may be reformed. The constituent power refers to those forces, subjects, and social processes that bring about the political order and which also define the conditions under which a constitution may be produced or reformed. The emergence of a constituent power implies a degree of fluidity in the existing social and political order and thereby creates the conditions for reconstituting the social order by means of a change in political forms. Another way of thinking about it is that change in political forms is part of a more global change in the social structure, or at least in an important part of it.

The constituted power thus tends to be identified with the constitution and with the various institutions that operate as a state at a particular time and place. All constituted power has a history; it is a political, social, and historical accumulation that brings with it learning and experience, as well as conflicts and contradictions, leading (on occasions) to development in particular aspects or (at others) toward exhaustion and decay.

Constituent power refers to the subject and the process by which a political order comes about, whereas the constituted power is the structure that comes about as a consequence: in other words, a constitution or an operating state. But if we look at things in dynamic terms, we see that the constituted power is not something that is static. Rather, it is exercised on a daily basis and in such a way as to reproduce structures through the laws, and in order to reproduce them it is necessary to introduce innovations. Furthermore, it is also exercised, maintained, and reformed by subjects. In this sense, then, constituted power is also something involving subjects, but in different ways and to different ends. At the same time, it is important to see that constituent power is also geared toward the production of a constituted power, or a constitution, with a social and political content that it will subsequently direct. In this sense, then, both axes end up intersecting one another.

This distinction between constituent and constituted power can be linked to another classic area of analysis in political theory. The constituted power, or constitution, can be seen as a form of conceptualizing the relationship between state and civil society over the long term, and this involves seeing where the boundaries between them are to be drawn, how arenas within the state are designed, how a whole set of arenas within civil society are formed and recognized, and how institutions and mechanisms are established to communicate between state and civil society.

I am disinclined to think of constituted power as identical with the state and, within the state, the political constitution. Equally, I think it is wrong to identify constituent power with civil society. I believe that both the state and civil society form part of the constituted power—in other words, the political order at a particular moment of time—and, at best, this is given visible form as a project and program for political and social life in the form of a constitution.

Constituent power is formed when there is a reconstitution of subjects outside the confines of the state and civil society: in other words, when projects or forces emerge that seek to change the relationship between the state and civil society, the arenas within them, the subjects involved, the relationships between them, and consequently the political form that society adopts. In this sense, a constituent power is something that emerges at points of crisis, or provokes a political crisis that, among other things, can lead to the reconstitution of a country.

At the same time, it is important to stress that constituted power is something complex. It contains the formulation for a constitution, a variety of in-

stitutions that give shape to the state, a variety of political practices and linkages between the state and civil society, and a variety of political discourses.
Additionally, it involves an array of political and economic forces that result
from the ability to wield political power, and different sorts of power depending on how it is defined by the constitution or by the way such institutions
operate. Constituted power also contains certain discursive elements, discourses of legitimation that nevertheless do not mirror or constitute the true
political order of a country.

It is frequently the case in Latin America—Bolivia included—that the
wording of the constitution does not reflect the way in which the state is constructed, how it actually works, how power is distributed within it, or the way
in which governance is carried out. Still less does it mirror the complexity of
the social and political order that lies beneath the form of government. Many
constitutions—or parts of them—thus serve to provide a juridical discourse
and to justify or erect a political image of a country that has little to do with
the ways in which power is actually wielded through economic, social, and
political structures.

We began this chapter mentioning the fact that one of the characteristics
of Bolivia's constitutions was the way they ignored the social diversity within
the country; they defined a mainly liberal institutional order that did not
reflect the way in which the country was actually governed. Much the same
could be said of other countries, inasmuch as states mostly do not operate
along the lines laid out in their constitutions. In this sense, the constitution
is a complex regulatory norm that seeks to provide rules for the effective
exercise of power and government within society but does not reflect the existing social and political order. Rather, it is designed to provide norms that
seek to push processes in the direction or in the form prescribed.

The Genesis of Constitutional Reform

Bolivia has been reconstituted in the last two decades; the state and civil
society have changed, as has the way in which they relate to one another
and the way that the state has been financed to the exclusion of much of
the country. The privatization of the economy, in particular the handover
of natural resources to transnational corporations, has created a situation
in which the Bolivian state has become increasingly dependent on external
indebtedness and so-called international cooperation. In this sense, constituted power has been reformed, and in more general terms the structures of

power within the country have changed, with foreign actors having a much larger presence than before. The power bloc that brought these to the fore includes the country's main business groups, closely linked to transnational interests and working in harmony with the policies advocated by global financial institutions.

Some changes to the constitution were made during the period of neoliberal reform in the 1990s, as well as in the first few crisis years of the new millennium. These constitutional changes were carried out in the wake of major changes to the property structure, as well as in the state's relationship both to the economy and labor. Some reflected a response to demands from lowland indigenous peoples. Reforms introduced in the early 1990s declared the country "plurilingual" and "multicultural," and, perhaps more importantly, recognized indigenous units of landholding (*tierras comunitarias de orígen*, or TCOs).

Other reforms had to do with the development of the new division of power and systems of controls between different areas of the state, such as the Ombudsman's office (Defensoría del Pueblo), the Constitutional Tribunal, and the various superintendencies. The extent to which these innovations have proved efficacious and acceptable to the public has varied. Probably the innovation that has become most consolidated—due in part to the efficient way it was originally run—has been the Ombudsman's office. The superintendencies have demonstrated less independence and capacity in regulating the privatized firms and the markets that resulted from capitalization.

What needs to be stressed here is that these reforms were not the product of pressures arising from the political life of the country or from ordinary people's demands for institutional change; rather, they tended to be adopted because they were part of the policy packages advocated by international financial institutions and agencies from within the international community. This, of course, does not mean that the reforms were bad as such, only that many of them were conceived beyond Bolivia's frontiers and therefore lacked social acceptance.

Conditions arose for what we call constituent power as a consequence of the reconstitution of Bolivia along neoliberal lines and the politically exclusive way these neoliberal reforms were imposed. A variety of political subjects opposed to this reordering began to give substance to the demand for a constituent assembly. They subsequently gained the strength required to ensure that this agenda was taken up by the state. Conditions were such that pressure for state reform took the form of the demand for a constituent assembly.

This constituent power stemmed from a number of sources, involving a range of territories and subjects and raising different issues. Three issues were of particular importance. The first was the attack against the monopolization of politics and the corruption (which had become widespread) it encouraged. The second was the way in which property ownership had been transnationalized, as well as the way this had influenced economic policy making. The third was the highlighting of the colonial character of the country and the deep inequalities between its peoples and cultures. The increasing interrelationship between these three elements or issues was what generated a force sufficient to produce change and drive it forward.

The most potent source of this constituent power emerged during the so-called water war in Cochabamba. The protest movement against the privatization of the city's water and sewer service, which came together as the Coordinadora por la Defensa de la Vida y del Agua, sought not only to restore property to the state but to broaden the public sphere by increasing public participation in the running and management of firms producing public goods and services like water. Following the water war, the coordinadora helped promote the campaign for a constituent assembly, a campaign first launched nearly a decade earlier by way of protests by lowland indigenous peoples. This campaign had little force at the beginning of the 1990s, when, for the first time ever, indigenous peoples from the lowlands launched a protest march on La Paz.[2] Even in 2000, the demand for a constituent assembly was perceived by the majority of party leaders involved in government as something antidemocratic and impractical.

In becoming a source of constituent power, the coordinadora was able to build a broad public arena. It became an exercise in direct democracy, in which there was a capacity to deliberate, to evaluate the situation as it developed, and to present alternative proposals and lines of action. The coordinadora thus worked as a sort of broader assembly in which the representatives of more specific nuclei of support were present as actors in confronting a transnational corporation and the Water Law (Ley de Aguas). Among the various forms of social organization that took part were rural unions, neighborhood committees, and committees of irrigators. Each component sent delegates on a rotational basis to represent them and to participate in wider political discussion.

The coordinadora became a form of constituent power because it opened up political spaces far broader and more dynamic than anything organized by the state or envisaged in the constitution. To make its voice heard, it developed links with civil society in ways that became stronger, more vibrant, and more representative. The very fact that it created a parallel political arena far more vigorous and dynamic than the party system or the arenas envisaged by state institutions was something that helped it become an element in building constituent power, not least because it provided the impetus to demanding a constituent assembly. The coordinadora ended by pushing for a thoroughgoing reform of the country's political institutions, an aim well beyond the narrower issues it had raised in the first place.

Another source of constituent power resulted from the coming together of peoples from Amazonia, the Oriente, and the Chaco. Assemblies are being established in individual communities which gave rise to coordination within ethnic groups, helping them achieve effective representation. Higher-level assemblies then bring together different peoples and cultures into a bloc, establishing coordination and strengthening the bloc's ability to fight the sort of exploitation and inequality that these people have suffered for centuries. So far, eight assemblies or *centrales* have been created to bring together different peoples and provide them with a platform on which to represent their views and to negotiate with the Bolivian state.[3] In some cases, these have been key to both unification and effective representation. Such was the case, for instance, of the Guarani People's Assembly (Asamblea del Pueblo Guaraní).

The third source of constituent power has a longer political history, arising as it did in the Altiplano and central valleys. The emergence of Katarismo stands out as a milestone in this respect. As an ideology, discourse, and political outlook, Katarismo has not only helped forge a moral and intellectual autonomy in the Aymara world but has had a certain pull in Quechua parts of Bolivia as well. Its political activities have included the organization of peasant unions (*sindicatos*), campesino political parties, and mass mobilizations and road blockages that became increasingly common after 2000. This is a separate political and social structure, distinct from the rest of Bolivian society; indeed, it is a society that has been submerged under colonial and liberal domination. However, it has become active and has mobilized against the various neoliberal governments and the economic and political structures they tried to erect. In some instances, this mobilization has been driven primarily by peasant *sindicalismo*, the product of *mestizaje*, which has one foot in the community and another in the more modern political arena that lies within the Bolivian state. Where Aymara and Quechua mobilization has the community as its nucleus (in other words, traditional and autonomous structures of authority), the assembly plays an important role in providing a public space in which the community can express itself culturally and act politically. Such mobilization has, indeed, placed previous governments under siege, bringing them to their knees. Where the nucleus is strictly speaking one of community, it constitutes a sphere that is external to the Bolivian state; where the *sindicato* predominates, it involves activity within the sphere of the modern, liberal state, instigated at the behest of rural workers.

These three different components typify the emergence of constituent power in Bolivia. What they have in common is the way in which politics runs through the assembly, a public arena that is open to direct democracy. Constituent power is characterized by the challenge to the existing constitutional framework and its insistence that politics be conducted solely through political parties and other such arenas legally prescribed by the state for the purposes of deliberation, legislation, and decision making. All three cases show how the political monopoly of the parties was challenged and broken down. In defying the constitutional order, they became expressions of constituent power. Beyond the politics of protest, the water war helped build an alternative political space; the other two resuscitated traditions of community self-government. As well, they involved modern forms of interaction with the Bolivian state through union federations and assemblies of indigenous peoples.

The story of how constituent power developed is therefore the story of how these elements emerged, how they developed, and how they structured themselves. Now, what is it that prevents the development of such constituent power leading to a process of revolution, in the classic meaning of the term? Alternatively, what is it that enables a constituent assembly to take place in such a way that is accepted and even convened by existing political institutions? Here a number of hypotheses suggest themselves.

First, although representative democracy has generally been associated with liberalism and, indeed, with the dominant class (whether national or transnational), in recent times it has been subject to popular conquest. Democracy in Bolivia, for all its limitations, has been the conquest of peasants, unionized workers, and popular movements. It was these that overcame the Banzer dictatorship in the 1970s, pressing as they did for the recovery of political rights and the restoration of constitutional order, itself seen as a condition for any subsequent transition to a fuller democracy along the lines that historically typified popular and indigenous communities. It was these sectors that resisted attempts to abort the transition in the period between 1978 and 1979 and during the early 1980s. It was these same nuclei that defended political rights when loss of influence led the dominant parties and groups to adopt an increasingly authoritarian posture, especially in mid-2005. And it was these that pressed for a widening of the institutional framework, supporting the referendum on gas nationalization and, especially, the convening of a constituent assembly. What we refer to as representative democracy is thus something that is part of the political culture of popular and community groups in Bolivia, although, of course, it is not the only form of democracy that people may have in mind, nor is it viewed as a basic precondition for a comprehensive reordering of the country.

The second factor has to do with the presence of a workers' party within the party system, which has proved able—at moments of government crisis and amid the popular mobilizations and blockades of recent years—to provide a channel, an outlet through the party system itself. In this respect, the shear size of the vote for the MAS (Movimiento al Socialismo) can only be understood as a product of the pent-up pressure of that constituent power, which brought the electoral victory of a majority of MAS representatives in both the Chamber of Deputies and subsequently in the Constituent Assembly. This implies a number of things, among them that it has been possible to generate modern ways of engaging in politics, through political parties, from within the peasant sector, and that in the last few years it has proved possible to invert the relationship between political forces so that these sectors now head up the state.

Changes in the Balance of Forces and in Institutions

These cycles of popular mobilization threw the party system into turmoil and increasingly eroded its legitimacy. It is important to remember that the party system had been suffering from problems of delegitimization for years. Parties enjoyed low levels of trust amid public opinion, even though electoral participation remained fairly high. Crossing these two sets of data—support for parties of between 2 and 5 percent and electoral participation rates of over 70 percent—it would seem that participation was directed much more toward upholding political rights than expressing confidence in the parties per se. Indeed, during the waves of mobilization in protest at the economic model, the thrust of public criticism was targeted precisely at the political parties, their monopoly over the system of representation, their performance, their leadership, and the role they played in instituting and implementing neoliberalism in Bolivia.

One of the peculiarities about Bolivia, especially compared to other Latin American countries, is that while the organizational capacities of civil society contributed to the growth of dissatisfaction with the party system and eventually produced a major recomposition within it, this happened without the system actually collapsing. Such a collapse would be something to be expected in view of the lengthy period of delegitimization in which the parties became targets for disaffection. But thanks to the presence of a party at the heart of the system which, for nearly ten years, spearheaded resistance to a series of policies that had undermined national sovereignty—not least those aimed at eradicating coca—this was not the case. In this sense, the party of the *cocaleros*, the MAS, managed both to defend a corporative interest as well as to stand up for national sovereignty. This enabled it to steer the country toward an outcome that preserved the existing institutional framework, notwithstanding the challenges from popular mobilization in 2000, 2003, and 2005. The MAS was able to articulate public dissatisfaction without destroying the institutional system.

In sum, the upsurge of constituent power in Bolivia, diverse in its nature, has brought about a major change in the relations between political forces within the country. It has accentuated the decline of the political parties—most of which cogoverned during the period of economic neoliberalism—and has produced a significant shift within both the legislature and the executive. From a small minority with only five deputies, the MAS became, in 2005, the majority party in both the Chamber of Deputies and the Constituent Assembly. The executive is no longer the plaything of the business leaders who, during the 1980s and 1990s, exercised strong influence over party leaderships and government appointments. Instead, we have a government made up of trade union leaders and workers from different sectors, which responds to the leadership of a party with peasant origins.

The 2005 elections thus mark a change in trends for the medium term, at least so far as voting is concerned. We have gone from a period in which pro-business parties with neoliberal programs predominated to one dominated by a party with a worker-peasant base but which enjoys wider electoral support around a nationalist ideology. Although the balance of forces has shifted and those at the heart of state power are a far cry from those that preceded them, this change has come about without major changes in institutions and political structures.

Changes in Constituent Power and in Constituted Power

The change in the relation of political forces that brought about change in the composition of the party system and those now in the executive implies a change insofar as the constituted power is concerned. This is at least the case of the majority, since those who represent the political Right in Bolivia continue to have a presence in the legislature. This change in the constituted power relates, basically, to those now running the state and to the make-up of the party system. Here it is worth highlighting some of the changes that have taken place within the constituent power, since it helps us define the nature and fate of the Constituent Assembly.

It could be argued that it is inappropriate to identify the constituent power with the elected members of the assembly. They were all elected as candidates of political parties, many of them for parties which had argued for years against holding a constituent assembly on the basis that it would be antidemocratic and not something contemplated by the previous constitution. They had also opposed such an assembly because it would mean revising the constitutional foundations on which the neoliberal economic order had been built. Many of those elected to the assembly had a good deal in common with the opposition congressmen elected in the December 2005 who—in opposing the system of private landholding—became a sort of anti–constituent power or part of the constituted power left over from earlier times. They are resistant to the agenda of change which the country is going through.

The same may be true of a significant number of those elected for the MAS. They were elected as a consequence of alliances or deals between the MAS and corporative or sectoral nuclei within civil society. Many are not (and never were) part of what can be truly described as the constituent power that had emerged in previous years. Even those elected from peasant and organized-labor backgrounds (the "popular" sectors) had not necessarily been a part of that constituent power.

A distinction can be drawn between three different positions. The first of these consists of those assembly members elected for the MAS on the back of such corporative deals with a range of organizations which played no part in the development of constituent power. The second are those who represent organizations that previously formed part of the constituent power but who then managed to negotiate their inclusion in the assembly through similar sorts of deals with corporative interests keen to ensure their interests were taken into account. The third category relates to those who continue to represent the main elements in the development of constituent power and articulate their agendas and proposals generated through a variety of different political organizations and arenas across the country. It is this third group which injected the proposals of constituent power within the Constituent Assembly (now part of the constituted power).

Another dimension, possibly more important, has to do with changes affecting the relationship between parties, organizations, and movements. One of the results of the political reconfiguration has been the MAS's strategy to become a party that singlehandedly represents the full range of popular, peasant, worker, and indigenous politics in Bolivia. Through the law convening the Constituent Assembly, among other measures, the MAS has sought to induce these organizations into negotiating with it as the main route to political inclusion. This has brought about changes at the heart of constituent power. While the MAS has made its aim to act as the leader of constituent power quite clear, it paradoxically subsumes aspects of constituent power to the constituted power of which it is now the executive authority. This may have had a disorganizing and disorienting effect at the heart of constituent power. Indeed, it helped fragment it, by including some sectors through electoral alliances and excluding others from the assembly precisely because they failed to establish alliances with the majority party.

Since this is a government of a workers' party—to put it generically—broad networks have yet to be constructed that mobilize against the government in ways that contribute to building on the constituent power developed in recent years. This is something that is latent, fragmented, and to all intents and purposes was beyond the confines of the Constituent Assembly working as if it were a constituted power. The assembly became closely linked to the presence of political parties, both those of the opposition (which were against it in principle) as well as that of the ruling party, which, as leader of the executive, tended to subordinate constituent power to constituted power. In so doing, it limited the scope for change which had previously emerged from the waves of protest and which might well come about if the new political order included the full diversity of social organization in the design of new political institutions of government.

PART V

ON STRATEGIES OF ECONOMIC DEVELOPMENT

The liberalization policies of the 1990s brought in new technology and led to the discovery of large reserves of natural gas in Bolivia. This has once again stimulated debate over priorities in economic development: between focusing on industries that bring with them substantial returns in terms of foreign investment, exports and fiscal revenues, and focusing on those that give rise to employment and therefore tackle problems of poverty and exclusion. The gas industry falls into the first category, substantially raising the quantum of foreign direct investment (FDI), annual exports, and treasury income. However, this gas bonanza has once again shown up the limitations of this sort of growth in achieving a more balanced sort of development in which the benefits can be widely shared.

This is not a new problem. In the years following the 1952 national revolution, the governments of the Movimiento Nacionalista Revolucionario (MNR) sought to use the country's mineral wealth as the mechanism for achieving a more broadly based pattern of growth that would foster the development of other sectors. As demonstrated in the chapters on regionalism (part 2 of this volume), the surplus achieved from mining was heavily invested in the development of agriculture in eastern Bolivia, a development that encouraged the migration of poor Andean peasants from the highlands into the tropical lowlands. The government also sought to increase the value added of the mining industry by encouraging investment in refining operations within Bolivia. This economic model presupposed a heavy degree of state intervention.

But unlike other Latin American countries, the degree of import-substitutive industrialization (ISI) achieved in Bolivia was extremely limited. Bolivia continued to meet its domestic demand for industrial goods largely from imports, much of them in the form of contraband. Industrialization was restricted to the provision of basic goods with a low technological content, sold largely on the domestic market, and the processing of a handful of export commodities. The structure of employment was such that those working in manufacturing represented only a very small proportion of the labor force. As industry closed or migrated out of La Paz, by 2005 the main centers of manufacturing were in El Alto, Santa Cruz, and (to a lesser extent) Cochabamba.

The impact of economic liberalization in the 1980s was therefore primarily to stabilize price levels and eliminate rationing and financial repression, whereas elsewhere it may have led to important changes in the structure of production, favoring the export sector at the expense of import-substitutive industries. The main social effects were felt through the shrinking of the public sector, particularly in the export-oriented mining sector. There were, however, important changes that took place in the structure of the export sector, with the decline of mining and metallurgy and the expansion of such exports as gas, soy, and (of course) coca derivatives. At the same time, there was the appearance of new manufactured export lines, such as clothing, textiles, furniture, and jewelry, mostly produced in small, semi-informal workshops using low technology but exploiting certain specific comparative advantages in terms of the materials used.

Although the protest movements that evolved in the late 1990s were highly critical of the neoliberal model, they tended not to hark back to an early era of ISI since there was no appetite for a return to the conditions of the early 1980s nor was such a restoration feasible. Rather they focused on the way in which Bolivia's experience with privatization had short-changed the Bolivian state and the Bolivian people more generally. The focus here was clearly on the hydrocarbons industry, where Gonzalo Sánchez de Lozada's "capitalization" strategy had led to an infusion of foreign investment (on very favorable terms) and this quickly revealed—some allege that it was already known—the true size of the country's gas potential. The contracts with foreign investors therefore became a target of public criticism, the analogy often made between this and the "plunder" of Bolivia's mineral wealth in the colonial period.

It was therefore not surprising that, on taking office, the Morales government spent much of its first year focused on the renegotiation of these gas contracts (against the wishes of the concession holders). The subscription of new contracts in October 2006 was widely seen as a victory for Bolivia in restoring national sovereignty over this key sector and in obliging investors to contribute substantially more than before to the national treasury. This was not an issue that invited political dissent, even among the government's most vociferous critics. Only a few wondered out loud (as Juan Antonio Morales does in chapter 12) whether Bolivia would live to regret its brazen treatment of the foreign investors if, as seemed possible, they would then be reluctant to invest more in order to develop Bolivia's gas-producing potential.

However, though not so much an issue of political dissent, the issue of economic development priorities poses a major dilemma. Despite its obvious attractions, the development of the gas industry as a monoproducer of foreign exchange raises important issues for the country's longer-term growth pattern. As well as having only limited spin-off effects with regard to the rest of the economy, reliance on a single commodity that cannot be openly traded on world markets has obvious dangers. There is also the role of the negative effects on other export sectors from a tendency to lead to currency appreciation. And perhaps, most importantly, it encourages a political economy based on rent seeking, both within the state and beyond it.

The policy dilemma for Bolivia therefore lies in how to mitigate these effects while using the resources generated from gas exports to develop employment and spread the benefits throughout the economy and society. For the MAS (Movimiento al Socialismo) government, this is particularly important, since much of its support base is to be found in those parts of Bolivia where there are no gas deposits. At the same time, there is the danger that the rents derived from gas will further sharpen (rather than reduce) conflicts over distribution, conflicts which in practice are very hard to manage. The gas boom is certainly one of the reasons why conflict over *autonomías* has become so bitter in recent years.

Chapters 10 and 11 therefore look at the two sides of the economic development debate. Carlos Miranda, an acknowledged expert in the hydrocarbons industry, maps out the opportunities that Bolivia has to expand its gas production and supply the gas-deficient markets of its neighbors in the Southern Cone. Fernanda Wanderley from the United Nations Development Program (UNDP) then poses the challenge facing policymakers in developing export-oriented industries for manufactured goods where the beneficiaries are among some of the poorest in Bolivia today. The two objectives are not mutually exclusive, but for reasons of political economy they are difficult to achieve in practice at the same time.

10

Gas and Its Importance to the Bolivian Economy

CARLOS MIRANDA

The Bolivian hydrocarbons industry surely must be one of the few industrial activities anywhere to have been nationalized three times in the space of the eighty years since it first came into existence. In 1927, the worldwide search for oil (whose strategic importance had become clear during the course of the First World War) produced the discovery of small quantities of this resource in Bolivia. Standard Oil of New Jersey, then the world's largest oil company, gained large concessions in Bolivia and successfully developed these in the years following its initial discoveries. Its activities were interrupted by the Chaco War (1932–1935) between Bolivia and Paraguay. In 1937, the Bolivian government took over Standard Oil's assets and annulled its concessions. These measures conformed to the legislation then in force, which contemplated such penalties in response to oil contraband and noncompliance with certain formalities in the handling of its contracts. The actions against Standard Oil won wide acceptance in Bolivia, where conduct of the North American enterprise during the war against Paraguay had been criticized. Military operations had been conducted largely on land included in its concessions.

Months before the concessions were withdrawn, the state oil company, Yacimientos Petrolíferos Fiscales Bolivianos (YPFB) had been established, and it took over Standard Oil's operations. Standard Oil refused litigation in the Supreme Court, withdrawing from Bolivia and claiming it had been "nationalized." This move was widely accepted in the international community, particularly given the spectacular nationalization of Mexico's oil industry in 1938. YPFB developed Bolivia's oil industry successfully, but without major breakthroughs. The targets it achieved were modest, although of major significance to the Bolivian economy. Bolivia achieved self-sufficiency in oil by 1953, and YPFB constructed two refineries linked by a network of domestic pipelines. Significantly, YPFB became a paradigm for a state company that was efficient, honest, and wholly Bolivian owned. This image has endured in people's memory.

From 1954 onward, participation by private capital in the oil industry was legalized and encouraged. The most important actor was the Bolivian Gulf Oil Corporation, which was successful in discovering new reserves of oil, as well as natural gas. The increase in oil output justified the building of an oil pipeline to the Pacific. Natural gas production likewise laid the basis for a long-term contract with Argentina and the construction of the country's first gas pipeline. The assets of Bolivian Gulf were taken over in October 1969, with its concessions reverting to the state, following an orthodox nationalization. This was accompanied by an indemnity that was agreed upon subsequently and complied with rapidly and scrupulously by means of a trust applied to Bolivia's exports of oil and natural gas.

By 1974, in the wake of this second nationalization, a sort of peaceful coexistence was achieved between YPFB and foreign oil companies that operated under contract with it. This lasted until May 1996. At that date, the state withdrew from its operational role, which it signed over to the private sector through shared-risk contracts between YPFB and private operators for upstream activities, as well as through authorized private transport and refining concessions. This system of "capitalization," which formed a key part the government's market-oriented economic reforms, was later rejected in a referendum held in 2004. This led to the new Hydrocarbons Law of May 2005, and then to the third "nationalization" of May 2006. Under this new system, foreign companies continue to act as contractors for YPFB, but without the right to dispose of their production, which is now marketed through YPFB. The industry has to pay 50 percent of its income (net of transportation costs) in tax, and YPFB participates in the profits from contracts.

It is interesting to note that, over this period, there have been five hydrocarbons laws: 1921, 1956, 1972, 1996, and 2005. All of these concur that income from the exploitation of hydrocarbons is crucial to the country's development, and none prohibits participation by private capital in association, in one way or another, with YPFB. For this reason, it would be risky to proffer a single explanation for the three nationalizations. The first, as we have seen, involved the application of existing laws. The second was justified as a political measure to eliminate an excess of power of foreign investors over the state. It should be noted that in these two cases, measures called "nationalization" were aimed solely at the largest company (first Standard Oil, then Bolivian Gulf). Other oil companies in operation at the time quietly closed down their business interests in Bolivia.

The third "nationalization" was the result of a number of factors that came together in a rejection of the market economy model that preceded it, but (as with the other two) it was carried out with a view to improving the use made of the income generated by the oil and gas industry, without proscribing the involvement of private capital through contracts. It recognized the importance of private-sector know-how and reiterated the hope of achieving substantial changes in the economy through the use of the income generated from oil and natural gas. On this occasion, "nationalization" involved fourteen companies operating in Bolivia, with seventy-one shared-risk contracts.

Finally, to understand the most recent nationalization, patterns of world consumption of energy consumption cannot be ignored. Over the last decade, humanity has been involved in the substitution of natural gas for oil, a process driven by the decline in the discovery of new oil reserves (as opposed to natural gas), global concerns about the environmental damage wrought to the environment through the use of oil and its derivatives, and increasing public criticism of transnational oil corporations on account of the size of their profits. The overall sense in Bolivia was that the country was not profiting from the oil and natural gas bonanza. Furthermore, it was becoming apparent that natural gas was the ideal fuel for generating hydrogen, viewed as the successor to hydrocarbons. In sum, Bolivia, a country rich in natural gas, entered the twenty-first century with important reserves of what seemed to be the new century's preferred fossil fuel, and with a new business structure in which the state—through YPFB—would take the lead.

Bolivia's Significance as a Producer of Natural Gas

With around eighty years of hydrocarbons activity behind it, Bolivia has accumulated an impressive amount of accurate and detailed knowledge on its geology. This information complements that concerning hydrocarbon deposits in northern Argentina and southeastern Peru and therefore contributes to the regional knowledge about the hydrocarbons potential of this whole sedimentary area, where there is clear alignment of fields with significant reserves of natural gas. Bolivia's geological potential is suggested in map 10.1 below.

Fields discovered to date have contained mostly a combination of natural gas and very light liquids (condensate) in commercially viable quantities, with a preponderance of gas over condensate. Generally speaking, the gas/oil ratio (GOR) is above 10,000.[1] Official figures on gas reserves for the begin-

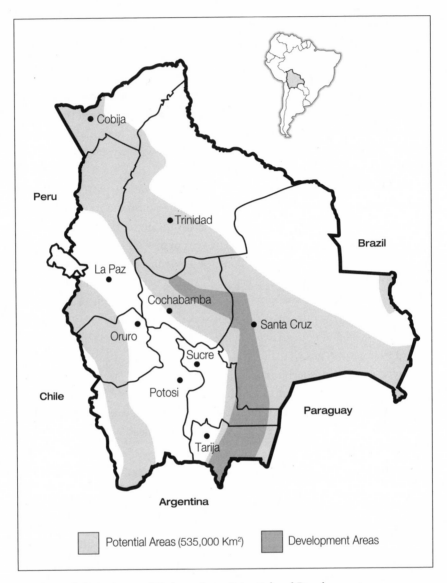

Map 10.1. Bolivia: Areas of Hydrocarbons Potential and Development.

ning of each year from 1997 to 2006 are set out in table 10.1.[2] Table 10.2 presents data for oil and condensate reserves.

It is interesting to note that as of 1997, discoveries led to a sharp increase in reserves. Investment both in exploration and in bringing new reserves into production are set out in table 10.3. The data include investment in a domestic pipeline (Gasoducto Yacuiba–Río Grande, GASYRG) built to connect production in newly discovered fields to the existing network of gas pipelines for export in order to reinforce current pipeline capacity and to comply with the volumes stipulated in the contract with Brazil between YPFB and Petrobras. From this it can be seen that the total investment made between 1997 and 2005 reached US$3.78 billion. The scale of this foreign direct investment (FDI) in a single sector is unprecedented in Bolivia.

How important is Bolivia as a gas producer in global terms? A schematic answer for 2005 can be made from the data of one of the most reliable publications in this area.[3] According to the *BP Review of Statistical Energy* (2006), Bolivia accounted for 0.46 percent of proven world gas reserves, totaling

Table 10.1. Gas reserves, 1997–2006 (trillion cubic feet)

	1997	1988	1999	2000	2001	2002	2003	2004	2005	2006[1]
Proven	3.8	4.8	5.3	18.3	23.8	27.4	28.7	27.6	26.7	31.2
Probable	1.9	2.5	3.3	13.9	23	24.9	26.2	24.7	22	25
Subtotal	**5.7**	**6.6**	**8.6**	**32.2**	**46.8**	**52.3**	**54.9**	**52.3**	**48.7**	**56.2**
Possible	4.1	3.2	5.5	17.6	23.2	24.9	24.2	24.1	15.2	19.2
Total	**9.8**	**9.8**	**14.1**	**49.8**	**70**	**77.2**	**79.1**	**76.4**	**53.9**	**75.4**

Source: YPFB (2005), p. 27, updated for 2006.
[1]Figures for 2006 are preliminary.

Table 10.2. Oil condensate reserves, 1997–2005 (millions of barrels)

	1997	1998	1999	2000	2001	2002	2003	2004	2005
Proven	116.1	141.9	151.9	396.5	440.5	477	486.1	462.3	465.2
Probable	84.8	74.8	88.6	295.5	451.5	452.1	470.8	446.5	391.4
Subtotal	**200.9**	**216.7**	**240.5**	**692**	**892**	**929.1**	**956.9**	**908.7**	**856.6**
Possible	110.2	43.6	96.5	345.1	469.8	473.9	454.8	437.7	254.7
Total	**311.1**	**260.3**	**337**	**1,037.1**	**1,361.8**	**1,403.0**	**1,411.7**	**1,346.4**	**1,111.3**

Source: YPFB (2005), p. 24.

Table 10.3. Gas investment, 1997–2005 (in US$ billions)

	1997	1998	1999	2000	2001	2002	2003	2004	2005
Exploration	130.38	374.56	372.2	256.79	168.99	113.47	108.58	86.66	86.61
Production	140.42	230.25	208.55	185.33	237.38	231.31	171.96	149.26	241.89
Subtotal	270.8	604.81	580.75	442.12	406.37	344.78	280.54	235.92	328.5
Other investments (GASYRG pipeline)						283	n/d		
Total	270.8	604.81	580.75	442.12	406.37	627.78	280.54	235.92	328.5
Cumulative	270.8	875.61	1,466.36	1,898.48	2,304.85	2,932.63	3,213.17	3,449.09	3,777.59

Source: YPFB (2005), p. 21.

6,338 trillion cubic feet. Bolivia's share takes on somewhat more relevance when we consider that Latin America's total reserves account for only 3.9 percent of world totals, and that Bolivia accounts for 12.44 percent of the region's proven reserves. If we add on probable to proven reserves, Bolivia accounts for 22.4 percent of the region's total, second only to those of Venezuela. It is also important to note that Venezuela's gas production is a by-product of oil-heavy reserves, with a GOR of less than 200. This means that for Venezuela to produce natural gas, it must also produce large quantities of oil; the opposite is the case for Bolivia. As we shall see below, Bolivia's true importance is as a natural gas supplier to the Southern Cone.

Could Bolivia become more important as a supplier of natural gas? Here, suffice it to say that the surface area of territory with the geological and petro-physical potential to produce hydrocarbons is 535,000 km^2, only 47,507 km^2 of which have been subject to exploration or are in production to date. It is therefore a developed but as yet immature area, since within it there are an indeterminate number of structures where drilling has yet to take place.

State of the Industry

To understand the importance of natural gas to the country's economy (beyond such geological considerations), we need an overview of the current state of the industry. As noted above, all fields contain natural gas and condensate. Therefore, once extracted and after water and sediments are removed, the mixture of natural gas and condensate has to be separated in special gas treatment plants. After treatment, it is separated into three elements: natural gas for export and for the domestic market, liquids to be refined into fuels, and liquid petroleum gas (LPG) to be exported and sold on the domestic market.

Table 10.4 shows how production of condensate and gas evolved between 1999 and 2005. The daily averages for each year indicate a rhythm of production that is continually rising. The production of natural gas multiplied fivefold over this period, and that of condensates nearly doubled. The figures underline the huge output of natural gas that accompanies the production of liquids.

In terms of geographical distribution, hydrocarbons output comes primarily from the southeastern and eastern part of the country, from the eastern flank of the Cordillera Real. Table 10.4 distinguishes gas production for 2005 in millions of cubic feet per day between the various producing departments, as well as the percentage breakdown and the number of fields. Although Santa Cruz has the largest number of gas fields, it is Tarija (second in terms of the number of fields) that accounts for 70 percent of the gas produced.

Up until 2006, all hydrocarbons were produced by private oil and gas companies under shared-risk contracts. Table 10.6 shows the percentage share of each in total production. Petrobras, working under the names of Petrobras Bolivia and Petrobras Energía, accounted for 60.8 percent. Repsol working under the names of Repsol-YPF and Andina, was in second place, contributing 21.1 percent of total output. The smaller shares also show up in table 10.6.

On May 1, 2006, the Bolivian government decreed the nationalization of hydrocarbons production, a process that is still under way. First it envisaged the conversion of all existing shared-risk contracts to service contracts. Secondly, it ruled that the capitalized firms should be nationalized. On October 28, 2006, YPFB signed service contracts with all those companies which previously had shared-risk contracts, and—in line with the present Hydro-

Table 10.4. Average annual hydrocarbon production, 1999–2006

	1999[1]	2000	2001	2002	2003	2004	2005	2006[2]
Oil (thousands of bpd)	31.05	31.39	35.78	36.28	39.55	46.44	50.65	48.03
Gas (millions of cfd)	497.50	549.94	691.85	861.24	991.17	1,224.15	1,419.46	1,374.39

Source: Author's elaboration on basis of YPFB data.

[1] July to December.
[2] Up to April 2006.

Table 10.5. Gas production, 2005 (daily average)

	Chuquisaca	Cochabamba	Santa Cruz	Tarija	Total
Volume (millions of cfd)	29.81	122.07	283.89	983.69	1,419.46
Percentage	2.1	8.6	20.0	69.3	100
Number of fields	3	7	21	17	48

Source: Author's elaboration on basis of YPFB data.

Table 10.6. Gas production, by company, 2005

Company	Percentage of Total Production
Vintage	1.5
Plus Petrol	1.8
BG-Bolivia	5.0
Chaco (BP)	9.8
Repsol-YPF, Andina	21.1
Petrobras Energía, Petrobras Bolivia	60.8

Source: Author's elaboration on basis of YPFB data.

carbons Law (Law 3058)—all these contracts have been approved by Congress. Furthermore, each one has been the object of a law mandating their fulfillment. Once registered by the government notary, the contracts come into force. Because the new contracts are with the same companies working under shared-risk contracts, the distribution of output indicated in table 10.6 remains unchanged.

How is Bolivia's gas used? Table 10.7 sets this out both in terms of physical volume and percentages of the total. As one can see, 70 percent of output is exported to Brazil and Argentina, 12 percent is used for domestic consumption, 16.9 percent is recycled or used for LPG for domestic consumption, and only 1.3 percent is lost through flaring. The low percentage of flared gas is indicative of the efficiency with which hydrocarbons are produced in the country. The figures underline, at the same time, Bolivia's enormous dependence on foreign export markets. As mentioned above, gas is produced in conjunction with production of petroleum. Table 10.8 details the volumes and uses of the oil (condensate) produced. We can say that up until 2006 at least, hydrocarbons were produced in Bolivia in such a way as to respect a delicate balance between meeting export commitments for gas as well as domestic needs, while generating sufficient condensate to supply the needs of local refineries. There are, however, doubts as to whether in the future supplies will be sufficient to meet both contractual export obligations and domestic consumption needs.

The pipelines that traverse Bolivia to some extent illustrate the evolution of the industry. The original idea that Bolivia could be a relevant oil-producing country was the justification for building a small export pipeline to Ar-

Table 10.7. Destination of gas produced, 2005 (daily averages)

	Percentage	Volume (mmcfd)
Flared[1]	1.3	18.45
Recycled[2]	13.6	193.00
LPG and others[3]	3.3	46.84
Exports to Argentina	9.0	127.75
Exports to Brazil	61.0	868.37
Domestic market[4]	12.0	165.00

Source: Author's elaboration on basis of YPFB data.

[1] Gas with very low pressure that cannot be used.
[2] Gas reinjected into well to maintain pressure of output and to avoid condensation of
   liquids in the subsoil.
[3] Gas consumed in the extraction of propane-butane (LPG) for domestic LPG consumption,
   gas used in the oil industry (compressors, pumps, etc.).
[4] Domestic consumption in thermoelectric plants, industrial use, household gas, and
   vehicular consumption as compressed natural gas.

Table 10.8. Destination of oil produced, 2005 (daily averages)

	Percentage	Volume (bpd)
Local refineries	91	45,464
Export to Argentina	—	124
Export through Chile	9	4.412
Export through Chile, refinery bottoms[1]	22	9,934

Source: Author's elaboration on basis of YPFB data.

[1] Volume left over in the refineries (bottoms) for which there is no market in Bolivia and therefore
   is exported.

gentina with a capacity of 12,000 barrels/day (bpd) and a large one of 50,000
bpd westward toward the Pacific. These export plans complemented the oil
pipelines built to supply domestic markets by linking the refineries with the
centers of output. The production of liquids from Bolivian fields tends to
be shipped westward, so that the expected output could be shipped to the
United States, the country of origin of most of the companies working in
Bolivia prior to the period of gas. By contrast, gas is pumped out toward the

south and east. The system of domestic supply is derived from the export gas pipelines. There are two major gas pipelines leading to Brazil, and three to Argentina.

Finally, it is interesting to note that the country's evolution from oil producer to gas producer has resulted in a major export pipeline being built almost every twenty years. The oil pipeline to Arica was built in 1954–1956 at a cost of around US$15 million, the gas pipeline to Argentina was built in 1970–1972 for around US$50 million, and the gas pipeline to Brazil was built in 1998–1999 at a cost of US$450 million. Costs have increased, in part, due to the increase in the price of materials and construction, but also because the dimensions of the pipelines (12 inches in diameter in the case of the Arica pipeline, and 32 inches in the São Paulo pipeline). From the foregoing, a valid generalization can be made: Bolivia's gas and oil output for export has to be transported at least 1,000 km through the internal pipeline system in order to then be shipped (by boat, oil pipeline, or gas pipeline) another 1,000 km to reach its market.

Fiscal Importance of Hydrocarbons

To demonstrate the importance of hydrocarbons as a source of tax revenue, table 10.9 is divided into three periods: 1990–1996, 1997–2004, and 2005–present (when the new hydrocarbons legislation came into force). Taxes are grouped as either direct or indirect: direct taxes are those paid by producers in the form of royalties, surface rights, taxes on profit, and other less important taxes such as those on bank transfers; indirect taxes consist of those paid by consumers as part of the final purchase price.

Using this matrix, we see that the state received, on average, US$407 million per annum for 1990–1996, a figure that increased to US$520.5 million per annum for 1997–2004. Finally, the new hydrocarbons legislation introduced in 2005, which raised taxes to 50 percent of the value of production, pushed up the tax yield to US$977 million. This last figure includes tax receipts for the months of January to May (under the previous tax legislation that set the tax rate at 32 percent of the value of production) and from May to December (subject to the 50 percent rate).

Taxation in the sector was increased as of May 1, 2006, when the nationalization decree was issued. This imposed an additional tax of 32 percent of the value of production in those fields with an average output of 100 million cfd over the preceding year (San Alberto and San Antonio), for an initial period of 180 days (the period established for the signing of new contracts). The new service contracts were signed within this deadline on October, 28, 2006. Law 3058 and Supreme Decree 28701 established that the contracts would take effect once approved by Congress and registered by the government notary. When the contracts were signed, it was established that the extraordinary tax contribution on San Alberto and San Antonio (32 percent) would continue until such point as all the contracts signed had come into effect.

The seventy-seven shared-risk contracts agreed to under Law 1689 were replaced by forty-four service contracts signed with the same companies for the same areas (the number is smaller because various areas for the same company were grouped into one and therefore came under a single contract). All the contracts are similar, whether with a single company or a consortium, and use the same model, but they are not identical, since they were all negotiated case by case. In many respects, the new contracts do not differ from the previous ones; for example, they extend for thirty-year terms and carry the same obligations regarding exploration, arbitration, and so on.

Where the main difference lies is in the marketing of output. When the contracts became effective (at the beginning of 2007), all production (gas and oil) was placed at the disposition of YPFB at the point where it is measurable in each field. YPFB then contracts out the transport of hydrocarbons and their sale on domestic and foreign markets, agreeing also on prices. YPFB, jointly with the production company, will instruct the purchaser to deposit monies from sale to pay the companies involved in transport. The value of sales is then distributed along the following scale of priorities: 50 percent for the payment of royalties, participations, and the direct tax on hydrocarbons (IDH). Of the rest, the costs incurred by the company for the volume delivered will first be covered. If there is then a surplus, it will be used to pay the company's profit, and any remaining money will then be paid to YPFB. The government anticipates that the state will take around 80 percent of the income.

The signing of the contracts brought a sense of collective relief, in view of the threat of Bolivia facing writs for arbitration and the possibilities of the companies' withdrawal. Both the government and the hydrocarbon companies showed a degree of realistic pragmatism in terms of economically exploiting the country's gas wealth, with the sale of gas to Argentina increased to a volume similar to that previously being supplied to Brazil.

Table 10.9. Taxes on oil and gas, 1990–2006 (in US$ millions)

Year	Direct[1]	Indirect[2]	Total	Avg./year
1990–1996	1,543.4	1,303.5	2,846.9	406.7
1997–2004	2,047.0	1,596.7	3,643.7	520.5
2005[3]	744	233.1	977.1	—
2006	1,442	247	1,689	—

Source: Ministry of Mines and Hydrocarbons, Ministry of Finances, YPFB, Mauricio Medinaceli (2006).

[1] Royalties, surface rights, income tax, etc.
[2] Tax paid by the consumer.
[3] With new law as of May, 17, 2005.

Importance of Hydrocarbons and Future Projections

Table 10.10 sets out the share of hydrocarbons in Bolivia's gross domestic product (GDP) and its exports. The figure for GDP was slightly higher in 2000 than in 1995, whereas the figure for exports was slightly lower. By 2005, the share in GDP had almost doubled from the 2000 level, and that of exports had quadrupled. The figures therefore show the enormous significance that the hydrocarbons sector had acquired for the economy as a whole.

The Southern Cone countries have not been exceptions to the overall global trend toward increased consumption of natural gas as the first step toward the post-hydrocarbons energy age. Over the last ten years—with the exception of Paraguay and Uruguay—the Southern Cone countries have seen the growth in gas consumption rates rise from 3.5 percent per annum to 7.5 percent. In view of this, the Bolivian hydrocarbons industry has acquired greater importance in the region, both on account of its geographical proximity and the size of its gas reserves. These high growth rates for gas consumption reflect the rising importance of this product vis-à-vis other energy sources in each country. Argentina is one of the most gas-dependent countries in the world, meeting 48 percent of its energy needs with this fuel. The 27 percent rate for Chile indicates that this country—albeit not a gas producer itself—is also reliant on this source for a large proportion of its energy needs. The contribution of gas in Bolivia's overall energy needs (22 percent) reflects the switchover to gas in many of its productive activities. The Brazilian case is perhaps the most significant. Although it is the country with the

Table 10.10. Participation of the oil and gas industry in GDP and exports, 1995–2005 (at current prices)

	1995	1996	1997	1998	1999	2000	2001	2002	2003	2004	2005 (est.)
% GDP	4.26	3.82	3.93	3.87	3.79	5.33	5.37	5.48	6.26	7.8	10
% Exports	12.9	10.9	8.4	7.3	5.3	12.1	22.4	25.2	30.1	37.6	47.3

Source: Muller y Asociados (2004); Medinaceli (2006).

highest energy consumption in Latin America, a mere 2 percent of its needs are covered by gas. This points to the enormous potential for exporting gas to Brazil, even though gas discoveries in Brazil may eventually reduce Brazil's dependence on Bolivian supplies.

Table 10.11 shows the reserves in each of these countries, their annual consumption, and (most important of all) a projection of the number of years over which they can sustain these levels of consumption, taking into account their population growth rates over the last few years. This is contained in the column R/C, and the figures are striking. It appears that Argentina, with its high gas dependency, can sustain only eight years of growth at current consumption rates without very large new discoveries that would lead to an increase in domestic production. Even if it manages to make such discoveries, the rhythm of domestic consumption, coupled with likely delays in bringing these reserves onstream, mean that it will need to import large quantities of gas over the next ten years. The Chilean case is still more striking. Since it has neither reserves nor production of its own to support its level of consumption and growth, it is wholly dependent on imports, either from neighboring countries or in the form of LNG (Liquid Natural Gas). In Brazil, reserves could cover current consumption for fifteen years into the future. Although Brazil depends on gas for only a small proportion of its energy needs, it—like other countries—is rapidly increasing the proportion of gas it uses as an energy source. This suggests that Brazil, too, will be a significant importer of gas, at least over the short to medium term. Bolivia has the largest reserves and the lowest domestic consumption (irrespective of the relative importance of gas as a source of its energy). This means that Bolivia has an almost limitless scope to sustain current levels of gas consumption within its own territory. A quick way of appreciating this is to look at the last column of table 10.11, which highlights energy consumption per capita. Argentina has the highest energy consumption per head, followed by Chile, Bolivia, and finally Brazil.

Table 10.12 sets forth a best-case scenario for the export of Bolivian gas. Current proven reserves suggest that, taking into account the domestic market and possible projects to industrialize gas, the maximum amount that Bolivia is able to commit itself for export is 90 million cfd. The markets to absorb this production are to be found in the region. The projection contained in table 10.12 takes on board the contract to export gas to Argentina agreed on October 19, 2006, as well as the doubling of volumes currently exported to Brazil. It assumes an average price of US$4 per million BTUs.

Since 2000, gas has come to play an increasingly important role as a source of fiscal income and export earnings, and its share of Bolivia's overall GDP has grown rapidly. The development of the hydrocarbons industry has come about by attracting the largest amount of FDI in the country's history. The contractual terms on offer for investors attracted investment, and this led to the discovery of large gas reserves. These are of major importance to the markets of the Southern Cone.

Table 10.11. Southern Cone countries: Gas reserves and consumption

	Reserves (billion m³)	Consumption (billion m³)	Projected duration (R/C)	Consumption per capita (m³/year)
Argentina	570	44.93	8	1,034
Bolivia	890	2.38	100 (2005)	265
Brazil	470	15.34	15	87
Chile	90	8.09	—	513

Source: Author's elaboration.

Table 10.12. Possible Bolivian export earnings, 2005–2015

	2005	2008	2010	2015
US$/year (millions)	1,294	1,950	2,500	3,900

Source: Author's estimates.

The oil and gas industry is characterized by a highly intensive use of capital and an inability to create many permanent jobs directly. Notwithstanding this, the industry, through service companies, has helped boost employment, especially in the construction of pipelines and/or other installations. There are no published studies on the number of jobs created in recent years. The only well-known work is that of Sturzenegger (2005), who shows that, in the 1997–2006 period, the industry generated two hundred thousand jobs.

The rise in the sector's likely income is due, in large part, to increases in prices in the international market. However, activity within the industry since 2003 has been in decline. The 2005 Hydrocarbons Law and the new contracts signed on October 29, 2006, suggest that activity would pick up again in 2007, particularly to meet the terms of the sales contract with Argentina, which adds greater certainty to the figures contained in table 10.12. As we have seen, Argentina is the country that faces the most serious problems in supplying its domestic gas consumption. The contract between Argentina and Bolivia gives it the time it needs to develop further its own national reserves or build terminals through which it can receive LNG imported from other countries.

The projections included in table 10.12 may experience several years' delay, but they are realistic, since they are based on the export agreement with Argentina and the intention of Brazil to double the quantum of its gas imports from Bolivia. A further opening of the Brazilian market is perfectly possible, in view of the size of that country's future market for gas and the fact that it will require imports in order to meet that demand. The signing of the new contracts provides reassurance that the development of current reserves will take place, particularly on the part of Petrobras for the Brazilian market.

The chances of directly supplying Chile seem remote, and it is for that reason that exporting to Chile is not considered in the projections. Chile has signaled that, with a plant at Quinteros to turn LNG back into gas and with the construction of another plant at Mejillones, it will be able to meet domestic demand from supplies of Argentine gas or through LNG from overseas. Peruvian gas may enter the Chilean market through a gas pipeline from Camisea. This would further complicate Bolivia's attempts to regain an access to the Pacific, but it would not represent competition for Bolivian supplies.

The positive position with regard to Bolivian gas (reserves, market, and investments) cannot necessarily extend to the long term. The present contracts are not that attractive for investors searching for completely new reserves in areas beyond those that have been traditionally developed in Bolivia. The major limitation will be prices, which would need to stay at their current high levels.

The projections do not include income from the industrialization of gas. The possibility of industrialization—converting gas chemically into other products—is a genuine possibility for the liquid products that accompany gas. The manufacture of polyethylene, for example, is a viable proposition if it can be done on a competitive basis and if there are sufficient markets. This is feasible in the case of Brazil. However, if it is not accomplished by 2010–2011, it will probably end up being postponed until there is another cycle of petrochemicals expansion in the region. Although the window of opportunity may be brief, it does exist.

As we saw in table 10.9, the size of the increase in state income as of 2005 is very substantial, leading to unprecedented fiscal inflows for Bolivia. The rational utilization of this income and the avoidance of such economic deformations as "Dutch Disease," which restricts nontraditional exports through a persistent overvaluation of the currency caused by gas (or other) primary exports, constitute major challenges for the future. Fortunately, the first symptoms of a surge in imports have yet to make themselves felt. In part, this is because 60 percent of the income consists of rents destined for regions and municipalities. Administratively, Bolivia is highly decentralized, and a good deal of the income from gas will go toward current expenditure in local government.

11

Beyond Gas

Between the Narrow-Based and the Broad-Based Economy

FERNANDA WANDERLEY

The exponential growth of proven and probable reserves of natural gas, the sharp increase in the tax take, and the emergence of a modern service economy in function of the main gas transnationals are the more visible symptoms of a progressive consolidation of Bolivia as a natural-gas producer. This renewed taste for exploiting natural resources revives a long tradition characterized by dependency on a monoproduction development model. Debate in recent years has centered, on the one hand, on the need to transform the political rules of the game and, on the other, how best to benefit from natural gas and its multiple uses. Beyond the conjunctural debate on the role of the state in the economy, it is worthwhile to evaluate what this increased importance of the gas economy actually means from an historical perspective. It is also important to discuss the conditions under which the "economy beyond gas" could be consolidated.

Bolivia's pattern of monoproduction development has sustained itself on different management models, and today the challenge lies in the state's ability to construct a more diversified and articulated economy that goes "beyond gas." The increase in export diversification in recent years presents a historic opportunity to engineer a transition to a broader economic base. The goal is to increase the number of productive sectors and actors with the potential to insert themselves into niches in the global market, and to create an economic dynamic in the input and service sectors. This will produce a substantial redistributive effect that will also encourage growth at the base of the productive pyramid. To understand the various means of achieving this goal, we analyze the effects of various export paths on income and employment, and on the linkages within the domestic market.

Patterns and Models of Development

Debate over the challenges confronting the Bolivian economy has revolved around the role of the state in the economy. However, rather than engaging in a discussion on the sort of state required and its role in building a commercially competitive and socially inclusive economy, we have gotten bogged down in a narrow debate over "more state" versus "more market." It was supposed that the supremacy of one or other of these mechanisms for assigning and distributing wealth would be sufficient to generate sustained and more-equitable growth. Today, we are at a new point in the political debate, and there are many who now argue that the *pattern* of development, rather than the model as such, is the structural problem of the Bolivian economy.

We share this view; if the pattern of development does not change—beyond just the liberal, mixed or nationalist variants—Bolivia will continue to be one of the poorest and most unequal countries in Latin America. The structural features of the Bolivian economy—low historical rates of economic growth, low productivity and competitiveness, a concentration on a handful of exportable products, lack of linkages between tradeables and nontradeables, and the persistence of poverty and social inequality—can be explained by its type of development, in which economic, social, and political logic is grounded on the export of natural resources. It is necessary to get beyond the more market/more state debate and understand that the type of state and the way it relates to the private sector has been key to the persistence of a development pattern based on monoproducing dependency.

Pattern of development refers to the way in which the factors of production in an economy link up, operate, and work together (or are prevented from doing so) in a context of competitive advantages (or disadvantages) that provide (or hamper) a dynamic to the productive structure. The pattern describes, on the one hand, the endowment of factors: Are we a country rich in capital, technology, labor power, or natural resources? On the other, it defines the future that we want for ourselves given the conditions we have in the present: Will we be a country that provides natural resources, or do we try to compete on a more diversified basis and with greater added value? This can be achieved by various models: an interventionist state, a market-driven one, or indeed by a mixed model that combines the state and the market. In this way, the pattern becomes the "what," while the model becomes the "how." In other words, the model is the form, while the pattern is the content or substance (Gray Molina 2006c).

Bolivia has changed the model a number of times, but it has never tried to change the pattern of development in any sustained way. Between 1900 and 1920, the country embarked on liberalism. The pattern of development was one of tin dependency, just as previously it had revolved around silver, rubber, and Brazil nuts. In 1937, with the nationalization of Standard Oil and the birth of Yacimientos Petrolíferos Fiscales Bolivianos (YPFB), the pendulum swung toward the nationalization of one facet of the extractive pattern. This was complemented in 1952 with the nationalization of the tin industry and the birth of the Corporación Minera de Bolivia (Comibol). In the 1960s, the pendulum swung back toward liberalization, with new private investments in mining, up until 1969 with the nationalization of Gulf Oil. This was the last move toward statism within the pattern of monoproduction. The years between 1985 and 2005 represented a lost opportunity to diversify the economy and multiply the number of actors in sectors that were competitive. The birth of the "gas pattern," with the promulgation of the 2005 Hydrocarbons Law, opened up a new change of model within the same pattern of extractive development tied to primary natural resources.

The Narrow-Based Economy

Whether more liberal or more statist, the models adopted served equally well to reproduce a development pattern founded on a narrow resource base. One feature that explains this narrowness is Bolivia's low average growth in the period between 1950 and 2005—2.8 percent, or an average per capita growth rate of 0.5 percent—which was inadequate in meeting the country's socioeconomic needs. In the last twenty years, a pronounced fiscal crisis translated into high levels of public sector debt, a low level of domestic savings further widened the gap between savings and investment, and fluctuations in the terms of trade, low productivity, and the negative effects of being landlocked contributed to rates of growth that were well below those of the 1960s and 1970s.

A second feature is a high degree of concentration on a few exportable products. Given the narrowness of the domestic market, insertion into foreign markets is critical for growth. This points to the need to improve entry conditions into international markets, thereby helping to make the contribution of the export sector in the overall growth rate more constant and less vulnerable to variations in the external situation. Historically, Bolivia has found it difficult to increase the value of its exports or diversify them.

A quick glance at the evolution of the structure of exports shows substantial changes as of the mid-1990s, when nontraditional exports increased as a percentage of the whole. However, this did not fundamentally change the underlying pattern of export activity, which remained highly dependent on the exploitation of a handful of natural resources and their limited transformation into manufactured goods. Since 2000, natural-resource exports have increased once again, reaching 75 percent of total exports in 2006.

A third feature is the low productivity of the factors of production. From a statistical viewpoint, growth can be understood as the consequence of the accumulation of factors of production and the productivity that these acquire. In this perspective, economic growth in the last twenty years is due more to an accumulation of factors than to any increase in productivity of labor or capital. Indeed, while labor and capital have contributed around 90 percent and 50 percent, respectively, the total factor productivity (TFP) has reduced that growth by around 40 percent.[1] Even though in the period between 1970 and 1980 TFP provided a strong impulse to growth, this fell back in the 1980s, with something of a recovery in the 1990s. Although the sharp decline of the 1980s can be explained by the macroeconomic imbalances that the country suffered at the time, the weakness of the contribution of TFP in more recent times can be explained by institutional weaknesses and the lack of a highly qualified workforce.

A fourth feature is the lack of linkage between the tradeable and nontradeable sectors of the economy. The structure of the GDP has changed over recent years, encouraging a growth in the nontradeable sector (primarily commerce and services), not just in employment, but also in generating output. Thus, while in 1980 the primary sector and manufacturing accounted for 29 percent and 14 percent of GDP, respectively, in 2006 their share had fallen to 21 percent and 13 percent. Whereas in 1980 nontradeables accounted for 47 percent of GDP, by 2006 this share had risen to 53 percent. Consequently, we can see three pathways being carved out with respect to GDP. The share of the primary sector has fallen; in manufacturing, there has been little change; and for nontradeables the path has been upward. Nontradeable sectors with an increased share include commerce and other services, while those sectors linked to energy and construction show no great variation. Employment has tended to decline in sectors linked to agriculture and mining, stayed fairly stable in manufacturing and those nontradeables linked to energy, gas, water, and construction, and it has increased in sectors such as commerce, transport, and other services. The inverse relationship between the nontradeable sector and the primary sector indicates that the former is a refuge for the latter at times of economic recession (UNDP 2005).

These features reveal a pattern of growth that is incapable of generating the trickle-down effects that would lift Bolivia from being one of Latin America's poorest and most unequal countries. According to the Survey on Improvements to Living Standards drawn from the MECOVI dataset (INE 2005), around 174,419 Bolivians fall into poverty each year. So, between 1999 and 2002, when annual growth rates averaged 1.76 percent, the number of impoverished Bolivians increased (in absolute terms) from 5 to 5.5 million, of which 3.5 million were classified as indigent. The rate of economic growth that would halt the increase in the impoverished population is estimated at 6 percent. So, with growth rates well below 6 percent and a Gini coefficient of inequality of 0.57 (countries with low-to-moderate levels if inequality have coefficients between .25 and .40, while countries with greater inequality have higher scores), the pattern of growth ends up contributing to poverty in Bolivia. A calculation based on projections of population and economic growth shows that with a per capita growth rate of just 0.3 percent, it would take Bolivia 178 years to emerge from poverty. Nine generations would fail to improve their living standards as defined by threshold levels of minimum income. At the same time, social mobility in Bolivia is very limited, and this acts as a disincentive for people to struggle to overcome poverty and raise economic growth over the longer term.

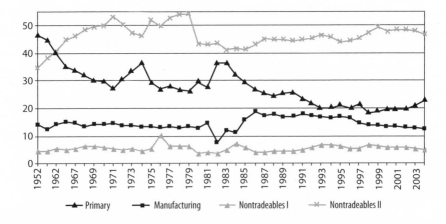

Figure 11.1. Less tin, more commerce: fifty years of GDP by economic sector. Author's elaboration from INE data.

The narrow base thus reflects a proportionately inverse relationship between the generation of wealth and the generation of income. In the manufacturing sector, 83 percent of the workforce is organized in family, peasant, or microbusiness units of less than five persons and produces barely 25 percent of the income. At the same time, just 7 percent of the workforce works in companies with more than fifty employees but generates 65 percent of the income. In the middle of this double pyramid, in which employment and income seem to diverge, there are medium-sized firms which produce 10 percent of output and recruit 10 percent of the workforce. This inversion in the proportionality between employment and income is what characterizes the Bolivian economy, making it one of the least equitable in Latin America. These data make it easier to see why such asymmetries persist between a few privileged people and an overwhelming mass of pauperized workers and farmers. Wealth in Bolivia is generated in a concentrated and exclusive form because there is no counterpart in the productive apparatus that acts to widen the range of opportunities.

Refocusing the Discussion from Sectors to Linkages

The inversely proportional relationship between the generation of employment and income is the consequence of the weak linkages between actors and productive sectors in the Bolivian economy. At one end of the scale there is the export of natural resources and a few products with value added; at the other is small-scale production of basic goods and services for the local market. So it was that from colonial times up until the first few decades of the twentieth century, domestic demand for primary goods like food, clothing, shoes, candles, wine, sugar, and the like was covered mainly by local production from small, family-based economic units.[2] In spite of the importance of this economic universe (in terms of numbers of firms, their employment generation, and their supply of goods and services to local markets), there were no sustainable increases achieved in productivity and efficiency. Consequently, the model did not transform into a motor of wealth creation. At the same time, the export of primary goods and one or two products with value added but without significant linkages to the rest of the economy failed to provide a source of growth with sufficient income distribution to overcome poverty.

The question we need to answer concerns the reasons for this lack of linkage between actors and productive sectors. Unlike those studies that point to the coexistence of opposing economies, here we would suggest that the popular economy and the export economy make up a single productive system: the narrow-based economy. The proliferation of precarious types of employment, the constant atomization of workshops of the same sort, or the chronic lack of any positive linkages between factors of production are all symptoms of the perverse effects of a pattern of development that links together all producers, big and small, in shared and reciprocal parameters that simply accentuate the narrowness of the country's economic base.

The coexistence of different practices and institutions in ways that produce an economic dynamic with few linkages has resulted in dualistic interpretations. Not only does this sort of approach cause people to think in terms of economic segmentation between separate systems, but also to define one as "good" that ought to replace the other which is "bad." The more influential schools of thought governing policy during the last three decades have tended to view large companies (whether private or public, Bolivian or foreign) as the motors of development. Modernization and economic takeoff are seen as necessarily coming about from a strategy of industrialization based on large-scale production, the intensive use of capital, and the application of modern technology. Proponents of this view suggest that large firms constitute the nucleus of the private sector and provide the basis for economic growth. They are alone in generating the necessary economies of scale, high productivity rates, and levels of efficiency. Small-scale firms have, at best, performed a transitory and therefore residual function in countries that have yet to reach the most advanced phase of development.[3]

Another interpretation of economic segmentation, also increasingly influential in recent years, takes a more culturalist approach. Small-scale production is linked explicitly to a set of alternative ethno-cultural norms and values that differ from those of modern rationality. This view stems from a conception that socioeconomic and cultural identities establish priorities and values other than those based on capital accumulation or efficient and competitive forms of organization. This line of interpretation suggests that the Bolivian economy is made up of two sectors—one modern, the other traditional—and that the latter is destined to remain outside the accumulation circuit, since it does not work on a logic of modern economic rationality. Two axes emerge on this interpretative matrix. One stigmatizes these alternative forms of social and economic organization as dysfunctional to growth (Laserna 2004), and the other romanticizes them as spaces immune to Western modernity, proclaiming that they contain the seeds of a new form of economic organization that could provide a substitute for the market economy (Medina 2001).

In contrast to such dualist perspectives—with their tendency to view the export economy and the popular economy as separate and closed systems—we suggest that we need to widen our field of vision and view the national economic structure as a multiplicity of linkages (or not) between actors and economic sectors. Only by understanding the levels and types of linkages that bind local, regional, and national economies together, as well as the institutional and political framework that provides support (or not) for such linkages, can we understand the vulnerability and precarious nature of Bolivia's insertion into the global economy, and the persistence of the high concentration of wealth.

Such attention to productive chains and institutional contexts arises from a new paradigm that postulates that the ability to place goods and services in the marketplace (whether national or international) does not depend entirely on the size of businesses and the factors of production on which they base themselves. Following the new institutional economics (Coase 1952; Williamson 1981 and 1993), a new line of empirical studies has shown that the distribution of firm size within an industry is the result of specific economic conditions (Levy 1991). Such studies underscore the importance of institutional and economic contexts in defining economic performance and competitiveness. The decision to organize production, and therefore the division of labor, within the firm (vertical integration) or between firms (organization via the market) responds to production and transaction costs in specific economic contexts (Uzzel 1994).

In the 1980s and 1990s, the discovery of clusters of successfully competitive small and medium-sized firms has given rise to another line of study that repositions the development of opportunities and constraints of different types of productive organizations (Sensenberger and Pyke 1991; Schmitz 1995; Saxenian 1994; Tendler and Amorin 1996; Biggart and Hamilton 1992). These studies showed the limitations of the paradigm which held that the road to industrial development is straight and narrow, passing only through the large-scale production resulting from the concentration of capital and labor. Work specialization, a condition for increasing efficiency and productivity, can come about from a division of labor either within a firm or between firms (Sabel and Zeitlin 1996; Sabel and Piori 1984). The division of labor between specialized and complementary economic units generates positive externalities for industry as a whole, such as the accumulation of skills and capacities for innovation, economies of scale, and the diminution of production and transaction costs and, consequently, the ability to conquer niches in the global market.[4]

Discussion of economic development directed the attention of policy-makers, economic actors, and researchers in the 1990s toward the linkages between firms and their institutional environment as the key element in determining competitiveness (Blair and Reese 1999; Blair and Gereffi 2001). Following this line of argument, it becomes clear that competitiveness depends a great deal on the level and quality of the linkages between economic units in adding value, as well as on the support provided by the legal framework, economic policy, and the way in which organizations as a whole shape the business environment. The contribution of these studies for developing countries is in the stress they place on meso- and microconditions, as well as on the structural constraints (being landlocked, poor-quality transport infrastructure, low human capital formation, high financial costs, and so on) affecting the development of product markets (see, e.g., Fairbanks and Stace 1997).

The Emergent Broad-Based Economy

Thanks to a fairly favorable external climate, Bolivia has made two historic achievements over the last decade. It has diminished the high degree of concentration of exports in a few sectors and products, and it has achieved a slight change in its export profile, with natural resource–based manufactures and low-technology products between 1993 and 1996 representing a fairly stable 40 percent of total exports.[5] Although the rate of open unemployment fell from 9 percent to 3 percent over this period, economic growth barely reached 4 percent, and relative poverty declined by one percentage point per annum, barely enough to return to the poverty levels that prevailed prior to structural adjustment.

Bolivia's exports totaled 4.07 billion dollars in 2006. Nearly half of these were derived from hydrocarbons (2.01 billion dollars), and a quarter from an emerging manufacturing sector linked to natural resources (1.11 billion dollars) (INE 2007). Only five years previously, the manufacturing sector accounted for exports worth 715 million dollars, a pattern that prevailed for some fifty years, with manufacturing accounting for between 14 percent and 17 percent of GDP.[6] In recent years, 160 of the 478 Bolivian export products with four digits on the United Nation's SITC (Standard International Trade

Classification)—that is, products in relatively general categories—achieved access to global markets, and 23 were consistent leaders.

To identify competitive Bolivian tradeables in recent years, we undertook an exercise with three different filters (Gray and Wanderley 2007). First we excluded products with an eight-digit SITC classification (which indicates a fairly narrow product classification) that have access to zero-tariff markets but that are not currently being exported. This includes more than 4,500 products with export potential. It suggests that the high structural costs of the Bolivian economy act as a barrier to entry to thousands of products. Second, we excluded those products that are not being exported to expanding regional or global markets. These include around 327 of the 478 products exported with a four-digit SITC classification. Third, we estimated Balassa indices for exports in expanding markets.[7] Only 23 export products remained after applying these three filters for the period between 1980 and 2005.

Of interest within this group are the "champions" (where Bolivia's exports of a particular product grew more rapidly than the global market) and the "underachievers" (where Bolivia's exports grew less than the global market). These two groups are the products for which Bolivia enjoys comparative advantages and can expect to improve its access to world markets. The main group is not very big, nor is it very diverse. Hydrocarbons and minerals are the leaders for the period between 2000 and 2004, with soybean products a distant third.

The implications here are revealing. Bolivia is, de facto, a narrow-based economy, grounded on the export of primary products highly vulnerable to price fluctuations. It is an economy with high structural costs in transport, low levels of human capital, and institutions that do little to promote growth. The returns that can be achieved from reducing structural costs are, therefore, high. However, a small group of nontraditional exports—including soy products, leather products, wooden manufactures, and jewelry—constitutes the emergent broad-based economy.

Four Paths to Exporting

To understand how some nontraditional products manage to conquer niches in the world market, notwithstanding serious obstacles, we need studies that disaggregate analysis to the level of the firm and to the linkages between the different actors providing goods, services, and labor. In earlier studies (UNDP 2005; Molina Gray 2006c), we suggested that the Bolivian economy is made up of four main sectors: the mining and hydrocarbons sector, the export sector, the popular/urban sector, and the popular/rural sector. We have explored the costs arising from the lack of linkages between these sectors with respect to growth, employment, and poverty reduction (Gray Molina and Araníbar 2006; Wanderley 2004 and 2005).

Here we go a step further and explore the opportunities and constraints presented by the various different ways of diversifying exports, both in terms of their growth and their linkages with other sectors and economic actors. We base this on Hurtado's work (2006) on cost structures, management strategies, and microeconomic dynamics among firms working in those tradeable sectors that have had most success in recent years: soy, jewelry, and manufactured wooden products. This complements earlier research (UNDP 2005; Wanderley 2004) on firms' strategies in the unsuccessful sectors of the export economy.

The first finding is the existence of at least four paths to exporting. The first two are the best known: traditional commodities, such as minerals and hydrocarbons, and nontraditional commodities like soy and oil seeds. The two others are not so well known and relate to manufactured goods: standardized products in price-sensitive markets (for example, products produced for mass-market retailers) and differentiated high-quality products (higher-cost products retailed under a well-known, desirable brand identity). We are particularly interested in exploring the competitive advantages and disadvantages confronting firms in the last three categories, forming as they do the nucleus of the "economy beyond gas," and looking at the effects that competitive strategies may have on their linkages with other activities and actors in the Bolivian economy.

In a recent study (INE et al. 2006) on the generation of direct and indirect employment by the Bolivian export sector, a preliminary reckoning was made of the links between the export sector and the rest of the national economy. The sectors that generate most employment are those sectors that are highly competitive in foreign markets (jewelry, textiles, leather goods, furniture made from certified wood, organic agriculture, among others).[8] According to the INE study, 887 exporting firms generate 32,000 jobs directly linked to manufacturing. These, in turn, generate 107,000 jobs indirectly in the urban popular economy (services, construction, commerce, transport, etc.) and 213,000 jobs in the popular rural economy (agriculture and nonagricultural services). The scale of the incipient broad-based economy is still quite small. It accounts for 352,000 jobs out of an economically active population of nearly 4 million. In other words, the dynamic new nucleus that is "beyond gas" accounts for a mere 9 percent of the workforce.

The quest for business strategies to boost productive linkages leads us to a second finding: the strategy of vertical integration tends to predominate both in the export sector and in the popular economy. This reinforces the low levels of coordination between sectors and productive actors. The low density of the Bolivian economy, as measured by the small universe of firms specialized and coordinated to add value, creates obstacles to the development of those export paths that depend heavily on coordination with other economic units, as we explain below.

The export of traditional products, such as minerals and hydrocarbons, is the first path, and the one that attracted foreign investment throughout the twentieth century; it accounts for about one-half of the per capita growth observed since 1950, and gave rise to modest amounts of treasury income. Almost two-thirds of Bolivian exports in 2006 came from this sector (2.8 billion dollars). Its limitations, apart from the foreign currency it generates, are well known. Extractive sectors work as enclaves, isolated from domestic markets and providing few jobs.

The second path consists of the export of commodities such as soy. Here, competitiveness is based on an aggressive industrial policy—cheap land, cheap credit, subsidized diesel fuel, and tariff preferences—that has helped sustain the soy industry for more than fifteen years despite falling levels of productivity. The impact of public-policy interventionism here cannot be understated. The main limitations are dependence on tariff preferences and the emphasis on reducing costs rather than raising productivity.

The third path is the export of standardized nontraditional goods and products that compete in market niches that are price sensitive. Key goods in this sector are jewelry and wood products. The main comparative advantages are cheap labor and an abundance of natural resources. The main limitations are the dependency on tariff preferences and a low level of linkage with other Bolivian companies. Nevertheless, these companies are responsible for the larger part of export income from nontraditional goods, and they are those that, on a unit basis, generate most employment.

The fourth path is the nascent export of nontraditional products, differentiated between themselves and competitive in market niches sensitive to quality. Among these products are jewels, furniture, craftwork, and organic products. Their main competitive advantage is their differentiation, their innovation in terms both of products and processes, their quality, and their relatively low price. This sector is built around coordination between suppliers of goods and services and a highly skilled workforce. Unlike the third path, markets are diversified and there is less dependence on tariff preferences like ATPDEA (Andean Trade Promotion and Drug Eradication Act). It stands out for its investment in innovation, a commitment to coordinating with other firms, and the degree of control and leadership it exercises over markets. However, these are the firms that currently contribute least to the total quantity of export earnings and, on a unit basis, produce less direct employment.

Our third finding is that the low level of linkage in the Bolivian economy has different effects for different sectors of the economy. The vertical integration of the productive process—from the provision of inputs and services through to product delivery—is the strategy that guarantees competitiveness for products that are standardized and price sensitive in international markets. Such firms have few linkages with others in adding value, even though this does not affect their capacity to compete. Although the absence of complementary goods and services weighs on their cost structure, these are companies that can reduce such costs with relative ease through vertical integration. Such firms manage to occupy niches in global markets because they can import technology and a proportion of the inputs, control the supply of raw materials, and make use of low-cost and nonspecialized labor.

So far as the popular economy is concerned, although the decision to integrate the productive process is a response to adverse economic conditions—serious structural barriers and failures in coordination and innovation—it does not lead to an increase in efficiency and competitiveness, as it does in the case of the firms exporting standardized products. Firms working in the popular economy find themselves caught in an economic dynamic where profit is under pressure in an increasingly saturated market. One of the characteristics of the popular economy is the proliferation of hundreds, even thousands, of productive units supplying the same sort of goods and services. Each worker aspires to reproduce his source of employment as soon as he has a chance to set out on his own. However, new units do not bring about specialization or complementarity in adding value. The consequence is therefore cutthroat competition without the capacity to supply goods or services to new niches, whether in the domestic market or abroad.

In contrast with those who export standardized nontraditional goods and those working in the popular economy, exporters who compete in market niches for differentiated products of a high quality and relatively low price stand out. Their competitive advantage lies in their capacity for innovation both in products and processes. Such firms rely on having highly qualified and stable workforces and being able to coordinate better with other firms in providing services, inputs, and in carrying out parts of the productive process. To compete in such market niches, the farming out of the productive process (market coordination) is very important. One of the main problems confronting such firms is precisely the absence or the unreliability of suppliers, as well as the low quality of complementary goods and services. Such problems have an impact on production and transaction costs, as well as restricting the number of firms able to insert themselves in markets demanding differentiated products and high levels of quality.

For the popular economy and those who export a variety of products, the low density of the production network is one of their main limitations. The consequences of such low density include bottlenecks (monopolies or quasimonopolies) at various levels of linkage, as well as a limited provision of goods, services, and inputs, thereby raising transaction and production costs. In an economic structure where the linkages are weak, other negative externalities arise as a consequence. These include poor capacity for learning, innovating, and developing activities that complement those of other firms. Our studies corroborate the hypothesis that managerial capacities depend not just on the personal qualities of business leaders. The probability of developing ongoing learning and innovation is higher when the transactions and linkages that structure the business environment help foster longer-term collaboration over the quality of goods and services provided, helping jointly to resolve possible problems such as the supply of raw materials and use of technology.

Our analysis suggests that the road to a broad-based economy does not involve just a single sector or export path. Policy is required that encourages a combination of approaches. Widening the base implies accelerating the rhythm of growth, multiplying the number of exporters with pulling power in the domestic market, raising the productivity of workers, democratizing the factors of production, and ensuring that those who generate most employment can also increase their income and position themselves in the global economy. In other words, it is a question of building linkages so as to grow, building bridges between different skills. It involves building a state that can promote conditions where stronger actors from the popular economy are able to benefit from the effects of redistribution.

We can see that different export paths may have different impacts on growth, employment, and the extent to which they can help develop linkages within the national market. No paths that lead toward diversification can therefore be ignored. Although the export of natural gas is the main source of economic growth, problems arise when it comes to encouraging diversification of exports and squaring the need to create employment and to generate income. Similarly, the contribution of different export paths varies between nontraditional manufactures. While firms that export commodities and standardized products generate more income and direct employment on a unit basis (albeit of variable quality), they contribute less to increasing the density of the production network as their competitive strategy is one of vertical integration. The situation for those that compete on innovation and quality is rather different; although they generate less income and less direct employment on a unit basis (albeit of a higher quality), they do most to maximize the use of inputs and services and thereby help build links with other firms.

Finally, building a broad base involves making profound changes to the way the popular economy works. It goes without saying that this economy incorporates the largest number of economic units and provides most employment. At the same time, the emerging export economy—principally differentiated products of high quality—depends on the linkages that are built with more competitive firms within the popular economy. No less important is the role played by the popular economy in incubating export firms. There is a huge productive potential in commercial sectors and in the domestic market for production and processing. The challenge is therefore to change the conditions in the economic environment in such a way that producers have the right incentives to exploit their existing capabilities to best effect and thereby enter the virtuous dynamics of market expansion.

Why Does the Narrow-Based Economy Persist?

Analysis of the different export paths shows that responding to the challenges of building a broad-based economy is not easy, but not impossible. Some difficult questions are posed. What conditions impede export diversification and the capacity of the more dynamic sectors of the economy to drive the domestic market and the sectors that provide inputs and services? What is it that pushes small-scale producers to seek to supply all the links of the productive chain, instead of specializing in one and thus raising their productivity in new markets? Why is the Bolivian economy unable to respond to existing demands?

In the popular economy, it is noteworthy that small-scale producers support one another in a family or wider social context, but that when it comes to production they prefer to work on their own. Research reveals a chronic lack of confidence between equals in the business setting.[9] In those sectors studied, we note the acute reluctance of producers to depend on one another in creating the conditions for their own survival and prosperity. The consequence is atomization into hundreds of economic actors, each with only the slimmest chance of building linkages as providers of goods and services to exporting firms. This sort of negative dynamic also affects firms that are capable of making the leap to becoming exporters.

Conventional wisdom has tended to drift between two main explanations as to the low growth trajectory of the Bolivian economy. The first is a structural explanation that sees growth constraints as a function of long-term factors—the effects of being landlocked, having high transports costs, low levels of technological take-up, low levels of human capital, high financial costs, and so on. The second is more idiosyncratic, locating problems more within the firm itself: the size of economic units, the low quality of human resources, the lack of capable management, limitations in the availability of capital, or the rudimentary nature of technology. Although both sorts of explanation are important, they fail to address the question of why linkages in the Bolivian economy are so weak. There are no magic bullets in explaining low growth in simplistic or overly straightforward terms.

We would argue that the atomization of nonspecialized units and the reluctance to engage in association is, to a large degree, a consequence of the institutional framework and of economic policy. These fail to give adequate incentives to creating an environment that favors different ways of producing and marketing goods and services. The continual preference given by the state to growth based on exploitation of natural resources has helped develop an institutional and economic policy framework aimed supposedly at strategic sectors, such as hydrocarbons, mining, and electricity. At the same time, a broad swathe of the Bolivian economy has lacked the sort of incentives and conditions that would help it become part of a sustained export diversification strategy. From this it follows that the main axes of change would include (i) a new and more variegated public policy agenda aimed at different types of growth, alongside standard policies to reduce the country-cost arising from such structural impediments as poor transport, lack of physical integration and low human capital development; and (ii) measures to extirpate the rent-seeking, clientelistic culture that accompanies a pattern of growth based on exploiting raw materials.[10]

To push forward with such an agenda, we would propose the adoption of a new methodological approach to identify the different effects of structural barriers, the institutional environment, and meso- and microeconomic dynamics of each growth path. Focusing on management strategies, organizational routines, and the transaction and production linkages in specific product markets would encourage analysis of the problems that confront businesses, as well as of the available alternatives in overcoming them. This sort of approach would achieve more than focusing only on the structural constraints afflicting the Bolivian economy in helping to identify more effective policies for each growth path.

Hydrocarbons and the Economy beyond Gas

There have been advances in the national policy debate that have helped put the pattern of development closer to the center of attention in responding to Bolivia's economic predicament. Still, there are continuities in the way that political, social, and economic dynamics lead to the wasting of opportunities to build a more diversified economic structure. The excessive attention given to issues of property and the management of natural gas, at the expense of a discussion about how to use the surpluses generated, is but one example. Such continuities reduce the chances of developing a new pattern for a more broad-based economy.

There can be little doubt that Bolivia's economic future can and should be built around natural gas. No other economic sector can compete in terms of the volumes of investment, the foreign exchange generated, and the tax revenues raised to finance development. In 2006, it is reckoned that the fiscal income derived from royalties and other taxes on natural gas would exceed US$1.63 billion (US$245 million from the Special Hydrocarbons Tax, US$474 million from royalties, US$703 million from the Direct Hydrocarbon Tax, and US$212 million in Value-Added Tax). Together, this is equivalent to about 20 percent of GDP, with one-half arising from the changes introduced under the 2005 Hydrocarbons Law. The lengthy national debate on the distribution of this new tax income underscores some of the fears raised in this chapter. Gas involves focusing on investments, but it also encourages fragmentation in the distribution of rents. The rent-seeking culture tends to predominate discussion at the national as well as regional and local levels. The gas economy promises to usher in a lengthy debate over rents, with much less attention being given to how best to take advantage of investments and rents to achieve a lasting transformation of the economy.

What role should gas play in the future? In this chapter, we have focused attention on the economy beyond gas, but without underestimating the importance of the new hydrocarbons axis. The shift from a narrow-based economy to a broad-based one implies a shift from not very sustainable sources of saving and investment toward more sustainable ones over the medium to long term, in ways that are less susceptible to external volatility and (so far as it is possible) less dependent on international aid. Some 8 percent of GDP currently comes from foreign assistance (grants, concessional, and semiconcessional lending), resources that help finance important projects in infrastructure, education, and health, as well as other areas of national, regional, and local development. These funds complement the significant but insufficient rates of domestic saving generated by households, firms, and the government.

Bolivia confronts two challenges in the next decade in the area of fiscal and financial strengthening. The first is gradually to substitute volatile sources of saving for more stable ones, within the context of more-aggressive trade and international integration. The tax revenues from natural gas will play a fundamental role here, as will new sources of savings and investment linked to foreign trade and investment in the more dynamic sectors of the economy. The second challenge is to transform public rents into instruments for public-private investment. This involves developing institutional linkages, such as a gas stabilization fund to save important rents at moments of growth and then invest them on the downturn or in times of recession.

Gas can therefore play an important role in changing the pattern of economic development in Bolivia. While it is not a substitute for the enormous potential to generate employment and income in the popular, export-oriented economy, and it can play a vital role in the multiplication of new actors. Either way, what is required is a development vision for the medium and long term that leads to linkages being built both within the domestic economy and between it and the outside world. With an economy capable of remedying its insufficiencies and overcoming its atomization, we can begin to be more optimistic about creating a better life for all Bolivians.

PART VI

The electoral victory of the MAS and the inauguration of the new government was bound to throw up major contradictions, both in terms of foreign policy generally and foreign economic policy in particular. The legitimacy of the new administration was, in large part, founded on the fact that—compared to its predecessors—it would stand up for Bolivia's perceived national interests. An important ingredient in the preceding crisis of confidence in the traditional elites had been that they had been accused of being more interested in doing the bidding of external actors than in protecting the interests of ordinary Bolivians. At the same time, despite some gains from high commodity prices, Evo's Bolivia remains a weak player in the international system, unable to set its own agenda and necessarily reliant on decisions made (or not made) in other centers of power, both in Latin America and beyond. So though the accent of policy would shift, such changes would be circumscribed by international realities.

Even so, the new situation afforded opportunities that had not existed previously and that increased Bolivia's scope for maneuver. First and foremost was the clear legitimacy that the new government enjoyed at home, and the authority that a sweeping electoral victory conferred on it to embark on a program of reform. The figure and personality of Evo Morales also aroused unusual interest beyond Bolivia's frontiers, not just in Latin America but in North America, Western Europe, and many other parts of the world. His much-publicized worldwide tour in early 2006 to Venezuela, Cuba, Spain, France, Belgium, China, South Africa, and Brazil attracted considerable attention from critics of globalization; seldom, if ever, had a Bolivian head of state roused such international media interest.

Morales was also elected at a time when Bolivia enjoyed an unprecedented opportunity in at least two other ways. First, the electoral battles in other Latin American countries threw up left-of-center governments in other countries of the region that challenged some of the suppositions of the so-called Washington Consensus. The presence of President Luiz Inácio "Lula" da Silva in Brazil and Nestor Kirchner in Argentina meant there were reasonably friendly governments in the two countries that had reason to share some of the reservations the MAS (Movimiento al Socialismo) had about the Washington Consensus, but which, in the past, had maneuvered to conspire against left-wing governments in Bolivia. Further afield, the Chávez government in Venezuela, the Rafael Correa victory in Ecuador, and finally the return of Daniel Ortega in Nicaragua provided some cover for a government in La Paz which sought to adopt a line critical of Washington and the United States. The declining standing of President George Bush as a consequence of the Iraq invasion and the fact that the United States had more important foreign policy priorities elsewhere made it easier to adopt such a posture without incurring excessive risks.

The second area of opportunity came about because of the unusually healthy economic circumstances that prevailed in 2006; these enabled the new government to embark on policy choices that would have been much harder in other circumstances. Not only did the boom in mineral prices provide unaccustomed surpluses on both the balance of payments and fiscal accounts, but Bolivia found itself able to benefit from international schemes for debt reduction and increased remittances from Bolivians living abroad. For the first time in many years, Bolivia was able to shake free from the economic policy strictures of the IMF and adopt an economic program based on national assertiveness.

The economic policies of the new government picked up on some of the economic nationalism that had been the prevalent economic doctrine in the 1960s and 1970s. It represented a rejection of the neoliberal policies that had prevailed since 1985, particularly with respect to privatization and trade liberalization, policies which the MAS had (convincingly) argued in the 2005 election campaign failed to serve the interests of the broad mass of Bolivian voters. The "capitalization" of former state companies in the mid-1990s, under the aegis of Sánchez de Lozada, had failed to bring the employment gains that its architects had originally promised. Trade liberalization had similarly proved disappointing in terms of the supposed benefits it would bring in raising efficiency and competitiveness. It was therefore with some ease that the MAS was able to campaign against the Free Trade Agreement of the Americas as being injurious to Bolivia's economic interests. Moreover, the so-called donor community in La Paz, which had come to be seen as broadly supporting the policies of the Washington Consensus, found itself relegated to the sidelines, with new foreign actors—notably Venezuela and Cuba—coming to the fore.

But how far could the new government go, in practice, in bucking the international system without bringing upon itself very real dangers? For Juan Antonio Morales, the president of the central bank during much of the preceding two decades and a key policymaker of the ancien regime, the answer is not very far: In chapter 12, he argues that Bolivia is not in a position to dictate to the rest of the world, and that the consequences of swimming against the tide will be a loss of trade, investment, and foreign assistance. Furthermore, he maintains that Bolivia's ability to negotiate with the rest of the world would be vitiated by the inexperience of policymakers and advisors. He finds the Morales government's economic blueprint, the 2006 National Development Plan, to be an uninspiring document with a strong isolationist imprint which, he feels, will serve Bolivia poorly over the medium to long term. In short, he is pessimistic about the country's medium-term economic prospects unless it embraces globalization.

In our final chapter, Carlos Arze, the director of CEDLA (a left-wing think tank) offers a very different analysis of the country's economic relations with the outside world and their contribution to Bolivia's problems. For him, globalization and the neoliberal policies that emanate from it were directly responsible for the social ills that contributed to the collapse of the previous regime. He argues that Bolivia's problems are a direct consequence of the predominance of transnational corporations and multilateral lending institutions, and that the reforms of the 1990s were the immediate reason for the erosion of living standards that reanimated the country's traditionally radical social movements. Reversal of some of these neoliberal reforms, particularly in key sectors like hydrocarbons and mining, is therefore a priority for the Morales administration in defending the country against globalization. As an institution, CEDLA has been critical of the Morales government for acquiescing to external pressures and for not adopting more explicitly socialist policies.

While the economic policies of the new government represent a departure from the Washington Consensus blueprint in important respects, in other areas—such as in aspects of fiscal and monetary policy—there has been less willingness to jettison the orthodox rulebook. The policy mix has been just that: a mix of policies concocted in a fairly pragmatic way, drawn from different ideological sources, and responding to different impulses and pressures. More than two years into the new government, it is still difficult to predict how economic strategy would pan out into the future and how it would fit into an evolving geopolitical matrix in Latin America and beyond. Will Bolivia be able to tap into nontraditional sources of investment? Will it lose its trade preferences into the U.S. market? Will Brazil continue to buy copious amounts of Bolivian gas? Will Venezuela provide a substitute source of development assistance?

12

Bolivia in a Global Setting

Economic Ties

JUAN ANTONIO MORALES

The way in which Bolivia inserts itself into an ever-more-globalized international economy is a question central to any discussion of the country's potential for economic growth. The conventional view is that if Bolivia wants to develop, it needs to take part fully in patterns of international trade and attract flows of foreign capital to finance the investment needed for future growth. Active participation in the world economy is seen as a necessary condition, but obviously not a sufficient one, for growth and development. A recent World Bank publication on Bolivia (Fretes-Cibils et al. 2006) states that "sustained high growth . . . would demand more investment and greater productivity than in the recent past. . . . [E]conomic growth will depend upon the capacity to expand exports and to integrate in the world economy."

Since its rise to government following the elections of December 2005, the MAS (Movimiento al Socialismo) has faced a changing international setting. It took office in the midst of a boom in natural gas exports (as well as of other primary commodities) that has created a different set of circumstances for economic management than had prevailed in the past. While the accent here is on current decision making, we will also devote some attention to developments in the recent past.

The view of the MAS government toward international economic relations differs in many ways from that of its predecessors. In its orientation it looks far more to the domestic economy, giving greater emphasis than previous administrations to state intervention and prioritizing the industrialization of the country's natural resources, although it has made some decisions that go in the opposite direction. The pertinent questions, therefore, are how economic sectors outside of hydrocarbons and mining will develop, whether dependency on natural resources will become more accentuated, and how much scope for maneuver there is in view of the trends observable among Bolivia's main trading partners and the main sources of international finance.

Linked to this is the extent to which the Bolivian economy is well prepared to operate under new guiding principles, and—critically—if it can steer itself away from the financial dependency it has experienced for so many years.

In recent years, the Bolivian economy has been characterized by a shift between first interventionist state-led development and then free-market neoliberalism. Coca as an export has become a central concern for Bolivia's relations with the United States and has implications both for the macro-economy and the international competitiveness of other economic sectors. To understand the MAS government's policies with respect to international trade and growth, particular reference must be made to the new economic nationalism, regarding both the hydrocarbons industry and trade preferences. The policies of the National Development Plan seek to modify policy in substantial ways, raising questions about the future role of trade and investment, as well as introducing new orientations in development policy that impact on international cooperation.

Initial Conditions and Some Lessons from the Past

Since the 1952 revolution, Bolivia has undergone several changes in the way economic policy is conducted.[1] Following the first years of revolutionary fervor, the country embarked on a development path that approximated to the recommendations of the Economic Commission for Latin America (ECLA) and the Inter-American Development Bank (IDB). This was a model of state capitalism, with a strong presence of state companies in the economy and a complex system of rewards and sanctions with respect to the private sector. Its objective was to achieve higher-value-added exports and to substitute for imports. We will call this an Interventionist State-led Industrialization (ISLI) model. Strong controversy persists about this model, in spite of the years.[2]

Bolivia achieved only meager results from this model, but it has to be said that it was never pursued with great vigor, except in the 1950s (when certain industries were created to substitute for basic industrial inputs) and during the first Banzer government (1971–1978). In the 1970s, access to foreign credit provided an added impulse to the ISLI model. This experience ended in notable failure, and many believe that the crisis of the early 1980s, which led to hyperinflation, was caused by both foreign debt problems and the inefficiencies of the ISLI model.[3]

At the end of 1985, the so-called neoliberal era began with the development of a market economy that minimized the role of the state. The stabilization program embodied in Supreme Decree (DS) 21060 was not just a set of policies designed to combat inflation, but involved important structural reforms.[4]

DS 21060 did not address privatization in any substantial way; such policies followed on only in the first half of the 1990s. These were carried out by means of a complex exercise in financial engineering known euphemistically as capitalization.[5] Coupled with the closure of state banks a few years earlier, Bolivia went from being one of Latin America's most statist countries (after Cuba) to being one of its most liberal.[6]

At the time, international financial institutions lauded Bolivia for its outstanding performance, even though the economy grew only modestly (around 4 percent) and investment was financed principally from external sources (whether official lending or, a little later, direct foreign investment). Bolivia also took advantage of debt relief. The pace of social development was faster, and Bolivia saw some improvement in its rating on the Human Development Index.

Pact-based coalition governments meanwhile, also seemed to have helped diminish political confrontation. Nevertheless, political parties failed to develop properly, and the coalitions tended to be heterogenous in nature. More importantly, party leaders failed to understand the depth of the disenchantment with a development model perceived as inherently unjust and benefiting a small minority.[7] The parties also failed to appreciate some longer-term trends, such as the increase in the indigenous population (due to improvements in health care and the fall in infant mortality), the rejection of policies of assimilation in favor of a pro-*indigenista* discourse, the growth in indigenous awareness as a result of the Popular Participation program, and—more fundamentally—the discontent caused by the exclusion from economic power of the majority of the population.

The regional crisis of 1999 (which followed on an international crisis that began the year before) substantially worsened an already precarious employment situation. This came on top of a severe crisis of governability that began under the Banzer government (1997–2001). The privatization (capitalization) program, as well as the whole neoliberal economic policy of which it formed part, therefore fell into discredit. With the ousting of the Sánchez de Lozada administration in October 2003, Bolivia entered a period of acute instability which, however, did little to affect the economy.[8] Evo Morales won the

December 2005 presidential election by an ample margin. When he took office, not only did he enjoy widespread political support, but the international economic situation had become far more favorable for Bolivia.

As can be seen in figure 12.1, GDP per capita, following several years of negative growth, underwent a recovery from 2003 onward. For 2006, a growth rate in per capita GDP of 1.7 percent was achieved. The end result, however, was a per capita GDP below 1998 levels and was barely 14 percent higher than 1990 levels (figure 12.2). Over the intervening period it had grown at an average annual rate of 0.8 percent.[9]

Bolivian growth would undoubtedly have been more dynamic but for the length and depth of the regional economic downturn of 1999–2002. The crisis of these years first began to affect Bolivia in the final months of 1999, almost a year after the larger economies of the region. The international and regional context began to improve as of 2003, and this is particularly notable from the strong improvement in exports.

Since the middle of the 1980s, the Bolivian economy has been reasonably open, a factor which has also encouraged exports. Export performance has benefited not only from high international commodity prices but also the policies taken between 1985 and 1997 to encourage economic opening and to attract foreign investment. Bolivia applies no quantitative barriers to imports. The average tariff is 9 percent, and tariffs are almost uniform (data for 2002; Corporación Andina de Fomento 2005).

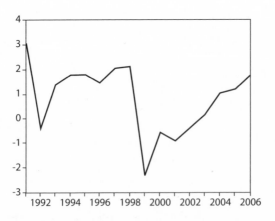

Figure 12.1. Annual rate of growth of per capita GDP, 1991–2006. Author's elaboration from INE data.

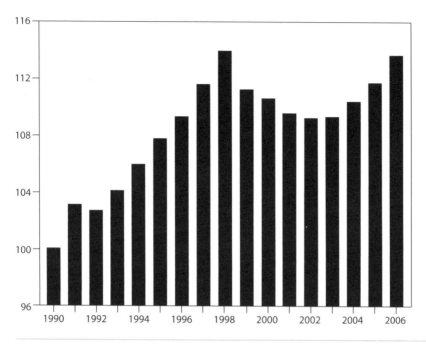

Figure 12.2. Index of evolution of per capita GDP (Base 1990 = 100). Author's elaboration from INE data.

The liberalization of imports brought about by Supreme Decree 21060 in 1985 had the immediate effect of forcing the closure of a number of firms, but these were replaced by others that were better positioned to take advantage of the new market conditions, particularly new export sectors such as soy and clothing. Although it is clear that exports have grown a great deal in value terms, they are highly concentrated in the hydrocarbons and minerals sectors, whose future performance could prove unstable. Notwithstanding the focus on primary commodities, the range of basic product exports has widened, and Bolivia has started to export manufactured products such as textiles and clothing. The increase in the exports of manufactures has been encouraged by the trade preferences contained in the U.S. Andean Trade Preferences and Drug Eradication Act (ATPDEA) and the maintenance of a competitive exchange rate. Also, the economies of Bolivia's neighbors began to grow significantly, and their own currencies have appreciated, which has helped increased the competitive edge of the Boliviano. All this translated into a widening of traditional export markets and a reduction in the competition between imports from these countries and domestically produced

Bolivian goods. Data for the Bolivian balance of trade in 2004 and 2005 were surprisingly good, not just because of the diversification of products but also markets. Not only did the number of export items increase, but the number of markets did likewise. Asian markets grew in importance, reducing Bolivia's dependence on exports to the United States, as shown in tables 12.1 and 12.2. On the current account of the balance of payments, not only was there a healthy trade surplus, but Bolivia also benefited from remittances. In 2006, remittances from Bolivians living abroad rose to the equivalent of 4.7 percent of GDP, double the figure for foreign direct investment.

Prices of Bolivia's main commodity export products, whether hydrocarbons or minerals and to a lesser extent soy, have experienced a sharp increase since the middle of 2003 (figure 12.3). The price of oil has risen fastest since 1980, especially in 2004 and 2005. However, it is natural gas that is most important to the Bolivian economy, and its price tends to rise with oil after a short lag. This is reflected in the contracts signed with Brazil and (more recently) Argentina. Figure 12.3 also shows minerals prices at their highest since 1980 in real terms, due principally to demand in India and China. This is complemented by the buoyant state of U.S. growth after 2003. It also illustrates how agricultural exports like soy have attracted higher prices than they did in the 1990s (although not in the 1980s).

Table 12.1. Exports by product group, 2003–2006 (in US$ millions)

	2003	2004	2005	2006[1]
Minerals	369.3	455.8	544.3	1,060.3
Hydrocarbons	490.9	838.9	1,427.5	2,039.8
Nontraditional exports	621.7	788.6	709.1	767.3
Other goods	203.5	177.8	240.4	365.9
Subtotal	1,685.4	2,261.0	2,921.4	4,234.3
Adjustments[2]	−87.5	−115.0	−130.3	−371.3
Total	1,597.8	2,146.0	2,791.1	3,863.0

Source: Central Bank of Bolivia. Compiled in accordance with the fifth version of the IMF Balance of Payments Manual.

[1] Preliminary data.
[2] Includes minerals processing and leased aircraft.

Table 12.2. Direction of exports, 2000–2006 (in US$ millions)

	2000	2001	2002	2003	2004	2005	2006
ALADI	652	787	808	1,069	1,450	1,922	2,691
Argentina	61	67	28	57	131	268	391
Brazil	166	298	333	504	714	1,118	1,592
Chile	31	33	33	44	51	41	68
Venezuela	52	99	175	176	244	160	196
Andean Community	315	367	391	438	507	311	414
Colombia	196	190	140	158	120	181	155
Peru	61	68	74	90	138	126	248
C.A Common Market	0	0	0	0		6	1
Canada	7	20	8	6	13	20	50
United States	354	187	193	237	359	408	405
European Union	252	141	96	112	163	163	247
Europe other	164	176	216	167	54	111	214
Asia	14	20	28	67	180	242	490
Japan	3	3	6	19	68	134	378
China	6	5	8	12	23	21	36
Rest of world	17	16	21	20	36	50	136
Total CIF	1,459	1,347	1,370	1,677	2,254	2,921	4,234

Source: Central Bank of Bolivia.

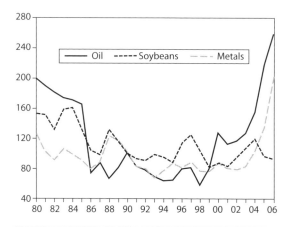

Figure 12.3. Real export prices, 1980–2006 (base 1990 = 100). Real export prices are nominal prices adjusted downward by Manufacturing Unit Value Index. Author's elaboration from IMF and World Bank data.

Figure 12.4 is interesting from a number of standpoints. We can see that real export prices and the terms of trade have followed a similar path, with only some years in which the latter exceeded the former. For both variables, there was a sharp fall between 1993 and 2003 in comparison with the early part of the 1990s. This fall helps explain why the structural reforms of the 1990s did not produce the positive results expected. Finally, we can see the recovery in both variables in the years after 2003.

Bolivia is the world's third largest producer of coca (after Colombia and Peru). In all its ramifications, then, coca has important implications for Bolivia's pattern of insertion into the international economy. To start with, Bolivia's relations with the United States and other industrialized countries have been stigmatized by coca for many years. The strategy of the United States, which has to an extent eluded its own responsibility for controlling demand, has focused on controlling supply through repression. Eradication was pursued vigorously with U.S. assistance during the governments of Hugo Banzer and Jorge Quiroga (2001–2002), but since then the intensity of the

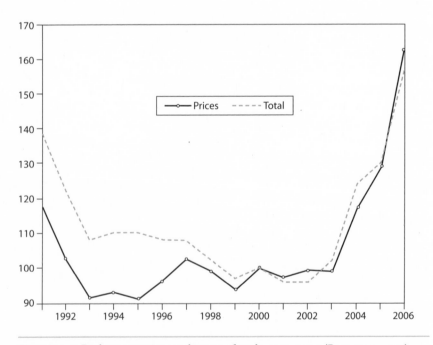

Figure 12.4. Real export prices and terms of trade, 1991–2006 (Base 1990 = 100) Real export prices are nominal prices adjusted downward by Manufacturing Unit Value Index. Author's elaboration of INE and World Bank data.

eradication campaign has diminished. Eradication has met with strong and sometimes violent opposition from coca producers—mainly poor peasants. The effects of eradication not only came to be felt at the local level but also had national implications with respect to the distribution of power nationally and the solidity of democracy (Van der Auwera 2004). In pursuit of the goal of coca eradication, the U.S. government—this time in conjunction with the countries of the European Union—launched a variety of alternative development plans in order to substitute coca cultivation with other cash crops.[10] Evaluations of these development programs have tended to be critical, suggesting that they were not very efficient and yielded only modest results for the effort involved (see, e.g., Farthing 2004). The Morales government has brought about a substantial revision in the coca eradication program, as well as of alternative development. There is greater toleration toward coca cultivation, and the program is geared more to fighting illegal drug trafficking. It is so far premature to gauge the results of this policy.

A source of significant foreign currency inflows, coca also has important macroeconomic effects, impacting on the way in which domestic resources for alternative activities are deployed. Unfortunately, estimates of its economic significance vary a great deal, and getting accurate information is well nigh impossible. Even so, income from coca has been and still is significant.[11] It is sometimes presumed that this income may have contributed to a lasting overvaluation of the exchange rate, thereby penalizing other exports and local industries that substitute for imports (in other words, the production of tradeables in international commerce). Coca incomes are therefore blamed for an antiexport bias, and it is argued that this helps explain Bolivia's poor export performance in the twenty years between 1985 and 2005. However, there is no solid evidence for such conjectures, and nor is it the case that there was a significant overvaluation of the exchange rate over most of this period.[12]

The Growth Policies of the Evo Morales Government

Exports of natural gas, and to a lesser extent crude oil, are the main prop of Bolivia's economic relations with the rest of the world. Not only have these grown in relation to the value of the country's overall exports, but—as we can see (table 12.3)—they have become the number one export line. There is, of course, a danger that Bolivia may become a monoexporter of energy, or even close to one, if high international oil prices persist (See chapters 10 and 11 of this volume).

Table 12.3. Hydrocarbon exports, 2000–2006 (in US$ millions)

	Natural gas	Petroleum and others	Total hydrocarbons	Total exports FOB	Share of hydrocarbons (%)
2000	122	44	166	1,246	13.3
2001	237	52	289	1,285	22.5
2002	266	65	331	1,299	25.5
2003*	390	101	491	1,598	30.7
2004*	620	219	839	2,146	39.1
2005*	1,086	342	1,428	2,791	51.1
2006*	1,672	368	2,040	3,863	52.8

Source: Author's elaboration from Central Bank of Bolivia data.
* Represents preliminary data.

Bolivia has the second largest reserves of natural gas in Latin America. Thanks to capitalization/privatization, as well as the other structural reforms of the mid-1990s, proven reserves grew from 5 trillion cubic feet (tcf) to 48 trillion.[13] Despite the magnitude of such figures, Bolivian reserves represent only a small percentage of proven world gas reserves. The discovery of these gas reserves had a highly divisive effect on public opinion in Bolivia, but even more so when it came to the possibility of exporting liquid natural gas (LNG) to the United States and Mexico via Chilean ports. It was during the Quiroga administration (2002–2002) that the idea arose of using natural gas as a negotiating tool with Chile to help Bolivia secure a sovereign access to the Pacific Ocean. It was the (false) belief that Bolivia would "sell its gas through Chile" that was to lead to the ouster of the Sánchez de Lozada government after the so-called gas war of October 2003.

The idea of using gas as a bargaining chip remains an issue, although it has passed to a secondary level of importance in a debate in which the main arguments were that (a) transnational corporations in the oil and gas sector were obtaining excessive profits and were despoiling the country of this natural resource; (b) to avoid what happened with silver and tin, it was necessary to industrialize gas; and (c) it was important to reestablish (*refundar*) the state oil company Yacimientos Petrolíferos Fiscales Bolivianos (YPFB).

The government of Carlos Mesa (2003–2005), which replaced that of Sán-chez de Lozada, called a binding but sui generis referendum in 2004. It con-sisted of five questions that were ambiguous and tilted toward greater state control of the oil and gas industry. A new Hydrocarbons Law (Law 3058) was approved in May 2005 amid considerable confusion and after Mesa had promised the international community that he would veto it. He did not do so, although he left it to the president of Congress officially to promulgate it. The new law created a hefty output levy, similar to a royalty, that raised tax payments sharply and distributed the revenues generously between de-partmental and municipal governments and universities. It also announced the strengthening of YPFB's role. However, it saddled YPFB with a complex corporative structure of governance which may yet render it unmanageable and make institutional strengthening impossible.[14]

The nationalization of hydrocarbons was a key campaign issue for the MAS. In fulfillment of this commitment, the government promulgated a nationalization decree on May 1, 2006 (DS 28701) which it turned into the focal point of its economic strategy. The promulgation of the decree was ac-companied by a military occupation of gas fields, a move that received sig-nificant media coverage.[15] The May 2006 nationalization decree had specific attributes that distinguished it from other nationalizations. The key point of the decree was that it involved new contractual terms for the investors in the industry, basically reducing their participation to fulfilling service con-tracts. At the same time, it granted YPFB control over the industry—from exploration and prospecting through production to marketing—by invoking the idea of state ownership up as far as the wellhead. It also increased royalty payments for larger fields, leaving smaller ones to subsequent negotiation.[16] Unlike previous nationalizations, the decree did not expropriate the physical assets (machinery and equipment) located in the oil and gas fields. However, it expropriated the profits and seriously constrained the business activities of the transnationals involved.[17] The decree has to be seen within a prevalent context of high international energy prices. These have led to the view, ex-pressed in many producing countries, that they are not receiving their fair share of the benefits of the oil bonanza, which remained predominantly in the hands of private companies. It thus encouraged nationalist responses in producer countries, and Bolivia was no exception.

At the end of October, the government agreed new contracts with the oil and gas companies, a mixture of operating contracts and shared production contracts. The new contracts are not so different from those in other oil and gas producing countries, and it was this that made them acceptable to the foreign companies. In a context of high prices, the state's share (under all modalities) can be as high as 82 percent of income (net of operating costs). The question that therefore arises is what happens if and when the current spate of high prices collapses.

In the third quarter of 2006, the government proceeded to enter into an agreement with Argentina to sell 27.7 million cubic meters of natural gas a day by 2010, on top of the 26 million cubic meters it had already set aside for sale to Brazil. Thus the country's main regional markets were covered, and the project of previous governments to export LNG to the United States and Mexico was abandoned. In order to comply with these export commitments to Argentina and Brazil, Bolivia needs to secure substantial investment in exploration, the development of new fields, and build new transport infra-structure, all of which require it to attract foreign capital. It is important to note that the contracts agreed on in 2006 do not involve firm commitments for fresh investment.

Bolivia belongs to two different regional integration arrangements: it is a full member of the Andean Community of Nations (CAN) and an associate member of Mercosur. It has been a member of the Latin American Integra-tion Association, known as ALADI, for an even longer period of time. It also has signed economic complementation accords with a number of countries outside the CAN and Mercosur. Furthermore, it benefits from ATPDEA and the European Union's Generalized System of Preferences (GSP). Membership in the CAN once seemed to hold considerable promise, particularly when this organization abandoned its highly protectionist vision and sectoral indus-trial development policies. Since the mid-1980s, the CAN has shifted toward a model of open regionalism whereby its members liberalize internal trade on a reciprocal basis but avoid erecting high external tariffs that produce dis-tortions in international trade. Sectoral industrial development plans were abandoned early on. At the same time, the CAN is able to negotiate trade agreements with other blocs elsewhere, giving it greater negotiating strength than if each country negotiated them on an individual basis. It should be noted, in addition, that the countries of the CAN provide a privileged mar-ket for Bolivia's soy production. Venezuela's decision to abandon the CAN in 2006, however, may severely wound it as a system of integration, and the full implications of Venezuela joining Mercosur are yet unclear. For their part, the CAN and Mercosur are looking toward merging into the South American Community of Nations, but this project is still at an embryonic stage. Chile rejoined the CAN in September 2006 as an associated member.

Although Bolivia is not a full member of Mercosur, the main advantage of Bolivia's relationship with this trade alliance is the exchange of information and, possibly, the coordination of policies that its participation can help foster. In trade terms, it does not give much by way of added advantage to what previously existed under ALADI and the economic complementation accords. Although Bolivia's exports to Mercosur countries are important, they consist of natural resources, mainly gas. Such exports would have taken place anyway, irrespective of the existence of Mercosur.

The CAN and Mercosur generated great expectations in Bolivia, but their full potential as markets has never been properly realized. This may be due, in part, to the fact that the members of these trading blocs never implemented trade liberalization with real conviction. They tended to operate under a prevailing protectionist mentality, as well being influenced of national lobbies. Trade negotiations were excessively slow and laborious. There was, furthermore, frequent recourse to administrative nontariff barriers that cancelled out what had been obtained through trade agreements. It is also important to note that the crisis years of 1999–2002 brought massive currency devaluations, and these had a significant impact on reciprocal patterns of trade.

The ATPDEA helped promote Bolivian manufactured exports, but it has a fixed expiry date.[18] Its continuation was in doubt during much of 2006 and 2007, reflecting difficulties in relations between Bolivia and the United States. Whereas other CAN members negotiated Free Trade Agreements (FTA) with the United States, as did Chile and the countries of Central America, the MAS government decided to discontinue FTA talks shortly after coming to office in 2006.

The government's opposition to the FTA, along with that of some social movements, was based on the view that it was not "fair trade" and that it would expose small-scale and community producers to foreign competition. Such concerns seem unjustified, and Bolivia stands to gain more than it would lose from an FTA. The costs of adhesion are minimal. Indeed, the costs of import trade liberalization were already borne back in the mid-1980s, and if anything has changed since then, it has been in the direction of increased trade opening. Also, it should be pointed out that those issues that are most frequently questioned—such as intellectual property and drug patents—are open to negotiation.

Failure to reach an FTA may mean the loss of a significant number of jobs, unless, of course, the ATPDEA trade preferences can be extended. At the same time, the tendency toward trade liberalization is likely to continue, although the speed of this was contingent on the eventual outcome of the World Trade Organization (WTO) Doha Round. Bolivia would not be in a position simply to ignore such an agreement.[19]

The MAS government's counterproposal to the FTA with the United States was an agreement on trade preferences with Cuba and Venezuela, the so-called People's Trade Agreement (PTA). It needs to be said right away that trade with these countries is modest. Exports to Venezuela in 2006 totaled US$196.2 million, and imports came to a mere US$56.6 million. It is interesting to note also that recent trade agreements between Bolivia and Venezuela include barter deals: Venezuelan diesel for Bolivian soy. Figures for Bolivian exports to Cuba and imports from it are insignificant for any practical purposes. The PTA, however, goes beyond a strictly commercial ambit. Venezuela—along with Cuba—has a cooperation program in Bolivia and with the Morales government, mainly in the areas of health and education. Furthermore, Venezuela has provided about US$100 million in finance for a program of microcredits and to support municipalities.

The Morales government's plan for economic development, the National Development Plan, is isolationist in its inspiration (Ministerio de Planificación del Desarrollo 2006). With this plan the Morales government sought to signal its intentions in the area of economic policy, as well as to influence the expectations of both the Bolivian public and those of the international financial community. The plan has been presented and debated in a number of different forums; nevertheless, it has failed to overcome the general skepticism with which all development plans tend to be received. It set out four key strategies for the 2006–2011 period: (1) an economic strategy to raise productivity and competitiveness; (2) a socio-communitarian strategy to improve living conditions and to overcome poverty by promoting education, health, and basic public health and by building a social security network; (3) a social empowerment strategy to strengthen democracy through social inclusion; and (4) an international relations strategy. It has has an evident bias toward the domestic market, with the exception of gas, and is based on a strong appeal to economic nationalism, with an isolationist imprint with respect to trade and investment. Many doubts remain about the industrialization of natural resources (including natural gas), especially taking into account the failures in policies of forced industrialization referred to above. Doubts also arise about the development of the economy in sectors other than natural gas. Excessive concentration on the hydrocarbons sector implies strong dependency on a volatile international market and also encourages the proliferation of rent-seeking activities and distributive conflicts.

In the realm of investment, the Morales government has also moved in a more nationalist direction. Historically, Bolivia has depended on foreign capital, in various forms, to finance investment and economic development. Between 1960 and the mid-1990s, foreign savings mainly took the form of official credit to finance investments in the nonfinancial public sector.[20] For a few years over this period—specifically between 1973 and 1982—Bolivia also drew down credit from private commercial banks to cover public spending. With the privatization program that began in the mid-1990s, the nature of foreign saving changed to one principally of foreign direct investment (FDI). Up until that time, Bolivia received only small quantities of foreign investment, but thereafter—partly but not entirely because of the capitalization program—FDI gained momentum. In certain years over the last decade, the ratio of FDI to GDP reached 11 percent, the highest in Latin America. This trend would have continued but for the political instability of the period after 2000.

In terms of absolute value and as a percentage of GDP (as shown in figure 12.5), FDI reached a peak in 1998 and then began to tail off until 2002. As of 2003, it stopped almost entirely. During the 1990s there was external credit to the Bolivian private sector, intermediated through the local banking system, induced to a large extent by FDI.

The regional crisis of 1998 to 2002—long lasting and profound—introduced some important additional modifications to this foreign finance panorama. It has to be borne in mind that this crisis brought with it major fiscal problems. As a result of the crisis and excessively expansive economic policies to mitigate it, the fiscal deficit jumped sharply. Thus it was that, as opposed to the preceding period, official credit came to be used not just to finance investment but also to cover current spending. Furthermore, governments had recourse to budget support donations. These foreign aid flows took place in a context of extreme political instability.

By mid-2003, the country's fiscal problems had begun to improve; this was particularly evident in 2006, when there was a surplus of 4.6 percent of GDP (due largely to taxes on hydrocarbons). It remains to be seen, though, if this was due mainly to the situation of high energy prices and if the high tax take may damage prospects for the sector in the longer term.[21] Bolivia's external

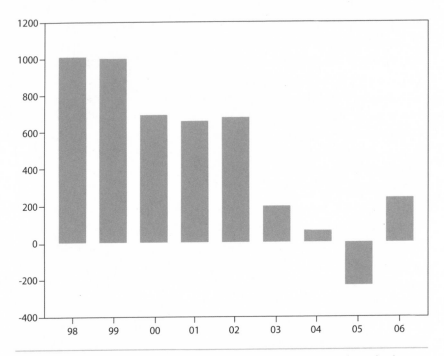

Figure 12.5. Foreign direct investment, 1998–2006 (in US$ millions). Author's elaboration from Central Bank of Bolivia data.

position was given further positive support by debt forgiveness from the IMF and the World Bank on the basis of terms set out in the Multilateral Debt Reduction Initiative (MDRI) in 2005 and the first half of 2006. This involved US$1.8 billion in debt relief: immediate in the case of the IMF, phased in that of the World Bank. Debt relief worth US$1.2 billion was also approved by the Inter-American Development Bank (IDB) in March 2007. The MDRI came on top of the debt reduction that Bolivia has enjoyed since 1999 (table 12.4), particularly as a result of the Highly Indebted Poor Countries initiative.

Bolivia has continued to seek access to foreign assistance in recent years, over and above the debt relief it has received, deploying the argument that it needed it in order to meet the Millennium Goals for human development set by the 2000 United Nations' Monterrey Conference. Thus it was that Bolivia was among the sixteen countries made eligible in 2004 for donations under the U.S. Millennium Challenge Account (MCA), which seeks to channel development assistance to deserving recipients.

The MAS government apparently has not given much priority to the potential benefits from MCA, even though it could mean US$500 million worth of financing, or around 4 percent of GDP. Bolivia's tense relationship with the United States makes it increasingly less likely that it will be able to access these resources. At the same time, the balance of payments bonanza, plus the country's limited capacity to absorb investment, has made the MCA less appealing, in spite of the fact that funding social spending remains problematic and the lack of basic services remains evident.

The high rate of domestic saving in the last few years is a reflection of the surplus on the trade account, and there is a strong possibility that this will not last. For the time being, these savings—well above the rate of investment in physical capital—are being used for the buildup of international reserves—for financial investment, in other words.

It is worthwhile examining the extraordinary recent buildup in reserves in a little more detail. The stock of net international reserves is a consequence of the surplus on the current account of the balance of payments and shifts in the composition of the public's borrowing in favor of bolivianos. One of the results of the favorable global context has been the amassing of current account surpluses, but these also reflective of low levels of investment in a context of high savings. The excess of saving over real investment is invested de facto in the buildup of reserves. This is one explanation for their high level. To this must be added the general public's perception that possibly the value of the boliviano will appreciate, as well as "bolivianization" moves by

Table 12.4. Foreign debt relief, 1999–2006 (in US$ millions)

	1999	2000	2001	2002	2003	2004	2005	2006	Total
HIPC[1] I	84.7	79.0	58.8	42.6	38.6	29.4	27.5	22.8	383.4
HIPC II	0.0	0.7	27.7	84.4	80.4	82.3	73.3	69.7	418.5
Total HIPC	84.7	79.7	86.5	127.0	119.0	111.7	100.8	92.5	801.9
Beyond HIPC			9.3	29.8	34.4	54.3	47.6	50.9	226.3
MDRI[2]								326.6	326.6
Total	84.7	79.7	95.8	156.8	153.4	166.0	148.4	470.0	1,354.8

Source: Central Bank of Bolivia.

[1] Heavily Indebted Poor Countries.

[2] Multilateral Debt Relief Initiative. Includes IMF relief and, partially, World Bank relief that began to come through in the second half of 2006 and will be spread over several years. IDB relief began in early 2007 and will be spread over several years.

Table 12.5. Central Bank reserves, 1997–June 2007 (in US$ millions)

	1997	1998	1999	2000	2001	2002	2003	2004	2005	2006	2007
Reserves	1,066	1,063	1,114	1,085	1,077	854	976	1,123	1,714	3,178	3,891

Source: Central Bank of Bolivia.

the central bank. This has led people to shift their dollar-denominated assets into bolivianos, thereby further pushing up the level of reserves.[22] Net international reserves play an important precautionary role and provide a safety net against externally induced volatility. However, they have a high opportunity cost, because their yield is low, and—what is worse—they tend to fuel inflationary pressures.

Bolivia is currently experiencing a difficult relation with transnational investors. Although the data are not very robust, it seems to be the case that investment (which was already lower than other Latin American countries as a proportion of GDP) has fallen even lower (figure 12.5). Rates of private investment, in particular, appear to have continued their downward trend. There is no doubt that the hydrocarbons nationalization harmed the investment climate, even though its negative effects were reduced by the signing of new contracts. The nature of relationships between the MAS government and investors—both Bolivian and foreign—remains under scrutiny. However, although attracting foreign investment has become more problematic, it is possible that firms from emerging market economies (such as China, India, Iran, Argentina, and Venezuela) may be interested in exploiting Bolivia's natural resources and may therefore displace companies from developed countries. The question is whether the government, desperate for the investment, will be able to negotiate better deals with these companies than with their traditional counterparts.[23]

As regards the IMF, Bolivia has been a member almost from the beginning, entering it at the end of 1945. Since the 1950s, it has had IMF programs

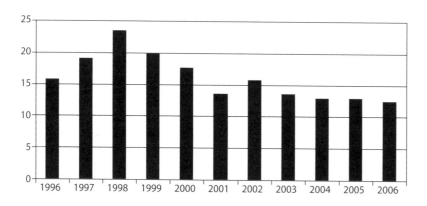

Figure 12.6. Investment rates, as percent of GDP, 1996–2006. Author's elaboration from INE data.

virtually without interruption, except that is during the first half of the 1980s. In the period between June 7, 2002, and April 2, 2003, Bolivia did not have a formal program, but it was subject to monitoring by IMF staff. Over these ten months, a new Poverty Reduction Growth Facility (PRGF) was painstakingly negotiated, although, unfortunately, no conclusion was reached. Pressured by the political events of February 2003, the IMF agreed to a Standby program, shorter in its duration and more costly than a PRGF, but more flexible. With the support of this Standby, important for the technical assistance it brought with it and the information it provided to the international community, it proved possible to weather the serious crisis of those years. The Standby program played an important role in ensuring economic stability at a time of grave political difficulty. IMF programs not only made resources available to Bolivia but also provided technical assistance and acted as seals of approval for the international financial community. An IMF program provides guarantees to donors. Bolivia has used such seals of approval to access other sources of finance, such as the World Bank.

The buildup in net foreign reserves in the central bank and the much improved fiscal situation enabled the Morales government to suspend negations with the IMF over a new Standby and, perhaps of more importance, a PRGF. Bolivia continues to submit itself to IMF oversight under Article 4 of its Constitutive Convention. That Bolivia no longer has an IMF agreement is not altogether bad news; it enables the country to take decisions in a more sovereign way, and it has managed to free itself from IMF conditionality. However, the lack of an IMF agreement may create difficulties in negotiations with donors, in particular the World Bank and the Paris Consultative Group.

Following the failure of the state capitalist model in the mid-1980s, Bolivia went for an open economy in which the private sector predominated and where the country inserted itself into international markets for trade and investment. The structural reforms of the 1990s had a major impact, but they took place at a time of unfavorable terms of trade and a progressive disenchantment among the public concerning the lack of results and the failure to honor promises to make the model acceptable. Notions about development and global insertion changed once again with the inauguration of the MAS government at the beginning of 2006, following a long crisis of governability. Changes in the international context during the last three years have been highly auspicious for Bolivia, providing some of the best opportunities for development in the last fifty years. Bolivia could finally be harvesting some of the fruits of the wide-ranging reforms of the previous decade.

Exports of natural gas and minerals have become the main props of GDP growth. As in other countries with a similar development profile, the question that needs to be asked is whether this growth will last. If it continues to depend solely on positive exogenous shocks, it will last only so long as those favorable exogenous factors endure. One of the challenges is to transfer the benefits of the hydrocarbons and minerals boom to the rest of the economy. It is at times of high prices and high returns that there should be clear signs of investment activity. Data for 2006, at least, suggest this not to be the case.

The MAS took office at the height of this improved international situation, but its main economic policy decisions—characterized by nationalism and isolationism—seem unlikely to take full advantage of it. Its economic policies, including those relating to international relations, run counter to international and regional trends and spurn the advantages to be had from international trade and foreign investment. The policies of the MAS are inspired by the old Bolivian tradition of economic nationalism that dates back to at least the middle of the twentieth century and further inspired by the so-called Bolivarian Revolution of Venezuela's president Hugo Chávez.

The country's international economic relations are heavily influenced by gas. The complex policy of gas sales not only influences FDI but also relies on the MAS government's limited administrative and negotiating powers. Aside from gas, there have been few initiatives in the area of trade policy. The FTA with the United States has been rejected and replaced with the PTA with Cuba and Venezuela. There has also been lobbying for the extension of ATPDEA.

The abundance of natural resources, especially gas and minerals, at a time of enormous international demand and consequent high prices, makes economic management easier, but creates new challenges for the not-too-distant future. In the short term, the boom has helped generate higher international reserves, an improved fiscal situation, and a moderate increase in the rate of GDP growth. The challenge lies in whether the benefits of this situation prove durable and sufficiently robust to confront the volatility that afflicts the prices of the raw materials that Bolivia exports.

13

The Perverse Effects of Globalization in Bolivia

CARLOS ARZE VARGAS

The discourse of neoliberalism presents globalization as the highest stage in the development of human society, a consequence of overcoming the barriers imposed by the technical limitations of the past and by the nation-state. Among its bolder exponents, it is seen as the arrival of a new postcapitalist phase, in which previous contradictions—indeed, the existence of social classes—are superceded and in which the means of production are neither capital nor labor but are "and will be knowledge." The free market will persist over the long term "as the only proven means of economic integration" (Drucker 1993, 7).

This growing integration of national societies, especially in the financial sphere, also involves "wider cultural, political and environmental aspects." But underscoring the supposedly objective nature of this process, it is argued that this integration of financial markets "has been possible thanks to modern electronic communications" (IMF 2000). Technical innovation, especially in computing, enables a "knowledge society" to be built that leads to more-flexible productive systems and helps firms to move across national frontiers. At the same time, it facilititates the extraordinary growth of trade, even more than that of production. The liberalization of capital flows thus becomes a factor in making production more agile.

With an orientation that is normative rather than explanatory, neoliberalism emphasises the supposedly unavoidable nature of globalization, repeating the suppositions of sociological and economic theories that see development as a historical process leading to the unchallenged rule of market forces. Thus, it is "the extension of market forces beyond national frontiers which for centuries has operated at every level of human economic activity: in rural markets, urban industries or financial centres" (IMF 2000). This capacity to do away with social contradictions and differences between countries stems from the fact that the increased liberalization of flows of goods, capital, technology, and labor brings convergence in key mercantile variables, such as prices and wages, leading to the elimination of the gap between rich and poor countries and between developed and backward economies (IMF 2000).

In spite of globalization's supposedly objective, nonintentional nature, huge efforts are made to justify its virtues, and political pressure is applied to align all states behind it; these affairs reveal its ideological nature.[1] This ideology is what is known as neoliberalism. In our view, globalization is simply a euphemism designed to conceal the capitalist nature of the economic integration of our times. Not wishing to deny the scale or specific attributes of this integration, particularly those derived from technological innovation, we would argue that it is nothing more than an expression of a recurrent trait of capitalism. It is therefore a concept that refers to the diffusion of the capitalist system in the world as a whole.[2]

Although globalization has reached new heights, largely because of its ability to impose itself in large parts of the planet in the wake of the collapse of true socialism, it has not overcome the main traits of monopoly capitalism. This phase, also referred to as imperialism, is identified by the preeminence of financial over productive capital, and its main actors are corporations— whether trusts or cartels—that exert hegemony by creating a global division of labor and splitting up the international market between the main powers. Globalization can thus be considered as a phase within imperialism, whose characteristics are revealed by the importance of technological innovation and financial capital to the process of capitalist accumulation.

The emergence and consolidation of this phase of capitalist globalization dates from the crisis of the 1970s, when the world economy experienced a downturn following the expansion of the postwar years (Sotelo 2001; Arrighi 1999). As in all such crises, difficulties in capital accumulation occurred due to such economic factors as a decline in profit rates and such political factors as increased class conflict. This gave rise to increased competition, capital concentration, and financial expansion, leading, in turn, to shifts in hegemony between different capitalist sectors and the emergence of new political leaderships.

Thus, the globalization that ensued from the 1980s onward is an intentional process, driven by certain dominant capitalist sectors and geared toward restoring conditions propitious for accumulation. As Samir Amin (2001) has argued, "It means the return of hegemonic blocks that are anti-labor and anti-popular. This logic works to the exclusive benefit of dominant capital, and particularly to its more powerful segments—which are also the most globalized—financial capital. 'Financialization' thus constitutes one of the principal characteristics of the present system, both in its national and its global dimension."[3]

The ideological underpinning of this recomposition of capitalism under the aegis of financial capital is provided by the monetarist and neoclassical theories that give pride of place to questioning state capitalism and any hint of state economic intervention, in this manner reviving liberal concepts that originated in the stage of competitive capitalism.[4] Neoliberalism promotes the notion that development will be achieved inasmuch as all countries integrate into a single, global market. Therefore, any action by nation-states that counters this or seeks to reject it will condemn them to backwardness and economic marginality.[5] Consequently, the main multilateral institutions advocate a series of propositions or economic policy recommendations—based on evidence that purports to be scientific—that systematize the views of the Washington Consensus.[6] In essence, the policies advocated under neoliberalism seek to establish conditions that favor the revival of profits in the dominant sectors—transnational corporations—by undermining the sovereignty of developing nation-states. This is made possible by the resoration of hegemony on the part of those local capitalists who are most closely linked to these interests.

Neoliberalism in Bolivia

We have seen, therefore, that the integration brought about by transnational corporations and driven by multilateral institutions through the imposition of neoliberal policies transcended national boundaries in developing countries and was accomplished through the presence of specific groups or fractions within local elites linked economically to those foreign interests and who supported the prevailing neoliberal discourse.

However, contrary to the idea that globalization would render the nation-state irrelevant, the state continued to fulfill its basic function of guaranteeing the reproduction of capital accumulation within a specific geographical unit.[7] The expiry of the state has not come about; rather, we have witnessed a change in some of its roles which favor (or not, as the case may be) the concentration of capital. One model of peripheral accumulation has been replaced by another, and one fraction of the dominant class running the state by a different one.[8]

The crisis of the early 1980s, which brought an end to the import-substitutive regime introduced in 1952, opened the way to a new sort of government which sought to restructure the way in which capitalism operated in order to revive a state that had been threatened by enormous social conflict. Those capitalist sectors which had been nurtured during the nationalist phase and had been supported by state policies designed to generate a national bourgeoise were the ones who led the attack that would impose the new neoliberal model. The coalition of these sectors, composed basically of businesspeople with interests in mining and commerce, as well as large-scale landowners and represented by the Movimiento Nacionalista Revolucionaria (MNR) and Acción Democratica Nacionalista (ADN), gave rise to what Lorgio Orellana (2006) has called "a regime of neoliberal accumulation." This New Economic Policy was initiated during "a cycle when class struggle was in decline, beginning with the conjunctural defeat of the working class in 1986" and entailed "a new correlation of forces which the financial oligarchy in power would support both ideologically and institutionally" (p. 17).

This new accumulation regime pursued policies to enable these fractions of capital to consolidate their hegemony. To this end, it was necessary to channel social contradictions within the legal order; this meant legitimizing the power of specific groups by a combination of incentives and coercion. Beginning in 1985, an attempt was made to impress on society as a whole the notion that economic freedom and political freedom were one and the same. The strengthening of the political system would legitimize economic power wielded by foreign capital and groups within the national bourgeoisie, thereby eliminating restrictions on market freedom. Political reforms sought to modify the juridical system and the institutionality of the state, removing the last vestiges of state capitalism.[9]

The relative stability of the political system, which some liberal analysts saw as a virtue of Bolivian democracy and a sign of strength, was achieved thanks to a series of governability pacts between the three main parties: the MNR, ADN, and the Movimiento de la Izquierda Revolucionaria (MIR). Built on the distribution of jobs in the public administration and acquiescence in acts of corruption among the parties involved, such pacts led to the formation of five successive governments between 1985 and 2002. However, in the longer run, they had the effect of bringing the political system into disrepute.

The neoliberal creed, written into structural adjustment programs, attacked state capitalism from all sides, seeking to create in its place the conditions that would enable the free-market economy to prosper and foreign investment to become dominant. For transnational capital to assume such dominance, neoliberal policies sought to get rid of the preexisting institutionality. They modified the way in which macroeconomic policies were designed and implemented and reformed the legal norms that governed different productive sectors.

Macroeconomic Management

Neoliberal macroeconomic policy sought to reduce state participation in the productive sphere, limiting its role to one of supervising and regulating private activity within the free-market economy. Structural adjustment involved the liberalization of different markets, although certain economic sectors continued to enjoy special treatment designed to promote foreign investment and export activities.

In the foreign-exchange market, a system of administered exchange rates was instituted by the central bank based on the availability of foreign currency. This sought to encourage competition between export sectors and to end distortions to internal prices by aligning these with international ones.

By the same token, restrictions on foreign trade were removed, with tariffs reduced drastically and nontariff barriers removed altogether. The argument here was that such policies would help modernize the capital stock and improve access to productive inputs. However, some sectors linked to agribusiness—with good political connections—obtained special treatment that protected them for a while from more competitive imports. Under the supposition that foreign investment would impact positively on innovation and technological modernization, management capacities, and marketing, measures were taken to encourage these through taxation, profit repatriation, and the lifting of tax restrictions on exploiting natural resources (Aguirre 1992).

The adjustment program imposed orthodoxy in fiscal and monetary management, under the argument that inflation was derived essentially from a lack of control over the money supply, itself a consequence of uncontrolled public spending and rising wages. New criteria for fiscal efficiency were therefore introduced that meshed with the monetary program administered by a fully autonomous central bank. This eliminated any possibility of providing credit to the treasury, the argument being that state intervention in the money markets reduced private-sector access to these resources, thereby reducing the efficiency of the system. Fiscal policy therefore made achievement of a balanced budget a priority. To this end, reforms were introduced to cut public spending drastically, primarily by liquidating and privatizing public companies, and generating "real" increases in income through higher taxes and a wider tax net.

However, the loss of sources of public-sector income as a result of the privatization of state industries, and the high costs this policy incurred, led to permanent problems of insolvency, further fuelling government concerns over how to finance the fiscal deficit. Current spending was thus cut back (and with it a tendency slowly to privatize public services) and tough tax reforms instituted that prioritized raising taxes on consumption. Whereas prior to the adjustment direct taxation (taxes on income and corporate profits) accounted for 69 percent of average tax revenues, from the late 1980s to date 75 percent of fiscal income has derived from taxes on consumption—which fall hardest on those living from labor income. Successive governments over this period reduced taxation on business profits, frequently providing companies with tax exonerations and amnesties.

The privatization of public companies—which took the form of "capitalization"—involved the transfer of state assets and control over the country's economic surplus to foreign capital. Furthermore, it brought no new fiscal income to the state, since it involved a sui generis type of association between the state and foreign companies. An amount similar to the value of the original capital was invested by foreign investors in exchange for a 51 percent share of the industries and control over their management. The value of the initial capital, in the form of shares, passed to pension fund administrators (Administradoras de Fondos de Pensiones, AFPs) as representatives of the Bolivian citizenry.[10]

Privatization further accentuated the duality of the national economy. On the one hand, there was an economy based on the domestic market in which Bolivian producers were in the majority. These were medium-sized and informal businesses, with low levels of productivity, unsophisticated technology, and large labor inputs who produced low-cost products for poor consumers. On the other hand, there was an economy composed of large firms who enjoyed monopolistic regimes protected by the state, who operated with high levels of productivity using the latest technology in order to supply foreign markets; these had with few linkages to the rest of the economy and a low demand for labor. This duality is made clear in the huge differences of productivity between the two sectors. Productivity in agriculture, manufacturing, and construction was, at the most, less than one quarter of that of mining, electrical energy, and banking (Arze 2001). It is here, of course, that hydrocarbons take on a special significance as an extreme example of enclaves in an otherwise backward economy.

National industry, already very weak and propped up by protectionist policies, after 1985 was faced with overwhelming competition from abroad, the supposition being that the trade opening would engender its transformation through the introduction of capital and technology. Twenty years later, Bolivian industry had not matched up to these expectations. Not only was its backwardness still in evidence, but it was more pronounced than before. Bolivian industry contributed barely 17 percent of GDP, and its share in exports was barely 15 percent, concentrated in the production of consumer goods (60 percent manufactured value-added goods, 37 percent intermediate goods, and 2 percent capital goods). Moreover, this low level of productivity was related to a growing participation by small businesses (less than ten employees) and microbusinesses, which made up 95 percent of the business universe and accounted for 49.5 percent of employment. On top of this, state companies, which amounted to 3 percent of total employment at the end of the 1980s, had disappeared; private businesses, which represented 36 percent of the total, were reduced to 26 percent by the end of the 1990s, and informal businesses had increased as a proportion from 61 percent at the end of the 1980s to 73 percent at the end of the 1990s (Escóbar and Montero 2003).

Faced by this declining competitiveness, the main option for a range of Bolivian manufacturing firms was to reduce their labor costs. This provided a spurious kind of competitiveness that brought huge social costs but which failed to bring technological modernization due to the lack of available investments. In the case of agriculture, the main source of supply for the domestic market and a source of employment for a significant portion of the population, trade liberalization brought virtual collapse in various types of production (for example, chile pepper, corn, and potatoes). This was mirrored by reduced local supply and substitution by imports (Pérez 2003). On top of this, Bolivia suffered constant pressure from the United States to eradicate coca cultivation, bringing major losses in economic resources and the elimination of jobs.[11] This gradual but sustained erosion in the productive capacities of peasant agriculture has led to the displacement of population (particularly in the Altiplano) through migration to urban areas and abroad.[12] According to the census data, the rural population shrank from 58 percent of the population in 1976 to 42 percent in 1992 and just 37 percent in 2001. This reflects the explosive rate of urbanization that has taken place in Bolivia.

Sectoral Reform

The sectoral reforms that have taken place, related mainly to the exploitation of natural resources, have facilitated the incursion of transnational companies in conditions conducive to high levels of profitability. A system for managing natural resources was construed that raised the capital values of transnational corporations. This led to the state being excluded from productive activities and to a weakening of its oversight functions. It also led to a fall in state income and negative effects on working conditions and living standards among important sectors of the population. Policy gave priority instead to foreign investment to develop extractive industries and transfer ownership of natural resources to these through contracts and concessions, with companies provided with guarantees and the means to generate large profits.

In 1990, an investment law was approved that favored foreign capital and removed privileges previously enjoyed by the public sector and local private firms. It provided for the free repatriation of proft and subordinated state sovereignty by transferring all negotiation of disputes to international forums. During the first half of the 1990s, new normative rules were introduced that privileged private capital investment (both national and foreign) in strategic areas such as forestry, mining, and hydrocarbons. The priority for the state was to attract and protect private investment in the exploitation and marketing of natural resources through the 1995 Forestry Law (Law 1700), the 1996 General Hydrocarbons Law (Ley General de Hidrocarburos), and the 1997 Mining Code (Código Minero).

In forestry, the passage of Law 1700 brought important changes. The period of concessions was extended from twenty to forty years, and the legislation included the possibility of the transfer of such rights to third parties, thereby speeding up the effective privatization of forestry resources. Similarly, it introduced a patent (a tax that serves as a means to control the exploitation of natural resources) of US$1 per hectare in lieu of payment for the right to clear forest on the basis of the volume of timber and secondary products removed (Pavez and Bojanic 1998).

The mining sector was the first to undergo neoliberal reforms. In order to change the legal norms (included the constitution) which prevented mining reserves being given over as property to private companies, in 1985, through Supreme Decree 21298, restrictions were lifted on 80 percent of the reserves that belonged to the Corporación Minera de Bolivia (Comibol), the state mining corporation, opening these up the private sector. Constitutional controls were further eased by means of shared-risk contracts, which removed, for example, the prohibition against foreigners owning properties lying within 50 kilometers of the frontier. The restrictions that previously obliged mining companies to sell to state-owned smelters were also eased. Subsequent changes ended up transferring all state assets to private ownership. Comibol ended up just signing contracts, effectively excluded from productive activities.

Reforms to mining taxation also brought changes that benefited private companies. The Complemetary Mining Tax (Impuesto Complementario Minero, ICM) was established as the only tax, with a variable rate of between 1 percent and 7 percent depending on the type of metal, which could be set off against Corporate Profits Tax (Impuesto a las Utilidades de las Empresas, IUE). Additionally, export products were made exempt from the Transactions Tax (Impuesto a las Transacciones, IT). This effectively ended the system of royalties payable on state property, while quicker monetization of reserves was promoted with the devolution of taxes on exports. The main result of this was that tax paid to the national state by mining companies became insignificant—some 4 percent of the value of sales—as well as the contributions payable to the departments where production took place.[13]

But it was in the hydrocarbons sector that the changes became a paradigm of neoliberal reform in extractive industries. The 1996 Hydrocarbons Law and other legal norms were geared toward granting transnational corporations the power to define their usage of resources and to set the rules of the game in the sector, depriving the state of sovereignty thereby. Law 1689 transferred to the oil and gas companies the right of free disposal of hydrocarbons under their own conditions—not necessarily those which were of benefit to the state or the country. The role of the state was reduced to a bare minimum, with Yacimientos Petrolíferos Fiscales Bolivianos (YPFB) becoming little more than an office that signed contracts and undertook to provide free services under the new export contracts. Regulation was put in the hands of the Superintendency of Hydrocarbons, with no authority over the firms and its functions limited to simply setting prices and tariffs within a free market.

To attract foreign capital, the new rules involved major changes in taxation. Although firms were subject to the payment of a Value-Added Tax (Impuesto al Valor Agregado, IVA), the IT, and the IUE, they did receive special tax concessions. These included exemption from IVA on all exports, exemption from IT on domestic sales of oil and natural gas, and the ability to set the IUE off against the Complementary National Royalty (Regalía Nacional Complementaria). More important, the rules introduced a new definition of hydrocarbons: hydrocarbons in existence on the date of the promulgation of the new law and "new" hydrocarbons from reserves where production began after that date. Subsequently, Law 1731 converted much of what had been considered existing hydrocarbons into new hydrocarbons.[14]

Thus, the payment of tax under the new regime was less, in unit terms, than it had been under the old one. Between 1990 and 1996, the state received US$7.77 per barrel of oil equivalent (BOE), compared with US$6.63 in the 1997–2001 period (Medinaceli 2004). This supports the contention that the main aim of the reform was to guarantee the quicker monetization of reserves through exports. The benefits to the state and domestic consumers from the increase in gas and oil output were effectively ignored as an objective of national policy by successive governments.

In September 1996, a contract was signed with Brazil to export 7.9 trillion cubic feet of gas over a twenty-year period and to build a pipeline linking Rio Grande, Corumbá, São Paulo, and Porto Alegre with a capacity to pump 30 million cubic meters a day. The volumes contemplated in the contract exceeded Bolivia's proven reserves, which were less than 5 trillion cubic feet at the time. The obligation to comply with the contract—which carried with it fines and penalties for noncompliance—therefore involved investment in exploration and development. This was subsequently presented by officials of the Sánchez de Lozada government (1993–1997) as the reason why such advantageous terms were offered to foreign investors (Miranda 2003).

The fixing of the price of gas exported also revealed the intention to favor Petrobras.[15] The calculations used in the negotiations gave a higher calorific value to the gas, and for this reason Bolivia found itself obliged to include in the flows of gas exported all the accompanying liquids, receiving a lower price for its main component, methane. For this reason, the exceptional quality of Bolivian gas sold as fuel enabled Brazil to obtain additionally between 90 and 100 tons a day of Liquid Petroleum Gas (LPG) and between 10 and 15 tons a day of gasoline at less-than-commercial prices (Miranda 2003). It is noteworthy that the prices obtained by the companies bore little relation to the very low costs, lower than those in many other countries. Thus, the estimated costs of Andina and Chaco, foreign oil- and gas-producing companies, were 73 percent and 74 percent less, respectively, than the average of twenty other international firms, exploration costs 96 percent and 46 percent lower, and administrative costs 45 percent and 59 percent lower (DPC 2003).

We therefore argue that the incursion of foreign investment into Bolivia came about because of the unusually favorable conditions in which state assets were transferred (in the case of the five largest companies "capitalized"), to the existence of enormous reserves (discovered previously by the state company), and (in the case of gas) to an assured market in Brazil previously negotiated by the state. Moreover, the supposed benefits brought by technological modernization, productivity, and improved management were only very limited, given the lack of linkages between these sectors and the rest of the economy. The consequence has been the existence of a modern sector geared toward exports and services alongside a wide range of technologically backward sectors lacking any help whatsoever from the state (see also chapter 11 in this volume). For many of those supplying the domestic market, trade liberalization and free-market policies have forced them into a spurious competitiveness based on reducing labor costs and eroding levels of job security.

Exploitation of Labor

Raising profitability involves increasing rates of surplus value by resorting to reducing the portion of value that corresponds to wage payments. This is achieved by various methods, such as intensifying work, extending the working day, and reducing wages paid (absolute surplus value), or by reducing the value of labor by raising the productive force in those economic sectors that provide goods consumed by the workers (or relative surplus value).

In Bolivia, adjustment policies were geared toward directly influencing levels of exploitation of the workforce by eliminating legislation that protected labor. These policies had the effect of increasing the numbers of people unemployed, making it easier to reduce wages through competition for employment from the informal sector. The increase in surplus value achieved by raising productivity in sectors that produce wage goods (goods consumed by workers) did not take place, given the scant incorporation of technological innovation. Instead of modernizing, firms adapted new forms of organizing the workforce (such as family workshops) employing traditional and even obsolete technical conditions. Use was made, for example, of "defensive strategies" (Gutierrez 1990) that raised the exploitation of the laborforce by using such organizational devices as involving workers in oversight, outsourcing of some of the costs incurred in different parts of the productive process, and buying in ancillary services. Similarly, the burden on the peasant economy was accentuated by unequal patterns of commercial exchange, with more use being made of informal-type arrangements within firms to lower labor costs.

Such strategies, backed by successive governments, encountered resistance from organized labor, leading, in turn, to coercion. Union leaders were deported, activists imprisoned, and, more generally, social protest was criminalized. This shows how economic liberalization, geared toward globalization, takes place within the framework of class struggle.

To understand the effects of such policies on the exploitation of labor, it is helpful to see how working conditions became increasingly precarious. The working day became longer over the period of adjustment, enabling employers to produce more surplus value. Average working hours increased by a couple of hours per day, with blue-collar workers most affected. The average hours worked per week were 49.6 in 1989, rising to 50 in 2000 (Montero 2003). The working day was also affected by the use of double shifts or by other secondary jobs which workers undertook to make ends meet.

The reduction of wages came about because of the elimination of elements within the nominal wage that supplemented it with the passage of time and protected its purchasing power. In August 1985, the whole gamut of labor costs was "reorganized" by reducing certain bonuses awarded for the number of years worked, as well as payments intended to cover specific items of spending that had been included in the monthly wage. The way they were calculated also changed. In the case of the bonus for years worked (a way of raising the nominal wage), the maximum level (payable after twenty years of employment) was reduced from 65 percent to 50 percent of the nominal monthly wage. For the purposes of calculation, the effective monthly wage was replaced as a base by the (lower) minimum national wage. Finally, the frequency with which part of the salary was adjusted was moved from yearly to triennieally; in a context of high levels of casual labor, this was a right that became ever more difficult to defend. The consolidation of bonuses on the basis of the minimum wage meant a substantial reduction in costs to the employer, who from then on was able to negotiate wage contracts on the basis of a lower amount (Arze 1999). Subsequently, governments adopted a mechanism for updating the nominal salary on the basis of an addition related to "expected inflation." In times of high inflation, this meant that real wages fell. This can be appreciated from the purchasing power required to buy a basket of basic food: in mid-1990, the average worker's wage was equivalent to 87 percent of the value of the basket, with more than 70 percent of workers in manufacturing receiving a wage lower than what it cost to purchase (Arze 2001).

Another way to reduce wages was to make increased use of short-term work contracts. These dodged various costs and reduced social benefits tied to the monetary wage. The spread of short-term labor contracts was rapid when compared with the period prior to adjustment. In the mid-1990s, a quarter of all contracts were short term, whereas previously labor stability rules were covered by official protection. Also, increased use came to be made of part-time and shorter shifts, affecting all sectors, including the public sector.

A key indicator for evaluating working conditions is the access workers have to some sort of social security, including health care and pensions. Access to health care underwent a sharp deterioration over this period. At the end of the 1980s, nearly half of all waged workers had access to health services, whereas by the mid-1990s this had fallen to less than 30 percent. The old pension system was scrapped, replaced by new system of private, AFP-administered pensions that excluded large numbers who previously enjoyed pension rights. It also made future pension entitlements much more subject to risk. The pensionable age was raised from 55 to 65, and the number of years that needed to be worked to claim a pension was increased. The worker's contribution was also augmented, while that of the employer was reduced by two-thirds, and the contribution previously made by the state was eliminated. Net wages were therefore reduced.[16]

Finally, the reforms made it easier for employers to avoid other labor costs (officially known as "social benefits," or *beneficios sociales*), because the oversight role previously played by the state was reduced. According to the legislation in force, wage workers should receive a number of collateral benefits, such as the *aguinaldo* (extra months' pay at certain times of the year), a premium for profits, production bonuses, and so on. At the end of the 1980s, a little more than one-third of wage workers did not receive any of these benefits, a situation that worsened in the 1990s, when the rate of those not receiving them reached 50 percent.

The sustained growth in the rate of unemployment has been the main factor containing wages and reducing their value. This is because competition between workers for jobs has become more acute, depressing wage levels. This is particularly the case for the least-skilled workers. The unemployment rate rose considerably after the stabilization measures, reaching an unprecedented 10 percent of the economically active population. Subsequently, by the mid-1990s, unemployment had fallen to around 3.5 percent, but it rose again to 10 percent by the end of the decade. Open unemployment rates, however, do not reflect the gravity of the problem, concealed as it is by high levels of underemployment in all sectors (where hours worked are more than the norm or income generated lower). Nearly 60 percent of a Bolivian workers are underemployed, a consequence of the absence of mechanisms to protect workers against unemployment and the persistence of very low wages forcing them to sell their labor at below its real value.

As in the rest of Latin America, neoliberal policies have inflated the size of the informal sector.[17] This fact is especially important in understanding the ways in which labor is exploited by capital. The linkages between informal units of production and the capitalist business sector, through such mechanisms as subcontracting and microcredit, enable surplus value to be extracted from the workforce in the backward sectors of the mercantile economy by financial and industrial capital. A number of studies carried out throughout the neoliberal period show how extensive this has been in different sectors, including various export sectors (Kruse 2000; Escóbar 2000; Poveda and Rossel 2003).

We can see, therefore, that adjustment policies have worked against the needs of the domestic economy and have increasingly eroded the living standards of the workforce.[18] This is made clear by the failure to increase the efficiency of the system, since the few positive examples of increased productivity stand in contrast to the enormous bulk of activities where productivity is very low but which provide most employment. These transformations resulted in higher rates of poverty and social inequality. Just by way of illustration, it is worth mentioning that 64.3 percent of the total population lives beneath the official poverty line (53.5 percent in urban and 82 percent in rural areas), compared to 62.6 percent in 1999. Similarly, inequality in income distribution worsened; in 1992 the richest 20 percent accounted for 55.8 percent of total labor income and the poorest 20 percent for 4.15 percent, whereas in 2001 the figures were 57.9 percent and 3.15 percent, respectively (Arze 2004).

The consolidation of a new regime of accumulation, led by those factions of the dominant class most closely linked to the dominant sector of international capital (transnational corporations) was made possible thanks to the temporary prostration of social movements. The country's rulers raised hopes of improvements in economic conditions and through popular measures such as municipalization, the extension of health services, and subsidies like the Bonosol. Also important was the achievement of a consensus in intellectual and academic circles, encouraged by the number of benefits that such sectors received from government. Their apologetic discourse focused on macroeconomic indicators—notably growth, inflation, and monetary reserves—as evidence of economic and social development.

However, the methods used to strengthen the presence of transnational capital not only failed to modify the dynamic and direction of economic growth (the behavior of GDP growth rates was irregular and never reached the levels achieved in the 1970s), but also ended up confirming the orientation in the pattern of capitalist accumulation that had been in force for decades. Strictly speaking, what neoliberalism achieved was to restore the domination of sections of the oligarchy which, economically and ideologically, subscribe to the notion that the country's only development option is to align itself to international capital, dedicated to the exploitation of raw materials and those industries requiring cheap labor, orienting them toward international markets.

As Orellana has pointed out, "the restoration of the oligarchy is evidence of the historical mode of capitalist development in Bolivia; in other words, the pattern of accumulation did not change substantially. If we start from the supposition that a pattern of accumulation is determined by the forms of subordination of the local economy to monopoly capitalism, the internal articulation between different economic sectors of social production and the specificities of the reproduction of capital which those relations determine, . . . we can conclude that in Bolivia the pattern based on the production and export of raw materials was in no way transformed" (Orellana 2006).

Throughout its history, Bolivia has had an economy dominated by sectors involved in the extraction of natural resources: silver in the nineteenth century, rubber in the first half of the twentieth century, and tin in the second half. This linkage with the international economy has brought about only a limited diffusion of capitalist relations in the rest of the economy. This has given rise to an economy that is unequal and mixed, where automated systems of production in mining and hydrocarbons coexist with traditional peasant forms of production that use the most decrepit of technology. The attempt at capitalist modernization undertaken by the nationalist regimes that emerged from the 1952 revolution ended up being frustrated by the incapacity of these to transcend that ideology. It was also, basically, because the global situation was dominated not by competitive capitalism, but by monopoly capitalism—which focused its pattern of accumulation not on the development of production but principally on the export of capital and the capture of rents.

The fate of the country to which the dominant classes have condemned it was reflected by that ideologue of the nineteenth-century mine owners, Mariano Baptista: "Bolivia should be, in the general market, a producer of raw materials, and minerals in particular. Its main contribution will be, for many years to come, the supply of metals. Its ongoing demand will be for manufactured goods, and its material progress will depend on this exchange. . . . To look for foreign capital, to knock at the doors of foreign banks, to bring in foreign interests to our main areas of production . . . , this is the key to national wealth: this is the desideratum of our situation" (quoted in Lora 1967).

Conclusion

Bolivia's Latest "Refoundation"

LAURENCE WHITEHEAD

This volume of essays reflects the divergent viewpoints currently in contestation in Bolivia. It is not designed to promote any one particular standpoint, let alone to denigrate alternative positions. Rather, the editors—as sympathetic but uncommitted outsiders—sought to collect the clearest and most cogent statements of the competing positions, in order to clarify for readers both within Bolivia and internationally, the foundational nature of the current debates and the deeper implications of gravitating toward one side or the other. Thus, we start with some fundamental questions of collective identity—first ethnicity and second regionalism. By reading Xavier Albó's eloquent presentation of the case for prioritizing the indigenous roots of Bolivia's social identities side by side with Carlos Toranzo's stress on the centrality of *mestizaje* and Diego Zavaleta's thoughtful presentation of the arguments for hybridity, the reader is able to grasp the full significance of this discursive controversy and to read more into each position than would be apparent if each essay were considered in isolation. Similarly, José Luis Roca persuasively foregrounds regional loyalties rather than ethnic identities as the driving force of Bolivia's underlying political dynamics, a position enriched by Rossana Barragán's historically informed focus on the natural-resource-base issues behind the various cleavages. This pair of essays complements each other well, and demonstrates the plausibility of an interpretation that treats ethnic rivalries more as a symptom than as the underlying cause of Bolivia's social divisions. But in any case, as efforts to rewrite the Constitution confirm, whatever the social economic or political bases of these clashes of viewpoint, institutions still matter.

It is through some combination of formal rules and informed brokerage practices that such disagreements will be processed and may (perhaps) be superseded. Former president Eduardo Rodríguez Veltzé, also former president of the Supreme Court, is ideally placed to illuminate the workings of the formal constitutional machinery, and Luis Tapia reflects a rich Bolivian tradition of social analysis in his discussion of the distinctive accompanying informal context. This prepares the scene for the next pair of essays on relations between state and society. George Gray has played a leading role in the UNDP's major research initiative on "the state of the state" in Bolivia, and this provides him with the evidence to support his view of a distinctive configuration. Bolivia is often described as a weak state with a strong society, but Gray's interpretation is more nuanced and brings into question the basic criteria of strength versus weakness. Franz Barrios tackles Bolivia's distinctive state/society relationship from a different angle, highlighting the incursions into the normal structure of state organization arising from what he labels "plebeian democracy" tendencies. From his standpoint, the role is not so much that the state will emerge weakened, as that it will remain "pathetic." Fernanda Wanderley provides an alternative focus for developing the country's economy to that of the simple export of raw materials, even though (as Miranda argues) gas exports provide Bolivia with a windfall that needs to be adequately managed. Finally, Bolivia remains highly constrained by its weak location in a highly competitive international economy, so it is essential to conclude these debates by outlining the alternative attitudes to globalization vividly expounded by Juan Antonio Morales (a former president of the Central Bank) and Carlos Arze. The upshot of this set of competing interpretations is to confirm that many of Bolivia's fundamental issues remain unresolved. These are serious and legitimate disagreements, dealt with in the Constituent Assembly and likely to continue to be debated subsequently. The outcome of the "refoundation" of the republic is still beset by continuing and deep-rooted tensions.

Rather than speculate about a still-shifting and unstable process of institutional change, this concluding chapter adopts a more comparative and historical perspective. Undoubtedly, the comprehensive overhaul of national structures and priorities initiated after the December 2005 election result constitutes a major effort to break with what are widely viewed as Bolivia's failings of the past. But this is being undertaken in a republic that already has almost two centuries of unbroken institutional history and in a political system whose institutions and informal conventions have developed incrementally over more than twice as long a period. Of course, there were also major upheavals and discontinuities, including a protracted war of independence, the federal revolution of 1899, and the national revolution of 1952. Another way to contextualize the current constitutional process is to compare it to its precursors. Technically, there were thirteen constitutions prior to the 2006/07 Constituent Assembly, although in some cases the innovations were only secondary. Among the major precedents, one might list Bolivia's original constitution of 1826; the liberal revisions of 1851, 1868, 1880; the economic and social nationalism of the 1938 *constituyente;* the redrafts of 1961 and 1967; and arguably even the neoliberal foundational decree (21060) of 1985, partly incorporated in 1994. These antecedents bring into question just how "original" the latest attempt to refound the republic can really be.

There is also a challenge posed from a comparative perspective. One influential line of analysis is to argue that Evo Morales and the MAS are, in fact, borrowing from abroad. Many of the themes under discussion in Sucre bore a distinct resemblance to innovations that were adopted in Venezuela following the election of retired Lieutenant Colonel Hugo Chávez Frias to the presidency in 1998. His Bolivarian Fifth Republic is said, by some critics at least, to be the model for Bolivia's most recent round of reforms. This assertion is reinforced by the convening of a constituent assembly in Ecuador, where President Rafael Correa appears to be operating on a parallel track. There is no doubt that Chávez takes an interest in these developments in neighboring South American republics, and that he has significant influence and means to project his preferences in these countries. Again, this line of argument would bring into question the "original" nature of Bolivia's current effort at refoundation. The next two sections of this chapter adopt comparative and historical perspectives to evaluate this skepticism.

A Comparative Angle: The Influence of External Models (Especially Chávez)

A potentially damaging criticism of the current experiment is that, far from representing the authentic interests and aspirations of a long-suffering and perpetually marginalized majority of the Bolivian population, it is, in fact, a transplant at the behest of external paymasters. One strand of such criticism highlights the role played by a variety of nongovernmental donors and aid organizations that have long supported projects and social movements that address issues of poverty and that are alleged to have transmitted their single-issue priorities and their antiglobalization ideas into the popular consciousness. There are no doubt some examples of them that can be marshaled to back up this interpretation, but it suffers from a variety of major flaws. First, as discussed more fully in section two below, these nongovernmental organizations (NGOs) never operated in a social vacuum. Quite to the contrary: Bolivia's *sindicatos* and popular organizations have an extremely rich and long tradition of struggle and self-expression. If they were supported and sustained by external donors during the two-decade-long supremacy of the neoliberal *partidocracia*, or government of party coalitions, they were never simply captured or subordinated. It would be more plausible to argue that in most cases it was Bolivia's social movements that attracted in and fired up the NGOs, rather than the reverse. Second, this took place in a context where many other international actors also felt free to project their preferences and utopias onto a vulnerable national community. If some NGOs supported movements of popular protest, other players—such as Western embassies, multinational corporations, and international financial institutions—felt no compunction about providing support, funding, and indeed leadership to their own counterparts and protégés, whose aims were directed to a very different model of societal and socioeconomic transformation. In fact, the intransigence of some "antisystem" NGO organizations can largely be understood as an escalated response to the vigorous and intrusive promotion of a neoliberal agenda by the dominant international actors. Third, neither of the Bolivian domestic coalitions that confronted each other over these questions (the liberal reforms of the 1990s or the social movements that came to oppose them) was content to serve as a transmission belt for foreign-originated models. Indeed, even the Sánchez de Lozada government of the 1990s may have been as determined to take the lead in designing and adapting external neoliberal and liberal democratic prescriptions as the MAS and Evo have been in selectively interpreting and applying the antiglobalization preferences of their NGO supporters. After long periods of donor dependency and the parcelization of the Bolivian state apparatus between rotating cliques of foreign advisers, it is understandable if many citizens now welcome the prospect of a restoration of domestic control, even though the new administration is bound to display inexperience and indeed some degree of incompetence. Bolivian nationalism, and the country's long history of managing the intrusive demands of foreign backers, ensure that all such external models are filtered and reprocessed rather than straightforwardly imported.

However, there is now also a more directly political attack on the national authenticity of the current project. The reelection of Chávez in December 2006, and the subsequent radicalization of the policy stances of his Bolivarian Republic of Venezuela, has refocused attention on the role played by Caracas in supporting—but perhaps also steering and even controlling—the course of decision making in La Paz. For example, it is noted that the Venezuelan and Cuban authorities have much better access to the highest levels of the executive than all other foreign partners, and even most domestic players. It is claimed that Evo exchanges views and has received advice from Fidel and Hugo on a direct, personal, and frequent basis. It is pointed out that the presidential plane (and accompanying bodyguards) are provided free of cost by the Venezuelan state. Some of the opposition connect these rather anecdotal observations with the more serious claims that on fundamental policy issues—such as Bolivia's relations with the foreign oil companies; the government's policies on land reform, health, and education; or, indeed, the proposal to use the new constitution as a foundation for the reelection of incumbent officeholders—Bolivia's choices are not at all original, but mere imitations of steps previously taken by the president of Venezuela. The strong version of this critique asserts that it is only a matter of time before Evo's Bolivia replicates the entire political trajectory followed by Hugo Chávez in his Bolivarian republic.

Caution is in order when assessing this critique. Of course, defenders of the Morales government insist on their autonomy and dismiss all such changes as hysterical propaganda. Some critics live up to that characterization by referring to the Chavista "power grab," without any qualifications. In early 2007, this polarization of opinion became particularly visible in disputes about the alleged infringement of media freedoms in Bolivia. Whatever eventually transpires, any reasonable observer would have to recognize that at least at that stage in the process, the press and the television continued to enjoy a degree of freedom to criticize the government that is unusual both by South American comparative, as well as by Bolivian historical, standards. Caution remains in order, because it is, of course, impossible to disprove the critics' contention that in due course harsher controls will be forthcoming. Neither Havana nor Caracas can be counted on to value the degree of media freedom currently available in Bolivia. However, it is also important to note that, for the most part, the Bolivian media still use their freedom with more moderation and responsibility than (say) was the case of the Venezuelan media earlier in the history of the Chávez administration. There is no "Aló Presidente" program on Bolivian television, nor would the response be comparable if one was attempted. The Venezuelan-financed channel Telesur is available to Bolivian viewers, but attracts no more than a modest audience, in part because the relatively poor quality of its production makes it hard to compete with other news channels. Some of the local radio networks are more likely to take a progovernment line, but their appeal depends heavily on the services they provide to their immediate catchment areas.

Any serious assessment of the influence of the Venezuelan experience needs to examine questions of timing and the differences of context that distinguish the Bolivian case. Castro and the Cuban Revolution have a very long-standing influence on the Bolivian Left. Ché Guevara was captured and killed in Bolivia when Evo Morales was only eight years old. The future president of Bolivia encountered Peronism during his period as a migrant worker in Argentina, and he was also exposed to Marxist and Maoist ideas in the course of his political ascent. However, it was not until 2002 (when he came in a narrow second in the first round of that year's presidential election) that he attracted the attention of the Venezuelan Left or came into contact with Chávez. By that time, most of his political commitments and structures of support were already firmly in place. When he first established contact with Evo, Chávez had already served for four years as the elected president of Venezuela and had recently survived the failed coup attempt of April 2002. His domestic power base was still precarious, the Bush administration was at the peak of its assertiveness, and Venezuela's oil wealth was far less in evidence. Instead of urging radical activism on his new Bolivian friend, he seems to have urged patience and caution. According to Evo's unauthorized biography, "Although the Venezuelan gives him good advice, at times he treats him [Evo] as if he were a child" (Pinto and Navia 2007, 188).[1] In summary, whatever the "Chávez model" turns out to be, it only arrived fairly recently in Bolivia and its influence in the long run remains uncertain. A reasonable assumption would be that the underlying foundation of Evo's current alliance with Caracas rests on the stabilizing and mediating influence of the Cubans.

Over the long run, the different structure and context of politics in the three countries makes it unlikely that Evo's Bolivia can be too tightly aligned with either Venezuela or Cuba. As concerns the first of these, there can be no comparison between the established oil wealth of Venezuela and its related geopolitical ambitions, and the more modest and underdeveloped hydrocarbon resource base of Bolivia, a country still landlocked and lacking external presence. After almost a decade in power, Chávez has established a personalist ascendancy far beyond Evo's intentions so far. His military background is quite unlike Evo's formation as a trade union and social-movement leader. The relationship between leader and followers within the MAS (or on the Bolivian Left more broadly) is much more tightly constrained than in Venezuela. Indeed, a key doubt overhanging the current Bolivian experiment is whether the loose coalition of protest movements that has unified around the present government will be able to maintain its cohesion and curb the tendencies toward internecine confrontation that have hitherto crippled the Bolivian Left each time it has attempted to exercise governmental authority. The ethnic, regional, and sectoral resistances threaten governability in Bolivia are of a different order from those confronting Venezuela's Bolivarian Fifth Republic. The nature of opposition is also more of a constraint than in Venezuela, given the economic power of the lowlands elites. Bolivia's traditions of protest mobilization and containment are also far removed from those of Venezuela.

It is hardly necessary to add that the differences are even more profound in comparison with Cuba. The centralization, the internal discipline, the curbing of market activities, the national security priority, and the ideological control that have long characterized postrevolutionary Cuban politics are all features diametrically at variance with Bolivia's political experience. It may suffice to recall that whereas Fidel Castro exercised unbroken supreme power for forty-eight years, and Chávez is gaining strength at the end of his first decade in office, no Bolivian president has ever lasted anywhere near that long. Since the establishment of democracy in 1982, there were only three presidents (Víctor Paz Estenssoro, Jaime Paz Zamora, and Gonzalo Sánchez de Lozada) who completed their full terms. Six other presidencies lasted for much briefer periods. Thus, for Evo to complete his current (five-year) mandate would represent a novelty. For him to establish a new constitutional system and to secure his reelection until 2021 (as some analysts have speculated may be the plan) would indeed be truly original within the Bolivian tradition of politics, and not just the imitation of some external model.

This section has so far focused on the alleged influence of the Bolivarian Republic of Venezuela, and to a lesser extent on that of socialist Cuba. But, of course, there are also other external models that might be considered. In particular, there is the example set by Lula (Luiz Ignácio da Silva) and the Workers Party (PT) government in Brazil. The Brazilian president has a background as a worker, a trade-union organizer, an antiglobalization campaigner, a Marxist party builder, and a democratically elected popular reformist leader, all features that resemble Evo's experience quite closely. His track record of advising and supporting the MAS is longer than that of the Venezuelans, and Brazil offers a more natural long-term partnership. There are short-run frictions between Bolivia and Brazil following Evo's showy nationalization-of-hydrocarbons exercise on May 1, 2006 (which deeply offended the higher echelons of Petrobras and embarrassed Lula on his presidential election campaign). But it would be very premature to assume that the pragmatic influence of the Brazilian model has been durably eclipsed by the showmanship of the Venezuelans. Indeed, there are definite signs that the temporary rift between Bolivia and Brazil may be narrowed as both governments focus more on what they otherwise stand to lose.

Other external influences could also prove significant in due course—notably Argentina, possibly Peru, and in some circumstances even Chile. In addition, the United States, the European Union, and indeed China may eventually turn out to play some role in steering and supporting a refoundation of Bolivia. And all these competing influences might be expected partially to offset each other, thus increasing the margin of maneuver potentially available to the authorities in La Paz to chart their own course. But—except in very exceptional circumstances—it is hard to see how any of these external models could become so preponderant that it would overwhelm the country's domestic political dynamics. Thus, the main conclusion of this section is that Bolivian society retains sufficient national autonomy and internal distinctiveness to chart its own course. Neither NGOs nor *chavistas* (nor any other external influence) have sufficient leverage to control the course of Bolivia's currently attempted refoundation. Therefore, in assessing the originality of this process, we now need to turn to comparing it with its historical precursors.

A Backward Look: The MAS and the MNR

From a long-term historical perspective, the current experiment seems yet another in an extended sequence of political reorganizations, not a few of which have also been accompanied by large-scale popular mobilizations justified in the democratic language of transferring power from a small exclusive elite to the broad mass of the Bolivian people. For the sake of brevity and clarity, this section focuses on just one episode of this kind, albeit probably the largest and the most transformative in the history of the republic. The national revolution of April 1952 led to the nationalization of the three dominant mining companies, the introduction of a sweeping land reform, the granting of universal adult suffrage, and the empowerment of a wide range of worker and peasant *sindicatos* that gained positions of key importance in the government and its state enterprises. The party that presided over this refoundation of the republic was the Movimiento Nacionalista Revolucionario (MNR), which held power for twelve years until the military coup of November 1964. The MNR remained the most influential training ground for Bolivia's political leadership for a further generation, only finally losing its preeminence when its last leader, Gonzalo Sánchez de Lozada (or "Goni") fled his presidential office in the face of the blockade and street violence of October 2003. With this precedent in mind, it seems worthwhile to compare the early MNR period (from April 1952 until the conclusion of the major reforms in the mid-1950s) with the current MAS-led program of transformations. The object of this comparison is once again to shed light on the originality of the latest project of national refoundation.

As in the previous section, it is important to start the analysis with a word of caution. Few observers in mid-1953 were able to assess with any degree of accuracy the nature and scale of the changes then underway. It is equally likely that appraisals made less than halfway through the Morales five-year term will be similarly incomplete. Nevertheless, there are some preliminary lessons from this comparison that may provide some guidance for the current conjuncture.

The shock impact of revolutionary mobilization of the early 1950s was of a different order of magnitude from the fears (let alone the practices) of 2006– 2008. There was a political police force with repressive powers, including "concentration camps," and opposition newspapers were liable to be seized and closed (for example, *Los Tiempos*, the leading daily in Cochabamba). The country's stock of weaponry was distributed in three equal parts to the security forces, the trade unions, and the peasant *sindicatos*. It led to a far more drastic redistribution of assets and power than anything attempted by the democratically elected and constitutionally constrained government of President Morales and the MAS. When his critics accuse him of importing totalitarian practices from Venezuela, they forget this more homegrown model of arbitrary power. Thus, the MNR, which now figures so prominently within the opposition, suppresses its own history and the popular origins of its power.

Nationalism was the dominant theme of the 1950s, whereas today the stress is on Bolivia's "multi" and "pluri" national identities. From a contemporary standpoint, the national revolution tried to impose a homogenous mestizo identity that falsified the ethnic, linguistic, and cultural realities of the society. The MNR relabeled the *indios* as campesinos and presented this as a liberation—the incorporation of the excluded rural masses into the dominant society. Today the MAS sees itself reversing this distortion, allowing the true majority of indigenous peoples and nations to free themselves from subordination to a European elite that had maintained its ascendancy through control of a centralized state. This is certainly a major contrast between the two projects of refoundation, but it can be overstated. The results of land reform, universal suffrage, and the spread of mass primary education in the 1950s were to open up new opportunities for social organization and political participation for the rural masses, most of which can be described as indigenous. The centralized state was not so powerful that it could suppress these identities; on the contrary, its stability depended upon striking a modus vivendi with the best-organized groups. The indigenous claims of today are based on the new opportunities and avenues for expression created through the national revolution. Moreover, they are largely articulated in Spanish (the principal language of the 2007 Constitution as well). So the current refoundation of the republic on "original" lines represents both an extension of an earlier tradition, as well as a break with some of its rigidities. It would seem that this is not an essentialist "Indian" repudiation of European exclusivism, but rather a renegotiation of the terms of the preexisting bargain, perhaps shifting some more opportunities from a white minority to a variety of indigenous claimants, but still with the mestizo mass of the population holding the balance.

Large-scale redistributions of social opportunity between competing collective identities are bound to produce impassioned debates and intense emotions, as rival claims to entitlement are asserted. However, by comparison with the zero-sum conflicts and polarized discourses of the 1950s, Bolivia's contemporary debates are remarkably open and thoughtful. Successive chapters in this volume have illustrated the extent to which alternative positions are being articulated with care and moderation, and on the assumption that the arbiter is a public opinion that can be swayed one way or the other according to the quality of the arguments. Evo and the MAS are capable of securing substantial electoral support even in the eastern lowlands; the voters of El Alto may at present seem the most radical, but not long ago they were persuaded to vote for Goni, and even for the ex-dictator Hugo Banzer. In short, there is now a real contest for the hearts and minds of an autonomous citizenry. No president of Bolivia can any longer afford to take the loyalty of his traditional supporters for granted. This was something the MNR learned quite slowly and painfully after 1952. It is a far more evident and pressing constraint on the current leadership of the MAS.

In 1952, the national revolution was often presented as a total break with all that had preceded it. Yet in truth, there remained major lines of continuity that both guided and constrained that refoundation. The policies of economic nationalism pursued after the revolution were in many respects just the application of principles already laid down in the Constitution of 1938, but not effectively implemented in the years that followed. The April revolution was a violent upheaval, but it conferred its mandate on a president and vice president who served for the four-year term to which they (convincingly) claimed they had been elected in the overturned elections of 1951. Crucial old institutions such as the Corporación Boliviana de Fomento (CBF) and Yacimientos Petrolíferos Fiscales Bolivianos (YPFB) coexisted with the new entities created by the revolution, like Comibol and the Central Obrera Boliviana (COB). In short, the refoundation welded features of the old order with creations of the new. The MAS has also innovated, reendowing YPFB with new assets and responsibilities, establishing a constituent assembly to run concurrently with the Congress, and so forth. But Evo did not come to power through a coup or an act of revolutionary discontinuity, and he has not (so far) been threatened by a coup (as happened to Chávez in 2002) or an invasion (Castro's Bay of Pigs). So the balance between continuity and innovation is tilted more toward the former than would be the case in more undemocratic settings. So far, at least, key bridging institutions like the National Electoral Court and the Central Bank remain intact. So Bolivia is attempting to refound its institutions within a democratic environment, with a substantial proportion of the citizenry supporting both the direction of change and a process of peaceful evolution. The originality of the current experiment could therefore reside in its potential to reconcile two tendencies which have never hitherto flowed together. In a previous volume, I argued, "The country has a long, rich and quite sophisticated tradition of liberal constitutional government, but one challenged at various points by mobilization from below, often at the behest of *caudillos.*" In general, the constitutional tradition "restricted participation to a social elite of *gente decente,* and the participatory tradition tended to overflow and swamp the formal channels set by constitutional proprieties" (Whitehead 2001, 21). For a viable democracy to emerge in Bolivia, it would be necessary to establish arrangements in which constitutionalism and participation would flow together rather than clashing and alternating. This is still a pending task, which could—in principle—be addressed by the Constituent Assembly.

Although the 1952 revolution seemed to have tremendous momentum at the outset, it ran into increasing difficulties by the late 1950s and was overthrown by the military in 1964. From the contemporary standpoint, the MNR regime is remembered not so much for its initial radicalism but for its subsequent stagnation, failure, and, indeed (many would say), reversal of direction. So much so that, on the fiftieth anniversary of the revolution, the leaders of the MNR chose to maintain a deafening silence about the earlier achievements of their movement. In fact, Goni deliberately vacated that ideological space, leaving a large gap in Bolivia's collective memory, a gap that was filled by the alternative narrative offered by the MAS. Naturally, Evo and his team have no reason to celebrate a precedent that belongs to their bitterest rivals. Moreover, comparisons between 1952 and 2005 raise the awkward issue of how to ensure that the MAS does not eventually replicate the reversals of the MNR. Nevertheless, from a nonpartisan point of view, it is worth considering why the national revolution faltered, and what lessons can be drawn from that experience.

Bolivia's international vulnerability certainly contributed to the disappointing trajectory of the 1952 revolution. The Korean War was coming to an end, and the associated temporary boom in commodity prices was about to go into reverse. So this was an unpromising time to pursue policies of economic nationalism that shut out international capital and expertise and weakened ties to traditional export markets. In addition, the accentuation of the Cold War left little space between Washington and Moscow for those who favored autochthonous policies of radical participation. The leadership of the MNR was soon polarized between those willing to pay the price for good relations with the United States and those drawn toward an anti-imperialist discourse. Initially the MNR could perhaps hope for assistance from neighboring Argentina's military populist protector, but Perón was overthrown in 1955, and after that the bipolarity became starker. The founder of the MNR, Víctor Paz Estenssoro, opted for the Alliance for Progress, while his trade union vice president faced a U.S. veto and gravitated toward Cuba following the Cuban Revolution. This sketch may contain some thought-provoking parallels with the present, but the Cold War is over, Chávez may fare better than Perón, commodity prices could stay high thanks to China, and perhaps the leadership of the MAS will prove more cohesive than that of the early MNR. In all probability, it is domestic, rather than external factors that will prove more decisive.

The internal processes that first bolstered and then undermined the national revolution could also have some contemporary relevance. There were problems with elite rotation, especially since the inherited rules specified a four-year presidential term with no immediate reelection. This meant that since a single party could count on an almost automatic electoral majority, the vice president in one term was the ostensible heir apparent for the next. Factions and patronage cliques were formed and pitted against each other according to this logic. Moreover, power within the ruling coalition was not just a matter of personal ascendancy; the revolution also created collective actors entitled to quotas and ministerial positions. It also encouraged direct democracy at the workplace and in the neighborhood. Thus strikes, demonstrations, and even armed versions of direct action became routine instruments of pressure on decision makers. After 1956, when repressive police structures were reined in, leaders of the revolution had to contend with mass protests from their own supporters, and with open clashes between rival revolutionary factions. This was what eventually opened the way to the restoration of military rule. Clearly, today's MAS government has the potential to head off such outcomes, but it also faces some similar dilemmas, as events in the mining camp of Huanuni and elsewhere have shown.[2]

The MNR's loss of momentum was not solely due either to adverse international pressures or to internal political factionalism. There was also the issue of effective policy making and competent administration. In the initial radical phase of the revolution, an already-overstretched state apparatus was assigned many additional tasks for which it was singularly ill equipped. There was a considerable loss of expertise, as officials associated with the prerevolutionary order were dismissed or left to go abroad, and the incoming cohort of public officials was often inexperienced and unprepared for the complex responsibilities they assumed. Between 1952 and 1964, the MNR's cadres were purged or selectively retrained, so that the ruling party became a more coherent instrument of government, but a less faithful representation of the social forces that had made the revolution. By the 1980s, the next generation of MNR leaders consisted of quite experienced technocrats or professional politicians, but they were also far removed in their outlook from their radicalized predecessors. This may help to explain why, half a century after 1952, the MNR seemed so completely out of touch with its own origins.

It remains to be seen how Evo and the MAS will cope with the challenge of forming a new stratum of public policymakers capable of handling the complex tasks of modern government. The MNR does not offer the only possible response—Brazil's PT, Cuba's Communist Party, and indeed the Chávez administration all had to grapple with comparable challenges. It may be that this time a substantively higher level of general education, a broader base of training and experience (including a relatively diverse and competent private sector), and a more pragmatic approach to policymaking can be combined to produce a more durable and socially responsible governing apparatus. Perhaps there are even some legacies from the MNR experience that can be rescued and incorporated into the new project. All this remains to be seen, and such evidence will be vital for any eventual assessment of the experiment in refounding the republic.

Although the prospects for Evo and the MAS remain open, it is worth recalling an underlying reality that did much to determine the relative failure of the previous MNR experiment. Neither public employment nor the private sector proved capable of providing stable job opportunities to the revolution's supporters during the 1950s and 1960s. That goes far toward explaining the bitterness of the party's factional infighting and the regime's difficulties in maintaining social control. Turning to the contemporary scene, whatever their legitimizing doctrines and intentions, Evo and the MAS will have to contend with a labor market overwhelmingly characterized by informality and benefiting relatively little from Bolivia's comparative advantages in the world economy. Only one-fifth of university graduates obtain stable employment. Out-migration is continuing on a massive scale, helping to generate income through remittances but depriving the country of a relatively educated workforce. A genuine and durable refoundation of the republic would have to turn this structural reality around.

Constrained Originality and the Prospects for a Bolivian Refoundation

In history and social life, complete originality is extremely rare. For political reasons, it may be expedient to magnify the discontinuity between a government's present intentions and a country's past experience, but in comparative terms there are few absolute break points or comprehensive refoundations. The Morales administration would do well to achieve a durable course correction, taking into account the lessons of various previous episodes, borrowing from elsewhere if appropriate, but concentrating above all on laying down the foundations for a robust and broad-based national agreement and for more reliable government performance in the future than has proved feasible in the recent past. This is a limited and pragmatic objective, but nonetheless worth pursuing for all that. It may need to be dressed up more grandiosely, with reference to a *"cosmovisión andina"* or to "twenty-first century socialism"—such embellishments can solidify support—but such phrases should not be allowed to obscure the essential test of success. The old rules of the political game were not producing satisfactory results, the economy was proving incapable of generating either the employment or the investment required for a prosperous future, and the mechanisms of social inclusion and popular participation lacked legitimacy.

Major improvements are possible in all these areas, and the majority-backed Morales administration has an unusual opportunity to bring these about. The international economic and political context for this experiment is also exceptionally favorable. The outcome could be called a refoundation of the republic, and it might rally sufficient support to sustain itself against some inevitable resistance and backlash. But the secret of success is not indiscriminately to discard or disregard all previous accomplishments. Not everything in the previous constitution was bad; much that was worth defending was simply never implemented. Not all the practices of bargaining and coalition building associated with the years of *partidocracia* were irredeemable; there is still a need for tolerance, compromise, and the invention of mediating institutions and procedures. Previous efforts at state building, decentralization, economic nationalism, macroeconomic stabilization, land reform, popular participation, plurinationalism, and even market development were not all entirely worthless. They can be reshaped and incorporated into the process of national refoundation. Admittedly, this would not be entirely original; instead, it would be a partial reformulation of ideas and experiences that are deeply rooted in the collective national memory. It would be a highly constrained expression of Bolivia's political originality. But that rootedness, that social legibility, is what could make the next round of national refoundation more durable, effective, and legitimate than its predecessors. Otherwise there is the risk—well exemplified in the country's previous history—that unrooted innovations will be rejected as the artificial imitation of foreign models, or the one-sided imposition of structures designed to serve a limited sector of the community at the expense of all the rest. Constrained originality could truly provide the foundation for a more consensual future, whereas a utopian dogma of unconstrained refoundation is more likely to recreate the vicious cycles of the past.

Chapter 1. *The "Long Memory" of Ethnicity in Bolivia and Some Temporary Oscillations*

1. This was the dual generic category that was used in the census when people were asked to identify if they belonged to a specific ethnic people. It was adopted because many (especially in the highlands) currently prefer to adopt the generic term *originario*, which they themselves coined, rather than the term *indígena*, a term used by others to describe them and which continues to have negative connotations (Molina and Albó 2006, 33). The statistical figures cited in this introduction are based on those published in the 2001 census.

2. In the lowland departments, this Andean presence is highest in Santa Cruz, where 17 percent of the population is Quechua, and 4 percent Aymara. Indigenous lowland peoples make up another 17 percent.

3. A survey by UNIR (2006), conducted only in departmental capitals plus El Alto, shows that 56 percent of those who identified themselves as Aymaras, 76 percent of those who identified as Quechuas, 79 percent of those who identified as Chiquitanos, 72 percent of those who identified as Guaranís, and 76 percent of those who said they did not belong to any indigenous people also referred to themselves as mestizos.

4. The *mita* consisted of compulsory periodic labor by the *ayllu* and community Indians in the mine of Potosí. They engaged in it to maintain their rights to their land.

5. In Jesús de Machaqa, a predominantly Aymara community to the southwest of La Paz, I have heard oral histories that refer to the "*Cacique* Party" as opposed to the "Liberal Party."

6. This was a personal comment dating from the 1970s, but it was also published in the press.

7. In Bolivia, the advent of bilingual education was slower in coming about.

8. The term *indiecito* was used in the testimony of a mineworker published by Nash (1976).

9. The ethnic factor had been used by some supporters of military dictatorships. The work of Fausto Reinaga (1969), for example, was read by influential military figures who went as far as asking him to help them write their speeches.

10. See Carlos Miranda's chapter in this volume.

11. I borrow the term *indio permitido* from current Mexican indigenous political literature (for instance, Hale 2004). The term *indio alzado* is very common throughout Latin America as a rebellious indian, with a wide range of connotations.

12. The Mexican presidents Porfirio Díaz and Benito Juárez were biologically *indígenas*, but so as not to appear as such they became known for their *anti-indígena* policies.

13. In the sense of the ethnic "nations" of Aymaras, Quechuas, Guaranís, etc. (as in the political thesis of the CSUTCB in 1983).

14. Tristan Marof is the pseudonym of Gustavo Adolfo Navarro, an influential writer and socialist politician of the 1930s. José Antonio Arze was one of the founders of the Marxist Partido de la Izquierda Revolucionaria in 1940.

Chapter 2. *Let the Mestizos Stand Up and Be Counted*

1. In addition, 2 percent were black, and the rest unspecified.

2. This lack of a mestizo option takes us back in history to the beginning of the colonial period, when mestizos were also excluded from the census.

3. The *media luna* (half moon) refers to the four "eastern" departments (Santa Cruz, Tarija, Beni, and Pando), although Tarija is geographically more southern than eastern. They are those that voted "yes" for departmental autonomy in July 2006.

4. Franz Tamayo is another important intellectual from the first half of the twentieth century. His book *Creación de la pedagogía nacional* (1944 [1910]) has become a classic.

5. Army commander Manuel Belzu Humerez led a military coup against elected president José Ballivián in 1848 and presided over the country until 1855. He championed the popular classes and indigenous majority in the political process.

6. The Kataristas, from the 1970s onwards, defended cultural diversity, respect for the languages and customs of indigenous peoples. One of its leaders, Víctor Hugo Cárdenas, was vice president from 1993 to 1997.

Chapter 3. *Oversimplifying Identities*

1. Clearly this is not always the case. There are ethnic groups whose members are distributed in a multiplicity of ways without this affecting their primordial identity. However, the diverse nature of Bolivia (large differences in levels and stages of development in different parts of the country, different levels of coexistence with other groups, different degrees of stigmatization, etc.) have generated important differences between individuals.

2. See, for example, Sen (2006), Blu (1980), or Carter Bentley (in Banks 1996).

3. Sometimes it is argued that while there may be a diversity of potentially relevant identities, not all have the same importance. This is highly relative and dependent on what we want to analyze. If the *desideratum* is to understand which identities are particularly relevant for war, then it will probably be the case that ethnic, religious, ideological, national, and regional identities will predominate, since these

explain a goodly proportion of violent conflicts throughout the history of mankind. But in other types of analysis being a member of a particular family or class will be the central identities, whilst others are of secondary importance.

4. The CRISE survey was carried out only in Achacachi, El Alto, Ascención de Guarayos, and in the city of Santa Cruz, and thus it is not nationally representative. However, in view of the ethnic make-up of these cities chosen and their particular characteristics (high ethnic politicization in the case of Achacachi, the fact that El Alto is the main receiver of migration flows), its findings are highly relevant.

5. See Rivera (2003) and Barragán (1992) for a discussion of the relation between class and ethnicity.

6. Inequalities in cultural status are understood as differences in recognition and hierarchical status (de facto) of norms, customs, and cultural practices of different groups (CRISE 2006). Most pluralist societies experience disputes between different cultural groups, not just in the distribution of political and economic power but also on issues of cultural status and recognition. Inequalities in cultural status are generally subsumed by the institutions and practices of the state, both implicitly and explicitly (CRISE 2006)

7. See Sanjinés (2004) for an excellent example of discourse analysis.

Chapter 4. *Regionalism Revisited*

1. As a result of the social rebellions that have taken place in Bolivia in the first few years of the twenty-first century, in some regions this oligarchic ideology has tended to change and become more popular in its nature.

2. A pertinent recent example that shows the sort of irrational pressure being exerted by the regions in the search to "be respected" is the structure of the state oil and gas company, YPFB (Yacimientos Petrolíferos Fiscales Bolivianos), in which all regions want a presence. Following impassioned debates, backed up by road blockades, civil strikes, and hunger strikes in the departments producing hydrocarbons, the Congress finally resolved the conflict by ruling that the executive presidency of YPFB should be in La Paz, while the vice presidencies should be situated in the province of Gran Chaco (Tarija), Santa Cruz, and Cochabamba, respectively. Furthermore, two management offices were established, one in Camiri (in the department of Santa Cruz) and the other in Sucre. See Article 23 of the Law of Hydrocarbons (May 2005). It seems improbable that this sort of institutional fragmentation will help YPFB prosper.

3. The best-known person to uphold of this point of view was Gonzalo Sánchez de Lozada, a bitter enemy of decentralization in any form.

4. For a pioneer study that elucidates this regional conflict, see Whitehead (1972).

5. See *Colección de Leyes, Decretos, Ordenes y Resoluciones Supremas*, 2nd cuerpo, tomo 1. Sucre, 1861.

6. For a broad discusión of this issue, see Roca (2005, 49–98). For a searching critique of Participación Popular, see Barrios Suvelza (2002, 69–116).

7. The Morales government at one point came up with the proposal to the Constituent Assembly to create forty-two autonomous regions that would be allowed to elect their own authorities. On the face of it, this sought to reduce the authority of departments and their prefects. *La Razón* (La Paz), November 2, 2006. The negative response to this was quick in making itself felt, and the proposal was shelved.

8. The main feature of Arguedas's work—his history, sociology, and narrative writing—is his analysis of regionalism. The same is true of G. René Moreno in the nineteenth century, who should indeed be considered the pioneer in the study of such problems. This cannot be said of the present-day authors working in the fields of historiography and the social sciences, who tend to ignore the problems to which regionalism gives rise.

9. For a comprehensive and lucid analysis of this, see Lynch (1962).

10. Swayed by the imperial arrogance of former times, Buenos Aires delayed several decades and only recognized Paraguay's independence after it had tried to crush it in alliance with Brazil and Uruguay. This was known as the War of the Triple Alliance, or in Paraguay as the "Great War" (1865–70).

11. Bolívar upheld the thesis of *uti possidetis*, meaning that the change of political regime should not alter the jurisdictions of the viceroyalties, a thesis that did not prosper on account of the nationalist feelings which had flourished during the period of Spanish colonialism. Thus, twenty Hispanic American republics emerged, not the four advocated by Bolivar.

12. In addition to its geographical proximity to the Pacific, La Paz was a very rich province. Its revenues came from the tribute paid by its sizeable indigenous population, from the production of coca (an indispensable input in the mining industry), and the commercial flows between the viceroyalties of Perú and Río de la Plata.

13. Sucre's claims to be the capital of Bolivia were given new force in 2007 by the Constituent Assembly. Sucre, supported by other opposition-dominated departments, resorted to demanding that the executive and legislature be restored to it. Should it fail to succeed in this respect, it is likely to continue with its rebellious stance, refusing to accept any solution that falls short of *capitalía plena.*

14. This new term has come to be used in the last few years. It takes its name from the geographical shape of the eastern part of Bolivia (which it compares with the phases of the moon). The new macroregion stretches in an arc from the northwest of the country, through the whole eastern areas, and ends in the extreme south in Tarija.

15. Along with the fact that Tarija has become the main department producing hydrocarbons, it shares similar racial and cultural characteristics with the other eastern departments (Santa Cruz, Beni, and Pando): a predominantly Hispanic heritage and a relatively small influence on the part of indigenous groups.

16. A sign of this tendency is the position adopted by David Choquehuanca, Evo Morales's foreign minister. Shortly after his appointment, he suggested that school-

children be given coca leaves as part of their school breakfast ration. He also announced that Bolivian diplomats should necessarily speak an indigenous language.

17. Kollasuyo refers to the southeastern quandrant of Tawantinsuyo, "The Four United Regions," as the Incaic state was called in its native terminology.

18. For many years, the term *camba* was used to denote the lower social orders in the *oriente*. It had a connotation that was both pejorative and racist. In recent years, it has undergone a radical change and is now employed as a proud emblem of *oriente* society as a whole, seeking to erase the differences between indigenous and nonindigenous peoples from Santa Cruz.

19. The term *colla* was born in the *oriente* as a generic label for all peoples from the west of Bolivia, whether of indigenous origin or not, and with the same pejorative and racist connotation as *camba*. It has gradually gained popularity and is ever more widely accepted among broad sectors of the Andean population.

20. The Massacre of Ayo Ayo took place in the church of this village, located in the Altiplano of the department of La Paz. A group of young recruits (all of them members of the Chuquisaca upper class) from the Sucre Battalion were killed by Aymara irregulars who were supporting the La Paz federal troops under the orders of José Manuel Pando. This act created deep regional resentment in Sucre, which was opposed to La Paz, which endures to this day. In Sucre's memorial cemetery, monuments to the "Martyrs of Ayo Ayo" stand prominently in the center of the park.

21. For a summary of the 1899 civil war, also known as the Federal War, see Jose Luis Roca (2005a).

22. Public opinion in the west, which inclines toward the indigenous position, neither understands nor accepts that large-scale livestock rearing requires between five and ten hectares to graze each head of cattle. Not only peasant leaders but also politicians argue, ironically, that it is better to turn oneself into a cow in order to gain rights to the land.

23. In recent years, a Landless Movement (Movimiento sin Tierra) has appeared, inspired by the Brazilian organization of the same name. It has urged its followers to squat on landed properties in the *oriente*. It fell into discredit after there were allegations that its main leader supposedly possessed large extensions of land in the Chaco.

Chapter 5. *Oppressed or Privileged Regions?*

1. Concepts used by Silvia Rivera and Alvaro García with reference to the indigenous population of the west. Sergio Antelo, the founder and leader of Nación Camba, reformulated the concept, applying it to mestizo *cambas* in Santa Cruz. The more precise term used by Antelo is "state colonialism" in the sense of the domination of the region/nation/culture/race by the state.

2. The term comes from the book by Fernando Mayorga (1997), *¿Ejemonías? Democracia representativa y liderazgos locales,* which deals with different types of leadership in the 1990s.

3. Not including Santa Cruz, since for that year we only have the voting population for the city of Santa Cruz alone and not for the department as a whole.

4. Here we include direct taxes on the profits of mining companies, tariffs on mining exports, export licenses, and various other additional taxes.

5. There were, however, important differences between the departments. In 1903 and 1913, in the case of La Paz, Cochabamba, and Tarija these signified less than 1 percent of their total income, despite the fact that they signified nearly 10 percent of the total income of Santa Cruz. In 1923, the tax on beer in La Paz represented 5 percent of total income, and in Oruro taxes on different types of alcohol constituted 14 percent of departmental income.

6. This distinction is based on that made for revenue since 1872. Under "central state" are all the expenditures of the national state relating to the workings of the central bureaucracy, mostly concentrated in La Paz after 1900. Under "noncentral" we would include the diverse and heterogeneous spending of the state bureaucracy in each department.

7. The budgets of 1949 and 1954 show a return to the proportions reached at the beginning of the twentieth century.

8. In 1923, the programmed total for tax receipts for mining in the departments of Oruro and Potosí were Bs. 298,324.17, the equivalent of 5.5 percent of national revenues.

9. A precedent for the system of royalties was contained in the Law of June 20, 1921, issued during the Bautista Saavedra administration, and in the Organic Petroleum Law (Roca 1999 [1979], 174; UNDP 2004, 8 and 41). Subsequently, ratification of the "Ley Busch" was promulgated in January 15, 1957, stipulating that "it corresponds to the producer departments in fulfillment of the terms specified in the Law of July 15, 1938" (Roca 1999 [1979], 189).

10. In the 1940s, Yacimientos Petrolíferos Fiscales Bolivianos (YPFB) achieved important increases in its productive capacity, tripling the output achieved by Standard Oil (Miranda 1999, 248).

11. The percentage for La Paz, by contrast, was 28 percent of the budget for regional administration, although it accounted for 63 percent of prefectural and 69 percent of municipal resources (UNDP 2004b, 47).

Chapter 6. *State-Society Relations in Bolivia*

1. See Joel Migdal (1988 and 2001) on strong states and weak societies Mark Granovetter (1973) coined the phrase "the strength of weak ties" to describe the effectiveness of weak social ties in socially and ethnically segmented labor markets.

2. See Whitehead (2002) and O' Donnell (1999) for critiques of the mainstream rational choice political-science literature on state/society relations in Latin America. Whitehead (1975) has focused specifically on the sectional nature of state rule in the Bolivian case.

3. Also see Barragán and Roca (2006) and Guillermo O'Donnell (1993) for a com-

parative discussion of the implications of discontinuous state development across regions of the world.

Chapter 7. *The Weakness of Excess*

1. Interestingly, Norbert Elias (1997) has revived study of the passions and their containment in macrosocial development with his theory of civilization processes.

2. As is well known, recent scholarship has also focused attention on the vertical division of powers, or checks and balances, that arises under both federalism and decentralization.

3. I refer to a specific example of Bobbio's work, as in other publications he appears to distance himself from this amalgamation (Bobbio 1985, 7–45). It is necessary to add that here another problem arises: the identification that Bobbio makes between liberalism and the rule of law (Bobbio 2004, 25).

4. Recall that Greek democracy was also not concerned with limitations on power, or with horizontal accountability, or with the protection of individual freedoms. Where contemporary Bolivia differs from Greece is in its commitment to equality before the law.

5. The doctrinaires of Popular Participation had declared that the Law of Political Participation was an "offering to the world." Here again we encounter the belief that Bolivia was generating a process of universal significance.

6. *La Razón*, September 12, 2007. When the judicial branch took this decision, the Constitutional Tribunal was facing the trial proceedings initiated by Evo Morales against four of its magistrates.

7. *El Deber*, June 2007.

8. *La Razón*, September 12, 2007.

9. *La Razón*, September 11, 2007

10. It is difficult to know just how conscious the vice president was of the Jacobin phenomenon when he compares himself with the Jacobins. The comparisons emerge from an interview with him in *El Mundo* on July 6, 2006.

11. *La Prensa*, January 24, 2007.

12. In October 2006, informal mineworkers clashed with unionized workers to gain control of one of Bolivia's most productive tin-mining centers. There were numerous casualties, and the dispute was only resolved when the government took most of the informal workers on to the state payroll.

13. *La Prensa*, August 12, 2006.

14. *La Razón*, August 28, 2006.

15. "Propuesta de un constituyente masista," *La Prensa*, August 12, 2007.

16. *Correo del Sur*, April 20, 2007.

17. Ibid.

18. *La Razón*, August 11, 2006.

19. *La Razón*, September 4, 2007.

20. Ibid.

21. See, for example, the declarations of the president of the commission dealing with the vision of the country (*visión del país*) in *La Prensa,* September 20, 2007. See also the position of the Confederación de Ayllus del Occidente Boliviano in *Correo del Sur,* April 20, 2007. Peasant and indigenous organizations from the lowlands and highlands upheld the argument of the treason of the MAS in *La Razón,* August 3, 2007.

22. *La Razón,* September 19, 2007.

23. *La Razón,* July 3, 2007.

24. *La Prensa,* June 13, 2007.

Chapter 8. *The Development of Constituent Power in Bolivia*

1. The assembly's commendation to Bolivar was that the constitution would be "the daughter of his enlightenment and experience," and that it should be the best and most liberal of its time. It involved some unusual institutions, such as the life-term presidency. The members of the assembly established a commission to temper certain discrepancies, taking care not to offend the will of the Liberator. One controversial matter was religion. The draft constitution made no mention of it. Bolivar sent a message justifying this, suggesting that "in a political constitution, the profession of religious faith has no place." This implied the separation of church and state. The issue of religion was of great importance to the elite of the time, which managed to overturn this stipulation, approving a text that declared the Catholic Church as the church of the state, to the exclusion of all others. See Baptista Morales (2005).

2. Article 230 reads:

I.   This Constitution may be partially reformed, once the necessity for reform is declared. This will be determined with precision by means of an ordinary law approved by two-thirds of the members present in each of the Chambers.

II. That law can be initiated in either of the two Chambers in the form laid down by the Constitution.

III. The law declaring the need for reform will be sent to the executive for promulgation, without its being able to exercise a right of veto.

Article 231 reads:

I.   In the new constitutional term, the matter will be considered by the Chamber which drafted the reform proposals and, if approved by a two-thirds majority, it will pass to the other [Chamber] for revision, which also will require two-thirds support.

II. The other procedures will be in accordance with those which the Constitution lays down regarding relations between the two Chambers.

III. The Chambers will consider and vote on the reforms, adjusting them to the dispositions set out in the Law Declaring Necessity for the purpose.

IV. Once approved, the reform will pass to the Executive for promulgation, without the president having the ability to delay it.

V. When the amendment relates to the constitutional term of the president or vice president of the republic, it will come into effect in the following constitutional term. Bolivia 2004, Constitución del estado (texto reformado). La Paz: Presidencia de la Republica.

3. The first partial amendment to the 1967 constitution came about with Law 1585 of August 12, 1994 (Constitutional Reform Law), and 1615 of February 6, 1995, both during the presidency of Gonzalo Sánchez de Lozada.

4. The second partial reform of the 1967 constitution was approved by Law 2631 of February 20 2002 (the Constitutional Reform Law), and by Law 2650 of April 13, 2004 (Law of Incorporation into the Constitutional Text), during the presidency of Carlos Mesa.

5. Congress widened the terms of reference of the Law of Necessity, whose Article 4 (which originally included only a citizens' legislative initiative and a constitutional referendum) stipulated that "the people deliberate and govern both by means of their representatives and by means of a Constituent Assembly, the citizens' legislative initiative and the constitutional referendum, established under this Constitution."

6. The constitution specifies the natural line of succession in the event of a president's resignation: the vice president, the president of the Senate, the president of the Chamber of Deputies, and, finally, the president of the Supreme Court. In this case, since there was no vice president (Mesa having occupied this role before he became president), the next in line were Vaca Diez, Cossio, and Rodríguez Veltzé.

7. Law 3089, of July 6, 2005, during the presidency of Eduardo Rodríguez Veltzé amended Article 93 of the constitution.

8. Law 3090, of July 6, 2005, interpreted Article 109 of the constitution, incorporating an interpretative norm in its text with respect to the presidential appointment of prefects following direct elections under universal suffrage.

9. See, for example, Domingo (2001).

10. Textually, this states that "the people deliberate and govern through their representatives and through the Constituent Assembly, the citizens' legislative initiative, and the referendum, established by this Constitution and subject to rules established by law."

11. Supreme Decree No. 27507, of May 19, 2004, defined the wording of the questions to be asked in the binding referendum.

12. Law 3058 on hydrocarbons was promulgated by the president of Congress, Hormando Vaca Diez, on May 19, 2005. He acted in lieu of President Carlos Mesa, who paradoxically had conducted the referendum on this issue. Disagreements arose between the executive and the Congress over how far this norm should be taken.

13. The question asked in the referendum on autonomies, and approved by Article 4 of the law convening it (Ley de Convocatoria) says: "Do you agree to giving the Constituent Assembly the binding mandate to establish a regime of departmental autonomy, to be applied directly after the promulgation of the new Constitution in

the departments where this referendum produces a majority, in such a way that the authorities are directly elected by the citizens and receive from the national state those executive powers, normative and administrative attributes, and economic and financial resources assigned to them by the new constitution and the laws?"

14. The Special Law 3091, of July 6, 2005, mandated the convening of the Constituent Assembly.

15. The text of Article 25 says, "The Constituent Assembly will approve the text of the new Constitution by two-thirds of the votes of members the Assembly present, in accordance with Title II of Part IV of the current Political Constitution of the State."

16. The participation rate in the election of assembly members was 84.5%. The MAS won 50.8% of the vote and 139 of the seats.

17. Article 1 of the rules declared that

the Constituent Assembly is *originaria*, because it is derived from the people's will for change, [the people being] the embodiment of national sovereignty. The Constituent Assembly is an extraordinary political event, emerging from the crisis of the state, derived from social struggles and installed by popular mandate. The Constituent Assembly, convened by Law 3364 of March 6, 2006, is unitary, indivisible, and it is the maximum expression of democracy. It is legitimately superior to the constituted power. The Constituent Assembly has full powers to write a new constitutional text and is mandated to transform and construct a New Bolivian State. Because of the characteristics of Bolivia's constitutional process, the Constituent Assembly does not interfere in the normal workings of the currently constituted powers until the approval of the new constitutional text and the new institutional design. This new constitutional text will be subjected to the approval of the Bolivian people in a referendum. From the moment it is approved, the mandate of the new text will come into force and [with it] the construction of the New Bolivian State.

18. Article 70 on the voting system to be adopted stipulated:

The decisions of the Constituent Assembly will be approved, as a general rule, by an absolute majority in commissions and in plenary. The Constituent Assembly will approve by two-thirds of members present in the following instances: a) the final text of the new Political Constitution of the State presented to the plenary by the Committee on Reconciliation and Style [Concordancias y Estilo]. b) the articles of the draft constitution that encounter objections and an alternative text being submitted by a third of the members present will pass to a second reading to be held once all the articles that have not been objected to are approved. The objections of minorities cannot exceed three articles. If these articles do not receive the support of two-thirds of the votes of those present in a second reading they will be submitted to the sovereign people in the referendum to approve the new Political Constitution of the State. c) in all those cases expressly determined by the Present Regulations.

Chapter 9. *Constitution and Constitutional Reform in Bolivia*

1. Here I use the preliminary distinction suggested by Antonio Negri (1993), although the reflections and the usage developed here are my own.

2. In 1990, lowland indigenous peoples staged a march from the Amazon region to La Paz demanding legal recognition for their territories, organizations, and systems of authority. They also demanded the holding of a Constituent Assembly.

3. See García Linera et al. (2004). These include the Asamblea del Pueblo Guaraní (APG), representing the Guaranís and Tapietes; the Central de Pueblos Indígenas del Beni (CPIB), representing the Bauré, Canichana, Cayubaba, Itinama, More, Movima, Moxeño-trinitario, Moxeño-xaveriano, Sirionó, and Tsiname; the Central Indígena de la Región Amazónica (CIRABO), which brings together the Araona, Chácobo, Cabineño, Esse-ejja, Machineri, Pacaguara, Tacana, and Yaminagua; the Central de Pueblos Etnicos de Santa Cruz (CPESC), representing the Ayoreo, Chiquitano, Guaraní, and Guarayo; the Organización de las Capitanías Weehnayek; the Central de Pueblos Indígenas del Trópico de Cochabamba (CPITCO), which includes the Yuracaré and the Yuqui; the Central de Pueblos Indígena de La Paz (CPILAP), representing the Leco, Mosetén, and Tacana; the Central Indígena de Pueblos Originarios de la Amazonía de Pando (CIPOAP); and the Central Organizativa de los Pueblos Nativos Guarayo (COPNAG).

Chapter 10. *Gas and Its Importance to the Bolivian Economy*

1. GOR is a coefficient used to show the quantity of gas in cubic feet obtained jointly from producing a barrel of oil. The wells known as oil wells have a GOR lower than 5,000. From this number upward, production is denominated as gas and condensate.

2. Official figures for each year are published in April. In 2006, publication of the data was suspended. For this reason, figures for 2006 could not be officially confirmed.

3. See British Petroleum (2005). At the time of writing, data for 2006 were still not available.

Chapter 11. *Beyond Gas*

1. Total factor productivity refers to the additional (and often invisible) impact that technological change has over (more visible) labor and capital inputs in the production of any good or service.

2. Rodríguez Ostria (1999) analyzes the changes in Bolivia's productive structure arising from the liberalization of the country's economy and the construction of the railway from Antofagasta to Oruro at the beginning of the twentieth century. In the author's words, the local production "began to collapse, which since colonial times had supplied the country with shoes, flour, sugar, wines and other products 'of the land' and substitute these with attractive products churned out by Chilean, British or US factories. The triumph of capitalist mechanization over local manufacturers—

a hybrid and rudimentary mix of family craftwork and small-scale manufacture—brought radical change. Various regions, such as Cochabamba, Santa Cruz, and Tarija, which had previously enjoys exclusivity in supplying the domestic market suddenly found themselves affected by competition from overseas" (Rodríguez Ostria 1999, 291). The publication of the *1915 Bolivian Economic Guide* (*Guía Económica de Bolivia de 1915*) describes clothing factories and manufacturing industries in La Paz as "property of mestizo individuals and some indigenous groups" (Cámara Nacional de Industrias 1981, 25).

3. In previous studies, Wanderley (2002 and 2005) explored the widespread acceptance of this view and its influence on economic policy in Bolivia.

4. For a critical review of the literature on small-scale firms, industrial districts, and the informal sector, see Wanderley (1999).

5. The Herfindhal index shows that the degree of concentration of Bolivian exports in 1999 (0.05) was well below what was the case before the collapse of the tin economy (0.32). For more details, see United Nations Development Program (2005).

6. See United Nations Development Program (2005) for a complete series since 1950.

7. The Balassa index measures revealed comparative advantage for a group or subgroups of products. It is a ratio of ratios composed of the domestic ratio of gains and losses in market share of a country with respect to a world ratio of gains and losses in world market share, over a period of time.

8. See the International Trade Centre-UNCTAD database (2006), which estimates the dynamic competitiveness of exportable products for 100 countries worldwide. The most dynamic sectors in Bolivia for the 2000–2004 period include Brazil nuts, jewelry, leather products, textiles, and processed wood products.

9. For a more detailed analysis, see Wanderley (2004).

10. For a more detailed analysis see United Nations Development Program (2005) and Prats (2003).

Chapter 12. *Bolivia in a Global Setting*

1. For a fuller analysis of the period between 1952 and 2002, see Morales (2003)

2. Cárdenas, Ocampo, and Thorp (2000) prefer, rightly, the term Interventionist State-led Industrialization to the more conventional notion of Import Substitutive Industrialization, a model to which they are sympathetic. Ocampo (2004), among others, highlights the achievements of the ISLI as against the results of postreform neoliberalism. Critical views of ISLI are numerous, including Edwards (1993, 1995), Easterly (2001), and the comparative work of Barro and Sala-i-Martin (1995). More generally, as Fraga notes (2004), there is a correlation between populism and the ISLI model between 1950 and 1970.

3. Morales and Sachs (1990) provide an analysis of the policies of forced industrialization between 1950 and 1980.

4. The literature on DS 21060 is abundant. See, for example, Morales and Sachs (1990) and the references it contains.

5. Capitalization was a complicated version of privatization. It was the brainchild of Sánchez de Lozada and implemented by his government (1993–1997). See Morales (2001).

6. Even so, state employment remained at high levels.

7. There were objective reasons for this perception. Income distribution deteriorated greatly in the 1990s.

8. Similar phenomena occurred elsewhere in Latin America.

9. At this rhythm of growth, it would take eighty-seven years to double Bolivia's per capita GDP. For comparative purposes, it is worth noting that the most dynamic Asian economies double their GDP per capita every ten years.

10. The countries of the European Union preferred not to involve themselves in eradication, adopting a risk-minimizing strategy with the accent on alternative development programs (Van der Auwera 2004)

11. In part, the U.S. government proposed to use ATPDEA to offset the loss of Bolivian national income brought about by coca eradication. It is noteworthy that Bolivia, among the Andean countries, was the one most affected by coca eradication (Van der Auwera 2004).

12. Aguilar (2003) finds that in the 1990–95 period, there were significant bouts of overvaluation and undervaluation, but these were of short duration. In the period between 1996 and 2002, he finds that the path followed by the exchange rate followed closely that of the real exchange-rate equilibrium. At the end of 2002, the boliviano was slightly undervalued, not overvalued.

13. These figures need to be derived from inventories; 2007 estimates (as yet not entirely confirmed) suggest values that are considerably lower.

14. YPFB also faced major financial challenges.

15. This was the third time that oil had been nationalized in Bolivia. The first time was in 1937, following the Chaco War, and the second in 1969 (see the chapter by Carlos Miranda in this volume).

16. A full description of the scope of the May 2006 nationalization decree is to be found in Miranda (2006). See also Medinaceli (2006a) for the crucial taxation issues, and Oporto (2006) for the political fallout.

17. This can affect the market value of their investments and, ultimately, the valuation of their equity.

18. ATPDEA had been due to expire at the end of 2006, but it has been extended for six months since then. At the time of writing, there were indications that it might be extended again.

19. In the case that ATPDEA is not extended, the government proposed a scheme to subsidize exports to the United States in order to avoid job loss.

20. Due to their small size or nonexistence, surpluses on current account of the nonfinancial public sector financed only a small fraction of capital spending.

21. See Catena and Navajas (2006), who carried out a simulation to establish what would happen if there was a decline in international prices of energy and a fall in demand for gas in neighboring countries.

22. It is worth noting that the reserves situation in Bolivia is not exceptional for the region. All Bolivia's neighbors, enjoying the same favorable international context, had also been accumulating reserves.

23. For instance, the Indian steel company, Jindal, has signed a contract to exploit the iron reserves of El Mutún, close to the frontiers with Brazil.

Chapter 13. *The Perverse Effects of Globalization in Bolivia*

1. "Markets promote efficiency by means of competition and the division of labor, that is, the specialization that enables people and economies to focus on what they do best. Thanks to globalization, it is possible to take advantage of ever larger economies across the world and to have better access to flows of capital and technology and to benefit from cheaper imports and larger export markets. But markets do not necessarily guarantee that greater efficiency will benefit everyone. Countries have to be prepared to adopt the necessary policies, and in the case of the poorest countries they will possibly require the support of the international community to that end" (IMF 2000).

2. Adopting a term used by Immanuel Wallerstein, Arrighi (1997) considers globalization as an "evolutive" model that has enabled capitalism to become "the first historical system to include the whole world in its geography."

3. More precisely, it is argued that the financialization of the economy had its origins in the 1970s, a consequence of important changes in the international economy brought about by the policies of developed countries. The decision of the United States to devalue the dollar in 1971 and end a system based on fixed exchange rates encouraged speculation in the money markets. Similarly, the increased capital flows in the form of loans to underdeveloped countries—petrodollars—and the actions of the United States to finance its high deficits through savings from other continents brought about a flood of capital that inundated the international market (Martner 1988).

4. "Once re-established, the unilateral logic of capital expresses itself in the implementation of policies that have the same characteristics everywhere: high interest rates, cutting public social spending, dismantling policies of full employment and the systematic pursuit of restoring unemployment, reducing taxation on the wealthy, deregulation, privatisation, etc." (Amin 2001).

5. "A recent report by the World Bank (Global Economic Prospects and Developing Countries, 1995) argues that the growing integration of such countries into the World economy offers an excellent opportunity, perhaps the best, to increase over the long run the wealth of developing and industrial nations" (Qureshi 1996).

6. These policies consist of measures geared to achieving macroeconomic stability, external opening to encourage the expansion of trade and investment, the stim-

ulus toward competitiveness and productivity, as well as the debt management to facilitate the availability of resources (IMF 2000).

7. "A convergence of processes that has taken place within the country and outside has placed the nation state in crisis. The new conditions of production, accumulation and exchange have intensified all the flows (capital, people, technology, information) and reduced the ability to exercise control over its jurisdiction, but at the same time these continue as fundamental reference points for social action and international policy" (Laserna 2002).

8. "We should remember that a regime of accumulation is the amalgam of strategies and structures through which a group of government agencies and individual businessmen promotes, organizes, and regulates the expansion or the restructuring of the capitalist economy (Arrighi 1999, p23). This group of capitalist and government agencies institutionalizes power and the hegemony of specific fractions of the dominant class and ruling political groups, whose community of interests promotes the restructuring of the institutions of the state and of the capitalist economy in the quest for power and profit" (Orellana 2006).

9. For some intellectuals linked to neoliberalism, the three axes of the new political landscape, initiated in 1985, were representative democracy, the market economy, and multiculturalism (Romero 1999).

10. Dividends are distributed among the elderly in the form of the Bonosol, a subsidy of around US$200.

11. Official calculations estimate a loss to the economy of US$610 million and 59,000 jobs in the Chapare region on account of the clampdown on coca and cocaine production between 1997 and 2000 (Udape 2001).

12. Telling signs are the spectacular increase of indigenous peasant migrants to El Alto and the rising number of Bolivians resident (mostly illegally) in Argentina and Spain.

13. Attracting capital brought, in addition, serious social problems. This was reflected by the destructuring of traditional forms of peasant agriculture where communities were subjected to new commercial relationships and/or forced to migrate to permit mining activity to take place. There were also conflicts arising from the environmental impacts of mining activity.

14. According to YPFB, of the total reserves of gas in 2001 (proven and probable), 97 percent were new reserves and only 3 percent were those that already existed. The situation was similar for condensates.

15. Transport charges also favored the companies. While the tariff for transporting gas for the domestic market was set at US$0.41 per thousand cubic feet, the export tariff was US$0.22.

16. The pension reform was, in reality, a financial measure aimed at generating a substantial volume of domestic investment to finance private activities. This objective was never realized because the insolvency of the state led governments that

administered the reform (through a series of rulings) to use employees' contributions to help fund the fiscal deficit (Arze 2003).

17. In changing the patterns of employment, a number of things stand out, including the reduction in public sector employment from 22 percent to 12 percent, the persistent inability of the private sector to generate employment, and the explosive growth of the informal sector, which has increased to over 70 percent of those occupied in urban areas (Arze 2004).

18. It is worth mentioning that this is also present within foreign capital, which, taking advantage of depressed wages and the lack of any government oversight, has acclimatized itself to conditions in the labor market to raise its profitability.

Conclusion: *Bolivia's Latest "Refoundation"*

1. More generally there is evidence that at key turning points both the Venezuelans and the Cubans have tended to advise moderation, advice that the Bolivians have not always accepted. Neither of these foreign powers can afford a collapse of the current Bolivian experiment. They certainly do not want Evo to become another Allende.

2. In October 2006, unionized mineworkers clashed with self-employed *cooperativistas* for the control of Bolivia's most productive tin mine. Seventeen workers lost their lives, and many more were injured. The incident showed how difficult it was for the MAS to exercise control over its own supporters.

BIBLIOGRAPHY

Aguilar, M. A. 2003. "Estimación del Tipo de Cambio Real de Equilibrio para Bolivia." *Revista de Análisis* (Banco Central de Bolivia) 6 (June): 41–72.

Aguirre, A., et al. 1992. *La intencionalidad del ajuste en Bolivia.* La Paz: CEDLA.

Albó, X. 1985. "De MNRistas a kataristas: Campesinado, estado y partidos, 1953–
1983." *Historia Boliviana* (La Paz) 5, no. 1–2:87–127.

———. 1993. . . . Y de kataristas a MNRistas? La sorprendente y audaz alianza entre
aymaras y neoliberales en Bolivia. La Paz: CEDOIN and UNITAS.

———. 1999. "Diversidad cultural, étnica y lingüística." In *Bolivia en el siglo XX*, edited by Fernando Campero P., 451–82. La Paz: Harvard Club de Bolivia.

———. 2002. *Pueblos indios en la política.* La Paz: CIPCA / Plural.

———. 2006. *Gama étnica y lingüística de la población boliviana.* La Paz: United
Nations System.

Albó, X., and F. Barrios. 2007. *Por una Bolivia plurinacional e intercultural con autonomías.* Informe de Desarrollo Humano, Cuaderno No. 22. La Paz: UNDP.

Albó, X., and J. M. Barnadas. 1995 [1984]. *La cara india y campesina de nuestra historia.* 4th edition. La Paz: CIPCA / Reforma Educativa.

Albó, X., and V. Quispe. 2004. *¿Quiénes son indígenas en los gobiernos municipales?*
La Paz: CIPCA / Plural.

Amin, S. 2001. *Capitalismo, imperialismo, mundialización.* Buenos Aires: CLACSO.

Anderson, Benedict. 1991. *Imagined Communities: Reflections on the Origin and
Spread of Nationalism.* London: Verso.

Arguedas, A. 1909. *Pueblo enfermo.* Barcelona: Vda. de Louis Tasso.

Arrighi, G. 1997. La globalizacion, la soberanía estatal y la interminable acumulación
del capital. http://www.globalización.org.

Arze, C. 1999. *Crisis del sindicalismo boliviano: Consideración de sus determinantes
materiales y su ideología.* La Paz: CEDLA.

———. 2001. "Ajuste neoliberal y mercado de trabajo en Bolivia." Global Policy Network. http://www.gpn.org.

———. 2003. "La privatización de la seguridad social: Una reforma financiera fra-
casada." In *Debate Social* (La Paz) 2.

———. 2004. "Las rebeliones populares de 2003 y la demanda de nacionalización de los hidrocarburos: ¿fin de la era neoliberal?" *Cuadernos del CENDES* 56:83–103.

Arze, R. D. 1988. *Guerra y conflictos sociales: El caso rural boliviano durante el conflicto del Chaco.* La Paz: CERES.

Ayo, D. 2007. *Democracia boliviana: Un modelo para desarmar.* La Paz: Friedrich Ebert Stiftung / ILDIS / Oxfam.

Banks, M. 1996. *Ethnicity: Anthropological Construction.* London: Routledge.

Baptista Morales, J.-L. 2005. "Supresión de la religión oficial del Estado." *Diálogo Jurídico* 2.

Barragán, R. 1990. *Espacio urbano y dinámica étnica: La Paz en el siglo XIX.* La Paz: Hisbol.

———. 1992. "Entre polleras, lliqllas y ñañazas: Los mestizos y la emergencia de la tercera república." In *Etnicidad, economía y simbolismo en los Andes,* edited by S. Arze, R. Barragán, L. Escobari, and X. Medinacelli, 85–127. La Paz: Hisbol / IFEA / SBH-ASUR.

———. 1996. "Los múltiples rostros y disputas por el ser mestizo." In *Mestizaje: Ilusiones y realidades,* edited by H. D. Ruiz, A. M. Mansilla, and W. I. Vargas. La Paz: MUSEF.

———. 2002. *El estado pactante: Gouvernement et peuples. La configuration de l'État et ses frontieres, Bolivie (1825–1880).* Paris: École des Hautes Études en Sciences Sociales.

———. 2005. "Ciudadanía y elecciones, convenciones y debates." *Regiones y poder constituyente en Bolivia: Una historia de pactos y disputas,* edited by R. Barragán and J. L. Roca, 275–448. La Paz: PNUD.

———. 2006a. *Las asambleas constituyentes en la historia de Bolivia.* La Paz: Editorial Muela del Diablo.

———. 2006b. "Más allá de lo mestizo, más allá de lo aymara: organización y representaciones de clase y etnicidad en La Paz." *América Latina Hoy* 43:107–30.

Barragán, R., and J. Peres. 2007. "De los pre-supuestos a los presupuestos: Fiscalidad y construcción estatal disputada, 1900–1954." Working Paper, Informe de Desarrollo Humano. La Paz: PNUD.

Barragán, R., and J. L. Roca. 2006. *Regiones y poder constituyente en Bolivia.* Informe de Desarrollo Humano, Cuaderno no. 21. La Paz: UNDP.

Barrios Suvelza, F. 2002. *El estado territorial, una nueva decentralización para Bolivia.* La Paz: Friedrich Ebert / Plural.

Barro, J. R., and X. Sala-i-Martin. 1995. *Economic Growth.* New York: McGraw Hill.

Biggart, N., and G. Hamilton. 1992. "On the Limits of a Firm-Based Theory to Explain Business Networks: Western Bias of Neoclassical Economics." In *Networks and Organizations,* edited by N. Noria and G. Eccles, 471–90. Boston, MA: Harvard Business School Press.

Blair, J., and G. Gereffi. 2001. "Local Clusters in Global Chains: The Causes and Consequences of Export Dynamism in Torreon's Blue Jeans Industry." *World Development* 29, no. 11: 885–903.

Blair, J., and L. Reese, eds. 1999. *Approaches to Economic Development: Readings from Economic Development Quarterly.* London: Sage Publications.

Blu, K. I. 1980. *The Lumbee problem: The Making of an American Indian People.* Cambridge: Cambridge University Press.

Bobbio, N. 1985. *Liberalismo y democracia.* Mexico City: Fondo de Cultural Económico.

———. 2004. *El futuro de la democracia.* Mexico City: Fondo de Cultura Económica.

Ministerio de Planificación del Desarrollo. 2006. *Plan Nacional de Desarrollo.* La Paz: Ministerio de Planificación del Desarrollo

Bolivia. 1901. *Censo Nacional de Bolivia: 1900.* 2 vols. La Paz: Oficina Nacional de Imigración, Estadística y Propaganda Geográfica.

Bouysse-Cassaigne, T. 1996. "In Praise of Bastards." In *Inside and Outside the Law: Anthropological Studies of Authority and Ambiguity,* edited by O. Harris, 98–124. London: Routledge.

British Petroleum. 2006. *Annual BP Statistical Review of World Energy.* http://www.bp.com.productlanding.do.

Calderón, Fernando, and Carlos Toranzo, eds. 1996. *La seguridad humana en Bolivia. Percepciones políticas, sociales y económica de los bolivianos hoy.* La Paz: PNUD-ILDIS-Pronagob.

Calla, R. 2003. *Indígenas, política y reformas en Bolivia: Hacia una etnología del Estado en América Latina.* Guatemala: Ediciones ICAPI.

Cámara Nacional de Industria. 1981. *Breve Historia de la Industria Nacional.* La Paz: Empresa Editora Gráfica.

Campero F., ed. 1999. *Bolivia en el siglo XX.* La Paz: Harvard Club de Bolivia.

Cañete y Domínguez, P. V. 1952. *Guía histórica, geográfica, física, política, civil u legal del gobierno e intendencia de Potosí.* Potosí: Armando Alba.

Cárdenas, E., J. A. Ocampo, and R. Thorp, eds. 2000. *Industrialisation and the State in Latin America.* Vol. 3, *The Post War Years, An Economic History of Twentieth Century Latin America,* New York: Palgrave Press and Saint Martin's Press.

Catena, M., and F. Navajas. 2006. "Oil and Debt Windfalls and Fiscal Dynamics in the Highlands: Bolivia in the Roller-Coaster." Mimeo. Buenos Aires: FIEL.

Choque, R., and E. Ticona. 1996. *Jesús de Machaqa: La marka rebelde.* Vol. 2, *Sublevación y masacre de 1921.* La Paz: CIPCA /CEDOIN.

Coase, R. 1952. "The Nature of the Firm." In *Readings in Price Theory,* edited by G. Stigler and K. Boulding, 33–56. Homewood, IL: Irwin.

Confederación Sindical Única de Trabajadores Campesinos de Bolivia. 1983. "Tesis política." In S. Rivera, *Oprimidos pero no vencidos,* 193–209.

Corporación Andina de Fomento. 2005. *América Latina en el comercio global.* Reporte de Economía y Desarrollo. Caracas: Corporación Andina de Fomento.

Crabtree, J. 2005. *Patterns of Protest: Politics and Social Movements in Bolivia*. London: Latin America Bureau.

Crabtree, J., and L. Whitehead. 2001. *Towards Democratic Viability: The Bolivian Experience*. Basingstoke: Palgrave.

CRISE. 2006. "CRISE Perception Survey: Results from Bolivia." Oxford: CRISE Working Papers.

Confederación Sindical Único de Trabajadores Campesinos Bolivianos. 2003 [1983]. "Tesis política." In S. Rivera, *Oprimidos pero no vencidos*, 193–209.

Dahrendorf, R. 2003. *Después de la democracia*. Buenos Aires: Fondo de Cultura Económica.

Dandler, J. 1984. "Campesinado y Reforma agraria en Cochabamba (1952–1953): Dinámica de un movimiento campesino en Bolivia." In *Bolivia: La fuerza histórica del campesinado*, edited by F. Calderón and J. Dandler, 135–204. Geneva and La Paz: UNRISD / CERES.

De Angelis, P. 1836–37. *Colección de obras y documentos relativos a la historia antigua y moderna de las provincias del Río de la Plata*. Buenos Aires: Imprenta del Estado.

Demélas, D. 1981. "Darwinismo a la criolla: El darwinismo social en Bolivia, 1880–1910." *Historia Boliviana* 1, no. 2: 55–82.

Domingo, P. 2001. "Exclusion, Participation and Democratic State Building." In Crabtree and Whitehead, *Towards Democratic Viability*, 141–59.

Delegado Presidencial para la Revisión y Mejora de la Capitalización. 2003. *Sector hidrocarburos: Datos comparativos*. http://www.dpc.gov.bo.

Drake, P. 1989. "Exporting Tin, Gold, and Laws from Bolivia, 1927–1932." In *The Money Doctor in the Andes: The Kemmerer Missions, 1923–1933*. Durham: Duke University Press.

Drucker, P. 1993. *La sociedad poscapitalista*. Buenos Aires: Editorial Sudamericana.

Durán Rivera, W. 2005. *El aporte del Tribunal Constitucional al fortalecimiento del estado de derecho y la democracia*. Sucre: Editorial TC.

Easterly, W. 2001. *The Elusive Quest for Growth*. Cambridge, MA: MIT Press.

Edwards, S. 1993. "Openness, Trade Liberalization and Growth in Developing Countries." *Journal of Economic Literature* 31:1358–93.

———. 1995. *Crisis and Reform in Latin America: From Despair to Hope*. New York: Oxford University Press.

Elías, N. 1997. *Über den Prozess der Zivilisation*. Vol. 1. Baden-Baden: Suhrkamp.

Escóbar, S. 2000. *Dinámica productiva y condiciones laborales en el sector minero*. La Paz: CEDLA.

Escóbar, S., and L. Montero. 2003. *La industria en su laberinto: Reestructuración productiva y competitividad en Bolivia*. La Paz: CEDLA.

Fairbanks, M., and L. Stace. 1997. *Plowing the Sea: Nurturing the Hidden Sources of Growth in the Developing World*. Cambridge, MA: Harvard Business School Press.

Farthing, L. 2004. "Rethinking Alternative Development in Bolivia." *The Andean Information Network. Special Update: Bolivia* (February). http://ain-bolivia.org/index2.php.

Fernández Segado, F. 2006. "Del control político al control jurisdiccional: Evolución y aportes a la justicia constitucional en América Latina." *Anuario de Derecho Constitucional Latinoamericano* 12, no. 1.

Foreign Policy Magazine. 2007. *The Failed States Index*. Washington, DC: Foreign Policy Magazine.

Foucault, M. 1995. *Microfísica del poder*. Madrid: Ed. Plante Agostini.

Fraga, A. 2004. "Latin America since the 1990s: Rising from the Sickbed?" *Journal of Economic Perspectives* 18, no. 2: 89–106.

Fretes-Cibils, V., M. Giugale, and C. Luff, eds. 2006. *Por el bienestar de todos: Bolivia*. Washington, DC: The World Bank.

García Linera, A., R. Gutierrez, R. Prada, and L. Tapia. 2000. *Retorno de la Bolivia plebeya*. La Paz: Muela del Diablo.

García Linera, A., M. Chávez, and P. Costas. 2004. *Sociología de los movimientos sociales en Bolivia: Estructuras de movilización, repertorios culturales y acción política*. La Paz: Editorial Plural / Oxfam / Diakonía.

Gill, L. 1994. *Precarious Dependencies: Gender, Class, and Domestic Service in Bolivia*. New York: Columbia University Press.

Granovetter, M. 1973. "The Strength of Weak Ties." *American Journal of Sociology*. 78, no. 6: 1360–80.

Gray Molina, G. 2004. "The Politics of Popular Participation, 1994–1999." DPhil thesis, Nuffield College, University of Oxford.

———. 2006a. "El estado como modus vivendi." Human Development Working Paper. La Paz: UNDP.

———. 2006b. "Harmony of Inequalities: Ethnic Politics in Bolivia, 1900–2000." Oxford: CRISE / University of Oxford.

———. 2006c. "La economía boliviana 'más allá del gas.'" *América Latina Hoy* (August): 63–85.

———. 2006d. "El estado del interculturalismo." *Revista Especializada del Defensor del Pueblo* (Bolivia) 1, no. 1.

Gray Molina, G., and A. Aranibar. 2006. "La economía boliviana en 2006: Una buena coyuntura para 'salir de la estructura.'" Working paper. Bolivia Human Development Report. La Paz: UNDP.

Gray Molina, G., and F. Wanderley. 2007. "Explaining 'Pockets of Growth' in a Low-Growth Economy." Mimeo. Cambridge, MA: CID / Harvard University.

Griesehaber, E. P. 1977. "Survival of Indian Communities in Nineteenth Century Bolivia." PhD diss., University of North Carolina at Chapel Hill.

Gutiérrez, E. 1990. "La crisis laboral y el futuro del mundo del trabajo." In *La ocupación del futuro*. Caracas: Nueva Sociedad.

Hale, C. 2004. "Rethinking Indigenous Politics in the Era of the *'Indio Permitido.'"* *NACLA Report on the Americas* 38, no. 2 (September/October): 16–21.

Hegel, G. 1986. *Vorlesungen über die Geschichte der Philosophie.* Vol. 2. Frankfurt am Main: Suhrkamp.

Huber, H. 1991. "Finanzas públicas y estructura social en Bolivia, 1825–1872." Master's thesis, Freie Universität Berlin.

Hurtado, G. 2006. "Estudios de caso de 'éxito en la adversidad': Madera y joyas." Working paper. Bolivia Human Development Report. La Paz: UNDP.

Hurtado, J. 1986. *El katarismo.* La Paz: Hisbol.

Hylton, F., and S. Thomson, 2007. *Revolutionary Horizons: Popular Struggle in Bolivia.* New York: Verso Press.

Instituto Nacional de Estadísticas. 2007. *Boletín estadístico* no. 6. La Paz: INE.

Instituto Nacional de Estadística, Unidad de Análisis de Políticas Sociales y Económicas, Cámara Nacional de Exportadores de Bolivia, and Instituto Boliviano de Comercio Exterior. 2006. *Empleo y percepciones socio-económicas en las empresas exportadoras bolivianas, Bolivia 2006.* La Paz: INE.

International Monetary Fund. 2000. *Globalization: Threat or Opportunity?* IMF Issues Briefs. Washington, DC: International Montary Fund.

———. 2006. Bolivia: Country Report 06/270 (July).

Irurozqui, M. 1994. *Armonía de las desigualdades: Elites y conflictos de poder en Bolivia 1880–1920.* Cusco: Centro Bartolomé de las Casas.

Kaufmann, D., A. Kraay, and M. Mastruzzi. 2007. "Governance Matters VI: Governance Indicators for 1996–2006." World Bank Policy Research Working Paper 4280. Washington, DC: The World Bank.

Kohl, B., and L. Farthing. 2006. *Impasse in Bolivia: Neoliberal Hegemony and Popular Resistance.* London: Zed Books.

Kranz, W. 1986. *Die Griechische Philosophie.* Leipzig: Dieterich'sche Verlagsbuchhandlung.

Kruse, T. 2000. "Procesos productivos e identidades sociales: Cambios en dos escenarios en Cochabamba, Bolivia." Paper presented at III Congreso Latinoamericano de Sociología del Trabajo, Buenos Aires, May 17–20.

Laserna, R. 2002. *Bolivia en la globalización: Estado y sociedad. Temas del presente.* La Paz: Universidad Católica.

———. 2004. *La democracia en el ch'enko.* La Paz: Fundación Milenio.

Lazarte, J. 2006. *La Asamblea Constituyente, un nuevo comienzo.* La Paz: Editorial Plural.

Levy, B. 1991. "Transactions Costs, the Size of Firms and Industrial Policy." *Journal of Development Economics* 34, no. 12: 151–78.

Lora, G. 1967. *Historia del movimiento obrero.* Vol. 1, *1840–1900.* La Paz: Los Amigos del Libro.

Löwenstein, K. 1994. *Verfassungslehre.* Tübingen: J.C.B. Mohr (Paul Siebeck).

Lynch, J. 1962. *Administración colonial española, 1782–1810: El sistema de intenden-cias en el virreinato del Río de la Plata.* Buenos Aires: Eudeba.

Martner, G. 1988. *Tendencias de la economía mundial.* La Paz: ILDIS.

Mayorga, Fernando. (1993). *Discurso y política en Bolivia.* La Paz: CERES / ILDIS.

———. 1997. *Ejemonías? Democracia representativa y liderazgos locales.* La Paz: PIEB.

Mcadam, D., S. G. Tarrow, and C. Tilly. 2001. *Dynamics of Contention.* Cambridge: Cambridge University Press.

Medina, J. 2001. *Suma Tamaña: La comprensión indígena de la Buena Vida.* La Paz: Deutsche Gessellschaft für Technische Zusammenarbeit / Federación de Asociaciones Municipales de Bolivia.

Medinaceli, M. 2004. *El régimen impositivo en el sector hidrocarburífero.* http://www.cbh.org.bo.

Medinaceli, M. 2006a. "Aspectos tributarios de la Ley de Hidrocarburos N° 3958 y el Decreto Supremo N° 28701." In *La nacionalización bajo la lupa,* edited by Fundación Milenio, 127–48. La Paz: Fundación Milenio.

———. 2006b. *Informe sobre el desempeño de la economía.* La Paz: Fundación Milenio.

Méndez, J., G. O'Donnell, and P. S. Pinheiro. 1999. *(Un)Rule of Law and the Underprivileged in Latin America.* Notre Dame: Notre Dame University Press.

Migdal, J. 2001. *State in Society: How States and Societies Transform and Constitute One Another.* Cambridge: Cambridge University Press.

———. 1988. *Strong Societies and Weak States: State-Society Relations and State Capabilities in the Third World.* Princeton: Princeton University Press.

Miranda Pacheco, Carlos. 1999. "Petróleo: Del descubrimiento petrolífero a la explosión del gas." In *Bolivia en el siglo XX: La formación de la Bolivia contemporánea,* edited by F. Campero P., 241–67. La Paz: Harvard Club de Bolivia.

———. 2005. "Cincuenta años de legislación petrolera en Bolivia." *T'inkazos* 18.

Miranda, C. 2003. *¿Podemos exportar gas natural?* La Paz: Fundación Milenio.

———. 2006. "Análisis global del Decreto Supremo N° 28701." In *La nacionalización bajo la lupa,* edited by Fundación Milenio, 97–110. La Paz: Fundación Milenio.

Molina, R., and X. Albó, eds. 2006. *Gama étnica y lingüística de la población boliviana.* La Paz: Sistema de Naciones Unidas.

Montero, L. 2003. *Los nuevos mundos del trabajo: El empleo asalariado en Bolivia.* La Paz: CEDLA.

Morales, J. A. 2001. "Bolivia's Economic Vulnerability: Crisis and Social Exclusion." In *Democratic Viability: The Bolivian Case,* edited by J. Crabtree and L. Whitehead. London: Palgrave.

———. 2003. "The National Revolution and its Legacy." In *Proclaiming Revolution: Bolivia in Comparative Perspective,* edited by M. S. Grindle and P. Domingo, 213–31. Cambridge, MA: Harvard University Press.

Morales, J. A., and J. D. Sachs. 1990. "Bolivia's Economic Crisis." In *Developing Coun-*

try Debt and Economic Performance, edited by J. D. Sachs, 157–268. Chicago: University of Chicago Press

Morrison, J. 2004. "Models of Democracy: From Representation to Participation." In *The Changing Constitution,* edited by J. Jowell and D. Olier. 5th ed. Oxford: Oxford University Press.

Müller y Asociados. 2004. *Estadísticas socio-económicas.* La Paz: Müller y Asociados.

Nash, J. 1976. *He agotado mi vida en la mina: Una historia de vida.* Buenos Aires: Nueva Visión.

Nava Gomar, S. 2003. "El Estado constitucional: Sinónimia positivizada entre constitución y democracia." *Anuario de Derecho Constitucional Latinoamericano* 9:13–31.

Negri, A. 1993. *El poder constituyente, ensayo sobre las alternativas de la modernidad.* Madrid: Editorial Libertarias / Prodhufi.

O'Donnell, G. 1993. "On the State, Democratization and Some Conceptual Problems: A Latin American View with Glances at Some Post-communist Countries." *World Development* 21, no. 8: 1355–69.

———. 1999. *Counterpoints: Selected Essays on Authoritarianism and Democratization.* Notre Dame: University of Notre Dame.

Ocampo, J. A. 2004. "Latin America's Growth and Equity: Frustrations during Structural Reforms." *Journal of Economic Perspectivas* 18, no. 2: 67–88.

Oporto, H. 2006. "La nacionalización mueve el tablero político y define el perfil del gobierno." In *La nacionalización bajo la lupa,* edited by Fundación Milenio, 9–18. La Paz: Fundación Milenio.

Orellana, L. 2006. *El gobierno del MAS no es nacionalista ni revolucionario.* La Paz: CEDLA.

Orlove, B., and E. Schmidt. 1995. "Swallowing Their Pride: Indigenous and Industrial Beer in Peru and Bolivia." *Theory and Society* 24:271–98.

Pavez, I., and A. Bojanic. 1998. *El proceso social de formulación de la Ley Forestal de Bolivia de 1996.* La Paz: CEDLA.

Peredo, Elizabeth. 1992. *Recoveras de los Andes: La identidad de la chola de mercado: una aproximación psico-social.* La Paz: ILDIS / TAHIPAMU.

Pérez, M. 2003. *Apertura comercial y sector agrícola campesino: La otra cara de la pobreza del campesino andino.* La Paz: CEDLA.

Petras, J., and H. Veltmeyer. 2005. *Social Movements and State Power: Argentina, Brazil, Bolivia and Ecuador.* London: Pluto Press.

Pinto, D., and R. Navia. 2007. *Un tal Evo: Biografía no-autorizada.* Santa Cruz: Editorial El País.

Platt, T. 1982. *Estado boliviano y ayllu andino: Tierra y tributo en el Norte de Potosí.* Lima: Instituto de Estudios Peruanos.

Popper, K. 1971. *The Open Society and Its Enemies.* Princeton: Princeton University Press.

Poveda, P., and P. Rossell. 2001. *Reestructuración capitalista y formas de producción.* La Paz: CEDLA.

Prats, J., ed. 2003. *Bolivia: El desarrollo posible. Las instituciones necesarias.* Barcelona: Instituto Internacional de Gobernabilidad / Gobierno de Catalunya / UNDP.

Quispe, F. 2000. "Entrevista con Felipe Quispe." *Pulso* (La Paz), October 2000.

Qureshi, Z. 1996. "La globalización: Nuevas oportunidades, grandes desafíos." *Finanzas y Desarrollo* 33, no. 1 (March): 30–33.

Reinaga, F. 1969. *La revolución india.* La Paz: Partido Indio de Bolivia.

República de Bolivia. 1926. Libro mayor de sesiones de la Asamblea de Representantes del Alto Perú, instalada el 10 de junio de 1825. La Paz.

Rivera Cusicanqui, S. 1983. "Luchas campesinas contemporáneas en Bolivia: El movimiento katarista." In *Bolivia hoy,* edited by R. Zabaleta, 129–78. Mexico: Siglo XXI.

———. 2003 [1984]. *Oprimidos pero no vencidos: Luchas del campesinado aymara y qhechwa de Bolivia, 1900–1980.* 4th ed. La Paz: Ediciones Yachaywasi.

Roca, José Luis. 1979 [1990]. *Fisonomía del regionalismo boliviano.* 2nd ed. La Paz: Los Amigos del Libro.

———. 2005a. "La estatalidad: Entre la pugna regional y el institucionalismo." In *Regiones y poder constituyente en Bolivia.* La Paz: PNUD.

———. 2005b. "Los prefectos, una mirada retrospectiva." In *Opiniones y análisis.* La Paz: Fundación Hanna Seidel / FUNDEMOS.

Rodríguez, G. 1993. *Poder central y proyecto regional, Cochabamba y Santa Cruz en los siglos XIX y XX.* La Paz: ILDIS / IDEAS.

Rodríguez, G., and H. Solares. 1990. *Sociedad oligárquica, chicha y cultura popular.* Cochabamba: Editorial Serrano.

Rodríguez Ostria, G. 1999. "Producción, mercancía y empresarios." In *Bolivia en el siglo XX.* La Paz: Harvard Club de Bolivia.

Rodríguez Veltzé, E. 2004. *Discurso del Presidente de la Corte Suprema.* January 2, 2004. Sucre: Editorial Judicial.

Romero, S. 1999. *Reformas, conflictos y consensos.* La Paz: Fundemos.

Russell, B. 2004. *History of Western Philosophy.* New York: Simon & Schuster.

Sabel, C., and J. Zeitlin. 1996. "Historical Alternatives to Mass Production: Politics, Markets and Technology in Nineteenth-Century Industrialization." In *Economic Sociology,* edited by R. Swedberg, 133–76. Gloucester, U.K.: Elgar Publications.

Sabel, C., and M. Piori. 1984. *The Second Industrial Divide: Possibilities for Prosperity.* New York: Basic Books.

Sachica, L. 1985. *Esquema para una teoría del poder constituyente.* 2nd ed. Bogota: Editorial Temis.

Saignes, T. 1995. "Indian Migration and Social Change in Seventeenth-Century Charcas." In *Ethnicity, Markets, and Migration in the Andes: At the Crossroads of History and Anthropology,* edited by B. Larson, O. Harris, and E. Tandeter, 167–95. Durham: Duke University Press.

Sánchez Albornoz, N. 1978. *Indios y tributos del Alto Perú*. Lima: Instituto de Estudios Peruanos.

Sanjinés, J. 2004. *Mestizaje Upside-down: Aesthetic Politics in Modern Bolivia*. Pittsburgh: University of Pittsburgh Press.

Sartori, G. 1995. *Teoría de la democracia*. Madrid: Alianza Editorial.

Sartre, J.-P. 1946. *Réflexions sur la question juive*. Paris: Paul Morihien.

Saxenian, A. 1994. *Regional Advantage: Culture and Competition in Silicon Valley and Route 128*. Cambridge, MA: Harvard University Press.

Schmitt, C. 2003. *Die Verfassungslehre*. Berlin: Duncker & Humbolt.

Schmitz, H. 1995. "Collective Efficiency: Growth Path for Small-Scale Industry." *Journal of Development Studies* 31, no. 4: 529–66.

Seligson, M., et al. 2006. *Auditoría de la democracia: Informe Bolivia 2006*. La Paz: USAID / LAPOP / Ciudadanía / Vanderbilt University / Encuentros y Estudios / Universidad Católica de Bolivia.

Seligson, M., and D. Moreno, eds. 2006. *La cultura política de los bolivianos: Aproximaciones cuantitativas*. La Paz: USAID, LAPOP, Ciudadanía.

Sen, A. 2006. *Identity and Violence*. New York: Norton.

Sensenberger, W., and F. Pyke. 1991. "Small Firm Industrial Districts and Local Economic Regeneration: Research and Policy Issues." *Labour and Society* 16, no. 1: 1–24.

Sieder, R., ed. 2002. *Multiculturalism in Latin America. Indigenous Rights, Diversity and Democracy*. London: Institute of Latin American Studies.

Soruco, X. 2006. "La inentiligibilidad de lo cholo en Bolivia." *Tink'azos* 21.

Sotelo, A. 1995. "Globalización del capital e inversión del ciclo económico en América Latina." *Estudios Latinoamericanos Nueva Epoca* 2 no. 4 (July–Dec.): 47–70.

Strauss, L. 1978. *The City and Man*. Chicago: University of Chicago Press.

Sturzenegger, F. 2005. *Empleo sector de hidrocarburos en Bolivia*. La Paz.

Szeminski, I. 1983. *La utopía tupamarista*. Lima: Pontifícia Universidad Católica del Perú.

Tamayo, Franz. 1944 [1910]. *Creación de la pedagogía nacional*. 2nd ed. La Paz: Biblioteca Boliviana.

Tendler, J., and M. Amorim. 1996. "Small Firms and Their Helpers: Lessons on Demand." *World Development* 24, no. 3.

Thomson, S. 2003. *We Alone Will Rule: Native Andean Politics in the Age of Insurgency*. Madison: University of Wisconsin Press.

Tilly, C., and L. A. Tilly, eds. 1981. *Class Conflict and Collective Action*. London: Sage Publications.

Toranzo, C. 1992. "Carlos Palenque y condepismo." In *Nuevos actores políticos*. La Paz: ILDIS

———. 2005. *Rostros de la democracia: Una mirada mestiza*. La Paz: Editorial Plural.

Transparency International. 2007. *2007 Corruption Perceptions Index*. Berlin: Transparency International.

Unidad de Análisis de Políticas Sociales y Económicas. 2001. *Bolivia: Evaluación de la economía 2000*. La Paz: UDAPE.

United Nations Development Program. 2004a. *Informe nacional de desarrollo humano*. La Paz: PNUD.

———. 2004b. *Informe de desarrollo humano en Santa Cruz, 2004*. La Paz: PNUD.

———. 2005. *Informe temático sobre desarrollo humano: La economía más allá del gas*. La Paz: PNUD.

———. 2006. *Cuatro millones de actores: Niños niñas y adolescentes en Bolivia*. Informe Temático de Desarrollo Humano. La Paz: PNUD.

———. 2007. *El estado del Estado en Bolivia: Informe nacional sobre desarrollo humano en Bolivia*. La Paz: PNUD.

———. In press. *La otra frontera: Usos alternativos de recursos naturales en Bolivia*. Informe Temático de Desarrollo Humano, La Paz: UNDP.

UNDP, IDEA. 2007. *El estado de la opinión: Los bolivianos, la Constitución y la Constituyente*. Encuestas para el Desarrollo Humano. La Paz: PNUD /IDEA.

UNIR. 2006. *Encuesta nacional Diversidad Cultural Hoy*. La Paz: Fundación UNIR Bolivia.

Urquiola, M. 1999. "La distribución de la población en el siglo XX." In *Bolivia en el Siglo XX*, edited by F. Campero, 193–217. La Paz.

Uzzel, D. 1994. "Transaction Costs, Formal Plans and Formal Informality: Alternatives to the Informal Sector." *Contrapunto*. New York: SUNY Press.

Van der Auwera, C. 2004 "L'incidence de la politique américaine en matière de drogue sur la politique intérieure bolivienne." Mimeo. Brussels: Université Libre de Bruxelles, Faculté de Sciences Sociales, Politiques et Économiques.

Vandergeest, M., and N. Peluso Lee. 1995. "Territorialization and State Power in Thailand." *Theory and Society* 24:385–426.

Verdesoto, L., and M. Zuazo. 2006. *Instituciones en boca de la gente: Percepciones de la ciudadanía boliviana sobre política y territorio*. La Paz: Friedrich Ebert Stiftung / ILDIS.

Wanderley, F. 1999. "Pequenos negócios, industrializacão local e redes de relacões económicas: Una revisión bibliográfica em sociología económica." *Revista Brasileira de Informação Bibliográfica em Ciências Sociais* 48, no. 2.

———. 2002. "Pequeñas empresas, sector informal e industrialización local: La sociología económica del desarrollo." *T'inkazos: Revista Boliviana de Ciencias Sociales* 11:9–30.

———. 2004. "Reciprocity without Cooperation—Small Producer Networks and Political Identities in Bolivia." PhD diss., Columbia University.

———. 2005. "La construcción de ciudadanía económica: El desafío del nuevo modelo de desarrollo." *T'inkazos: Revista Boliviana de Ciencias Sociales* 18:31–52.

Weingast, B. 2005. "The Political Foundations of Democracy and the Rule of Law." *American Political Science Review* 91, no. 2: 245–63.

Whitehead, L. 1972. *National Power and Local Power: The Case of Santa Cruz de la Sierra, Bolivia.* Cambridge: Cambridge University Press.

———. 1975. "The State and Sectional Interests: The Bolivian Case." *European Journal of Political Research* 3, no. 2: 115–46.

———. 2001. "The Emergence of Democracy in Bolivia." In Crabtree and Whitehead, *Towards Democratic Viability,* 21–40.

———. 2002. *Democratization: Theory and Practice.* Oxford: Oxford University Press.

Williamson, O. 1981. "The Economics of Organization: The Transaction Cost Approach." *American Journal of Sociology* 87:548–77.

———. 1993. "Calculativeness, Trust, and Economic Organization." *Journal of Law and Economics* 36 (April).

Ybarnegaray, R. 1999. "La incorporación del oriente a la economía boliviana." In *El desenvolvimiento económico de Bolivia en el siglo XX.* Vol. 3. La Paz: Nueva Economía.

Zavaleta, R. 1986. *Lo nacional-popular en Bolivia.* Mexico: Siglo Veintiuno.

———. 1987. *El poder dual: Problemas de la teoría del Estado en Latinoamérica.* La Paz: Los Amigos del Libro.

Zuazo, M. 2006. "Qúeste los mestizos: Diálogo con tres estudios sobre mestizaje y condición indígena en Bolivia." *Tink'azos* 21.

Xavier Albó is an anthropologist, a Jesuit priest, and one of the most prolific and distinguished writers on Andean rural society. He is a researcher at the Center for the Research and Promotion of the Campesinado (CIPCA). His many books and articles cover linguistics, education, rural politics and sociology, as well as anthropology.

Carlos Arze is currently director of CEDLA (Centro de Estudios para el Desarrollo Laboral y Agrario). He studied economics at the Universidad Mayor de San Andrés in La Paz. He is an expert on labor economics and has worked on statistics to do with employment and labor conditions in Bolivia.

Rossana Barragán is a historian, the director of the Bolivian National Archive, and a teacher at the Universidad Mayor de San Andrés (UMSA) in La Paz. She was the director of the intellectual journal *T'inkazos* until 2005. Her doctoral thesis was on the development of the Bolivian state in the nineteenth century. She has recently been involved in a study for the United Nations Development Program on fiscal management in the twentieth century.

Franz Barrios is an economist and holds a PhD from the Technical University of Berlin. He has been working on state and public sector reform, as well as constitutional designs for territorial structures in Bolivia and elsewhere. His most recent published work is on the theory of constitutional systematics.

John Crabtree is a research associate at the Latin American Centre, Oxford, and senior member of Saint Antony's College. He has written widely on the politics of the Andean countries, particularly Peru and Bolivia. In 2001, he coedited (with Laurence Whitehead) *Towards Democratic Viability: The Bolivian Experience* (Palgrave) and in 2005 was the author of *Patterns of Protest: Politics and Social Movements in Bolivia* (Latin American Bureau).

Carlos Miranda is one of the foremost authorities on the hydrocarbons industry and has worked as consultant on this sector. He is an engineer by training, with a masters degree in petroleum engineering from Stanford University. He is the author of *Gas and Geopolitics in the Southern Cone*. Currently he is Academic Director of the Masters Program in Gas Management at the Universidad Andina Simón Bolívar in La Paz.

George Gray Molina heads up the research unit of the United Nations Development Program (UNDP) and is chief editor of the Human Development Report for Bolivia. He received his doctorate in Oxford, where his research focused on Popular Participation. He has worked on poverty, decentralization, and public policy for the Inter-American Development Bank. Prior to his job at UNDP, he headed the the Unidad de Análisis de Políticas Sociales y Económicas, a government socioeconomic think tank.

Juan Antonio Morales was president of the Central Bank of Bolivia (1995–2006). He obtained his bachelors, masters, and doctoral degrees in economics at the Université Catolique de Louvain. He has taught at the Universidad Católica, La Paz, for more than thirty years, and is currently teaching on the masters program in development there.

José Luis Roca is the pioneer of regionalism studies in Bolivia, and he has written extensively on the economic development of Santa Cruz. Probably his best known work is his *Economía y sociedad en el oriente boliviano* (2001, Cotas Ltda). He has also written an important critique of the privatization policies of the Gonzalo Sánchez de Lozada administration. He has been a journalist, ambassador to the United Kingdom, minister, and senator.

Eduardo Rodríguez Veltzé is a former constitutional president of the Republic of Bolivia (2005–06). Before becoming president, Rodríguez Veltzé was president of the Supreme Court, to which he was first appointed as justice in 1999. He is a professor of civil and administrative law at the Universidad Católica and the Universidad Andina Simón Bolívar. He studied law at the Universidad San Simón in Cochabamba and the Kennedy School at Harvard University.

Luis Tapia holds a doctorate in political science. He is coordinator of the Doctoral Program in Development Science at CIDES–Universidad Mayor de San Andrés and the Universidad Nacional Autónoma de México.

Carlos Toranzo has a doctorate in economics and a masters degree in political science. He is also a prolific journalist and has worked for many years as a political analyst at the Friedrich Ebert Stiftung–ILDIS in La Paz. He has taught in universities in Mexico, Chile, and the United Kingdom.

Fernanda Wanderley is a researcher and lecturer in the Graduate Program on Development Studies, CIDES–Universidad Mayor de San Andrés. She holds a PhD in sociology from Columbia University, where her research focused on small-scale producer networks and political identities in Bolivia. She contributed to the UNDP's Bolivian Human Development Report with a study on the exercise and meaning of citizenship.

Laurence Whitehead is an official fellow in politics at Nuffield College, Oxford. He first published on Bolivia in the 1960s and has written numerous articles and other contributions since then. In 2001, he coedited (with John Crabtree) *Towards Democratic Viability: The Bolivian Experience.* He has also published widely on democratization in Latin America.